Katie Herzog

Object-Oriented Programming

Katie Herzog

Object-Oriented Programming

January 13, 2012 - March 30, 2012
Palo Alto Research Center (PARC, a Xerox Company)
Essays by Amelia Acker and Andrew Choate

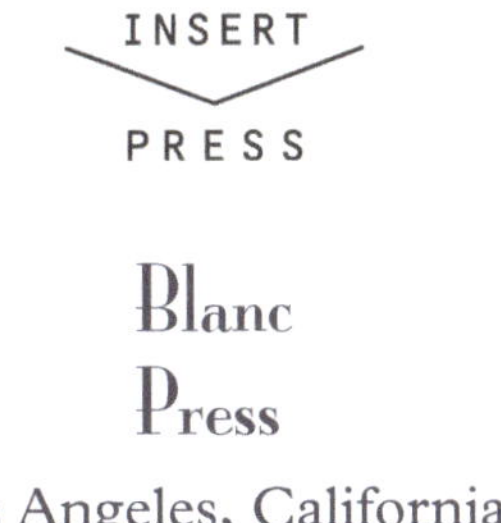

Los Angeles, California

Katie Herzog: Object-Oriented Programming
January 13, 2012 - March 30, 2012
Palo Alto Research Center (PARC, a Xerox Company)
Insert Blanc Press January, 2013

ISBN: 978-0-9814623-6-3

PARC (Palo Alto Research Center)
3333 Coyote Hill Road
Palo Alto, CA 94304

All photos in the Plates and Installation View sections by: Kerry Hiroshi Paul

Book design and layout by Mathew Timmons. Text set in Plantin and Myriad Pro.

Front cover image "Quarry," Plate 30, 2009. Back cover image "Freedom (Richard Stallman Folk Dancing)," Plate 31, 2008.

All quotes on the cycling for libraries jerseys are from the book "Archives of Library Research from the Molesworth Institute" by Norman D. Stevens.

Acknowledgements: Lisa Fahey, Susan Rosenberg, James Kennard, Norman D. Stevens, Computer History Museum, Center for Cultural Innovation, Palo Alto Research Center, and MediaGoblin.

Table of Contents

Essays

Landscapes of Information

Amelia Acker

Figure 1. *Melvil's Rib (Dewey)*. Acrylic on canvas.

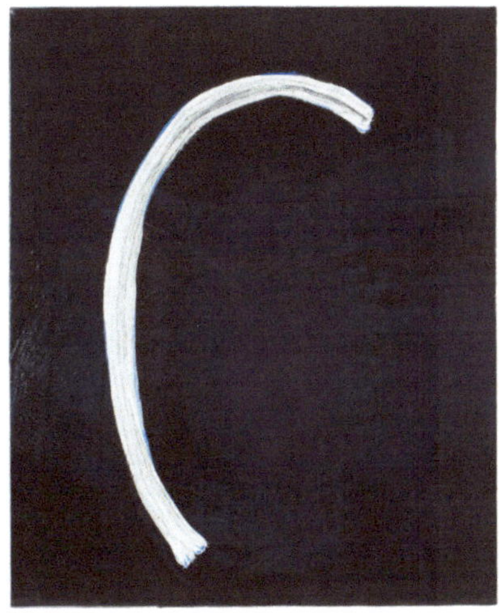

Figure 1, Plate 8, 2011.

In an artist's talk on her recent retrospective, Katie Herzog identifies x-rays as an entry point for considering the construction of information narratives and the historicity of images. For different readers, x-ray images may be technical data read through a diagnostic gaze, where for others they may simply be soft tissue and bones. Information narratives construct expectations of what to see and how to interpret data. For example radiologists must learn how to see pathologies by reading the body rendered through diagnostic imaging techniques. Herzog's retrospective reminds us that the way we read information has epistemic consequences, and that all information communication technologies, like x-ray radiograph images are "crafted products in particular historical circumstances."[1]

Herzog's current work is at the nexus of critical information theory, disjunctive librarianship, and gender and technology studies. Given the impact that the Palo Alto Research Center (PARC) has had on information technology and user interface design, it is a provocative/well suited space to experience her work.

Figure 2. *C is for Cookie*. Acrylic on Wool Blanket.

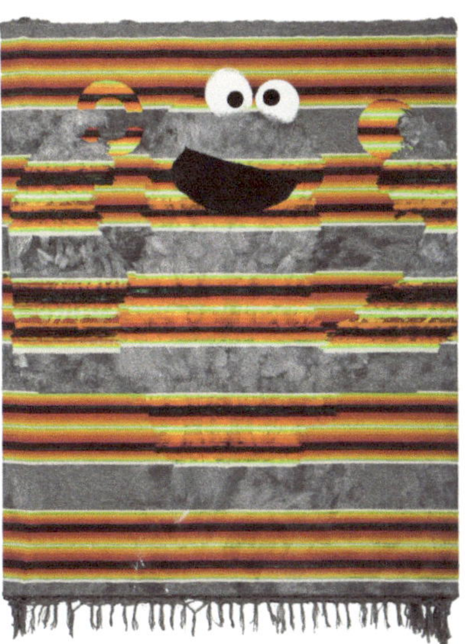

Figure 2, Plate 1, 2011.

I. Visual Information Systems

The impact that PARC has had on modern computing in the digital age cannot be underestimated. Founded in 1970 as a research and development division of the Xerox company, PARC has a distinguished reputation for developing information systems and hardware that have fundamentally changed the way we work, play and experience information in our everyday lives. PARC is credited for developing a range of information communication technologies, from the laser printer and Ethernet networking to the personal computer.

Arguably, the largest influence PARC has had on digital culture has been in the ability to enable consumers to copy and paste information on our desktop PCs, to visually orient objects, and to graphically overlap and switch between "windows." Herzog's retrospective at PARC entitled, Object-

Oriented Programming plays with many of the traces that PARC has left in shaping our information infrastructures.

We experience the semiotic power of digital materiality in graphical user interfaces through gestures of control: drag and drop, click and copy, opening a new window with the mouse. The ideas moving from one document space to another, cutting and copying electronic text was first introduced by Douglas Engelbart at the Augmentation Research Center at PARC in the late 1960s. Most origin stories of early graphical user interfaces reference the first bit-map picture of Cookie Monster. It was the first image to be summoned by Alan Kay on a Dynabook prototype using Smalltalk in April of 1973.[2]

C is for Cookie illustrates one of the earliest, inaugural moments of seeing an image in a digital, visual information system: Cookie Monster, with his C and his cookie. Yet, both Cookie Monster's C and cookie are also symbols for the word, the word as image, and as mimetic tools for learning how to read. As Bruno Latour reminds us, when all parts of an artifact are digital, written in software code, they are "writings all the way down."[3] *C is for Cookie*, like *Melvil's Rib (Dewey)*, contains multiple information narratives at the material, symbolic, and experiential levels of writing and information processing.[4] In each, the 'object' as an image is oriented, anchored by a variety of information narratives that circulate in an age of instant communication and carry layers of significance all the way down.

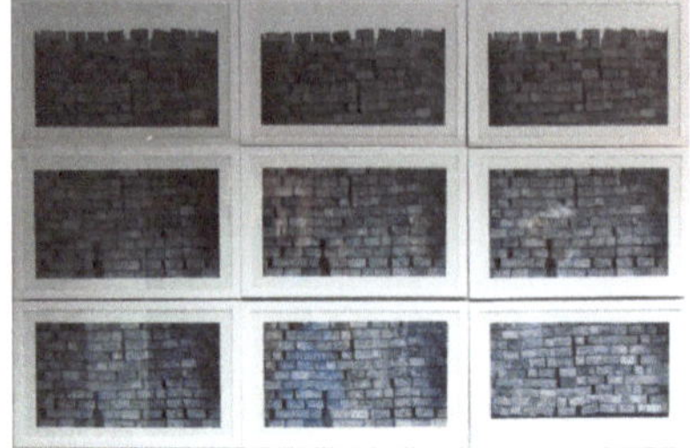

Figure 3, 2004.

Figure 3. *Haystack*. Photocopy installation.

II. Design, Copy, and Failure

"The fundamental meaning of a mark is that it's there."—Alan Kay

"If I make a mark it is a political act ... it has it's own narrative." —Katie Herzog

Alan Kay developed "object-oriented" programming with the conceit of the desktop GUI in the 1970s when he was working on the Dynabook at PARC. Kay, the inspiration for the video game programmer played by Jeff Bridges in the 1982 Disney classic *Tron*, was attempting to develop with his team the first personal computer.[5] He called it a "learning and thinking amplifier" (Ibid). While the desktop metaphor for personal computing is still pervasive in most operating systems (Mac OS, Window, Ubuntu), the Dynabook failed.

In many ways, the failure of the Dynabook is a mark of its great influence on the present narrative and everyday experiences of personal computing. As a sign, it points to something more. For American semiotician C.S. Peirce, the sign is an "instruction for interpretation."[6] Herzog's *Haystack*, like Kay's Dynabook, is an example of a sign that instructs interpretation and speaks to something more.

Haystack refers to Claude Monet's Haystacks series. Photocopied, reversed, and enlarged, Herzog's *Haystack* points to the power of copying and printing in the information age while bringing the status of an original work into stark relief. What is the political economy of original copies, derivatives of expression, and signs in the digital age?

In 1989, Xerox sued Apple Computer, contending that software originally developed by scientists at PARC was unlawfully used in Macintosh software and Lisa, Apple's first commercial PC with a GUI. According to an Apple spokeswoman at the time, "The Xerox complaint seems to confuse the distinction between ideas and expression; copyright protects expression, not ideas [...] Apple intends to prove in court that the audio-visual expressions in the Lisa and Macintosh interfaces were wholly original to Apple and duly registered with the copyright office."[7]

Computers and their information systems transform artifacts into signs, but those variables without the context of a wider information narrative such as an indexical system of "original works" and "original authors" often become void and unprotected. A copyright lawyer consulted in the New York Times article about the Xerox complaint in 1989 said that their case would be weakened because of the likelihood that there was a lack of copyright on the GUI, "in those days nobody put c's in a circle on computer screens."[8]

For copyright lawyers in a juridical context, the absence of a mark on a screen allowed the most salient features of PARC's GUI to be cut and copied. Today few people who use personal computers read the narrative of failure, or the missing mark on a screen, into the success of Apple's Lisa. However, in the information landscape of the market and copyright law, the narrative of failure in the design and experience of personal computing is buried, and re-buried each time we cut and copy. In the landscape of art works, the narrative of authorship, design and copy carry a different purchase within the fair use doctrine of free expression.

Figure 4. *Mr. Watson Come Here I Need You*. Acrylic and garnets on canvas.

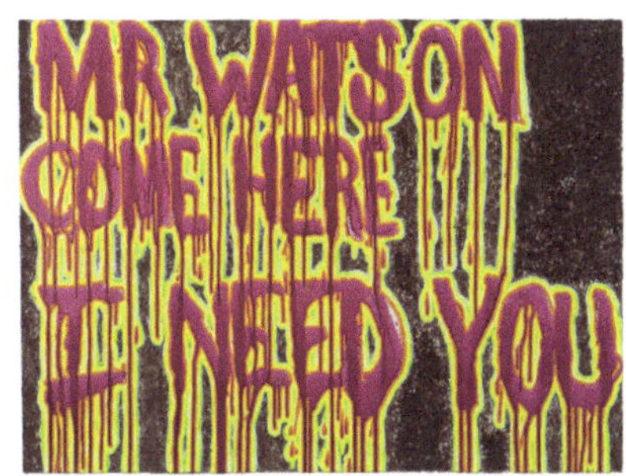

Figure 4, Plate 4, 2011.

III. Invisible Work

As we learn to read information landscapes in different ways, sometimes narratives of context fail, intersect, or create fissures. Many social science researchers in gender studies, science and technology studies, and information science have described information landscapes by looking at the materials and practices of work. Coincidentally, another area where PARC has influenced our experience of information technology has been in workplace studies.

In workplace studies, ethnographers look at how work is socially and materially organized in information technology-intensive workplaces (e.g., libraries, air traffic control towers, and laboratories). After two decades of workplace research, ethnographer Lucy Suchman and her colleagues at

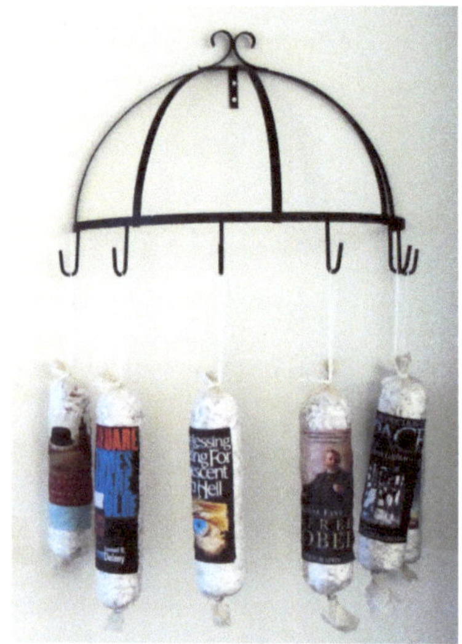

Figure 5, 2011.

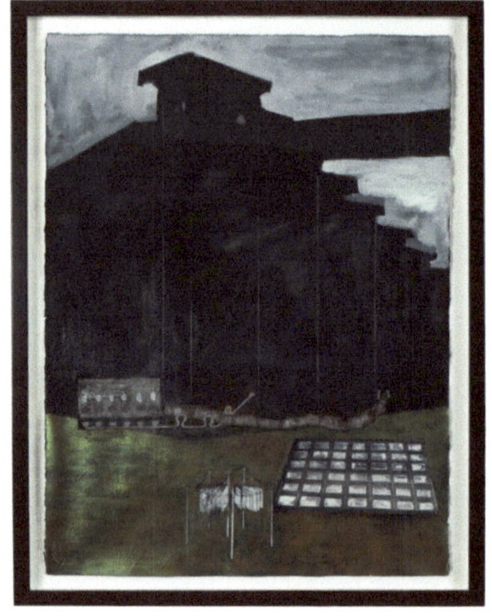

Figure 6, Plate 44, 2005.

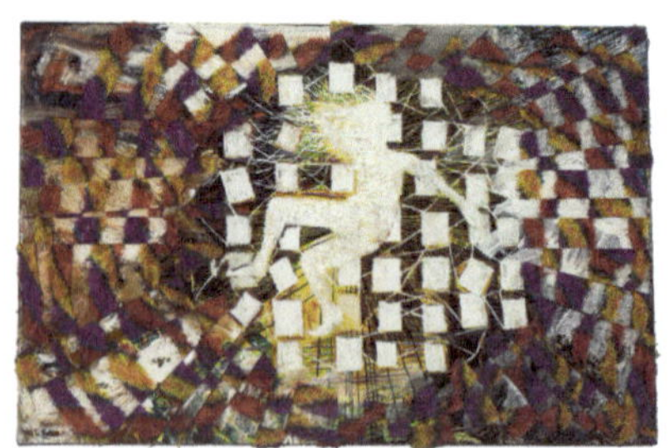

Figure 7, Plate 29, 2009.

PARC described workplace research as "reconstructing technologies as social practice." [9] By studying work empirically, Suchman and her team were not only able to look at work in order to computerize or simplify process and see why system implementation fails, but to make work visible (Ibid). In *Mr. Watson Come Here I Need You*, the artist underscores the social and material 'structuring' of Alexander Graham Bell's assistant, Mr. Watson, in the next room, as well as the infrastructure of transmission in the first successful telephone experiment.

Failure can often be understood and read into invisible work and infrastructures. The juridical context of copyright of the GUI in Apple machines tells one story, while the market or the labor conditions of the workers that manufacture machines may tell another.[10] We take the artifactual nature of information technologies for granted because they are in the service of other things (such as communication, consumption, and commerce). In the structuring of space the people occupying it can disappear into the background. Because they are in the service of other things, other practices and work, they are often rendered materially and conceptually invisible; but, as Paul Dourish and Genevieve Bell have written, "everyday space is not experienced neutrally."[11]

The same week that Object Oriented Programming was being de-installed at PARC, all but one member of PARC's library staff were terminated. Herzog offered the last librarian a choice of one of the *Literaturwursts* (Figure 5) which were installed outside the entrance of the library, known as 'the information center'. The *Literaturewurst* is a direct reference to the development of the information center: both speak to the decline of print, the rise of information-as-immaterial objects, and the power of spaces that structure our information experiences. It was a providential intervention that works such as *Mr. Watson Come Here I Need You* (Figure 4), *Paper Factory* (Figure 6), and *Information Entropy* (Figure 7) that explore the experience of invisible work appeared in the hallways, corridors and copy rooms of PARC. In each piece the social relationships of communication and material consequences being obscured by information infrastructures are referenced.

IV. Cyborgs

In addition to the infrastructure of invisible work, Herzog engages with 'identity work' that is often tied to information communication technologies. Identity work, like invisible work, covers the range of practices that people do to create, present and maintain personal identities. In *Gender Circuits*, Eve Shapiro describes how the gendered self is constructed through processes of identity work with information communication technologies, as a discursive practice.[12] Herzog's paintings illustrate how the transmission of information is politicized, but they also show the viewer that gender is both a technical discourse and a practice of identity.

Herzog's fascination, perhaps obsession, with information contexts can be read in virtually all her pieces. Further, there is an anxiety of gender;

perhaps erstwhile reflections of a damaged gendered subjectivity that we all carry. She sees gender as a technical discourse and practice in information environments all around us. Each piece speaks to the cyborgs that we have become, and "the information machines" that we are becoming, according to Donna Haraway.

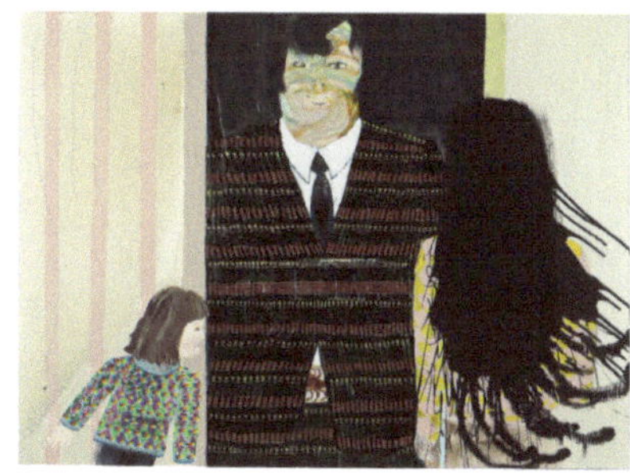

Figure 8, Plate 3, 2011.

In *Door to Door Encyclopedia Salesman* (Figure 8), a daughter and mother are greeting a salesman wearing a scorpion belt buckle at the door. The piece speaks to the end of an age—closing the door on the circulation of print and analog information, while the belt buckle conjures a treachery, with the transition to electronic communication, the inevitable decline of face to face encounters. While *Library Wedding* (Figure 9) points to the institutional import that library's play in our social lives—they are a place, real and tangible in an illusory sea of digital information. Herzog's retrospective speaks to multiple information landscapes and the experience of cybernetic organisms, or cyborgs, at the beginning of the 21st century.

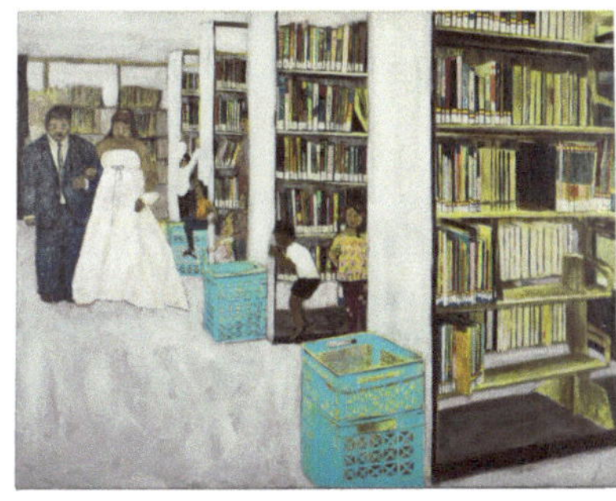

Figure 9, Plate 39, 2006.

Cybernetics is the study of social structures, systems and information. Established by Norbert Wiener in the late 1940s, the term comes from kybernētēs in Greek, meaning steersman, pilot, or rudder. In Virgil's *Aeneid*, the helmsman is Palinurus. As the ship's guide, Palinurus observes the direction of the ship, the sea, and the wind to steer Aeneas' ship. He responds, adjusts, shifts, and steers in reaction to the flow of information. Adjusting his gaze, the steersman reads the seascape, the coast, and the weather as informational elements, and like all good cyborgs, navigates accordingly. Herzog's work is a cybernetic handle for us to use, like Palinurus' rudder, to cut through information landscapes across time and space.

V. References

"COMPANY NEWS; Xerox Sues Apple Computer Over Macintosh Copyright - New York Times", n.d. http://www.nytimes.com/1989/12/15/business/company-news-xerox-sues-apple-computer-over-macintosh-copyright.html.

Dourish, Paul, and Genevieve Bell. "The Infrastructure of Experience and the Experience of Infrastructure: Meaning and Structure in Everyday Encounters with Space." Environment and Planning B: Planning and Design 34, no. 3 (2007): 414–430.

Eco, Umberto. Semiotics and the Philosophy of Language. Bloomington: Indiana University Press, 1986.

Hiltzik, Michael A. Dealers of Lightning: Xerox PARC and the Dawn of the Computer Age. HarperBusiness, 2000.

Kay, Alan C. "The Early History Of Smalltalk", n.d. http://propella.sakura.ne.jp/earlyHistoryST/EarlyHistoryST.html.

Latour, Bruno. "A Cautious Prometheus? A Few Steps Toward a Philosophy of Design (with Special Attention to Peter Sloterdijk)" (2008): 2.

Myers, Margaret, 1933- & Scarborough, Mayra & Rutgers University. Graduate School of Library Service (1975). *Women in librarianship : Melvil's rib symposium : proceedings of the eleventh annual symposium sponsored by the alumni and faculty of the Rutgers University Graduate School of Library*

Service. Bureau of Library and Information Science Research, Rutgers University Graduate School of Library Service, New Brunswick, N.J

Saunders, Barry F. CT Suite: The Work of Diagnosis in the Age of Noninvasive Cutting. Duke University Press Books, 2008.

Shapiro, Eve. Gender Circuits: Bodies and Identities in a Technological Age. Routledge, 2010.

Star, Susan Leigh. "The Ethnography of Infrastructure." American Behavioral Scientist 43, no. 3 (November 1, 1999): 377–391.

Suchman, Lucy. "Making Work Visible." Commun. ACM 38, no. 9 (September 1995): 56–ff.

Endnotes

[1] Saunders, CT Suite, 305.

[2] Kay, "The Early History Of Smalltalk."

[3] Latour, "A Cautious Prometheus?"

[4] Melvil's Rib references a women in librarianship symposium by the same name held at Rutgers University Graduate School of Library Service in 1975.

[5] Kay's wife, Bonnie MacBird wrote the story for the movie's director Steven Lisberger.

[6] Eco, Semiotics and the Philosophy of Language, 26.

[7] "COMPANY NEWS; Xerox Sues Apple Computer Over Macintosh Copyright - New York Times."

[8] Ibid.

[9] Suchman, "Making Work Visible"; Star, "The Ethnography of Infrastructure."

[10] Star, Susan Leigh. "Invisible Work and Silenced Dialogues in Knowledge Representation." In Inger V. Eriksson, Barbara A. Kitchenham, Kea G. Tijdens, Women, Work and Computerization: Understanding and Overcoming Bias in Work and Education. Amsterdam: Elsevier Science Publishers, 1991, 81- 92.

[11] Dourish and Bell, "The Infrastructure of Experience and the Experience of Infrastructure."

[12] Shapiro, Gender Circuits.

Technology Hurts

Andrew Choate

Technology hurts. And not just the stick we first used to beat each other.

It's a continuous shock to me that *lol* is more frequently transmitted than *ow* (ouch wow). Because it is always a surprise that communication technologies end up emphasizing distance rather than closeness. Ouch. It's because of the technology. Wow.

Art objects are fundamentally communication devices that function at a distance. That can hurt. It can also heal. I don't want art without a living tension like that. Technology, however, is about resolving problems and tensions. But only the conscious ones. So of course advances in technology ultimately generate more unforeseen and unpinpointable tensions below the surface of our consciousness. *Tweet: I'm fine with the collective unconscious; it's the collective consciousness that troubles me.* The goals of art are in tense opposition to the aims of technology: one seeks to address our level of inner attunement to the objects, spaces and people of our time, while the other is manufactured to help us get ahead. There is tension in that opposition too, and technology wants so bad to solve it, and it whines and throws temper tantrums about human fallibility and the inefficiency of biology and the chaos of conscience, but it is the practice of art that actually inserts itself into a seeping, infesting, affect-laden dialogue with the self that has either been *gotten ahead of* or is *getting ahead of other people.*

Herzog's art thrives in the confrontation of these tensions. Her painting *Mr. Watson Come Here I Need You* (Figure 4) directly addresses the essence of communication at a distance. The title phrase is painted in bright yellow and pinkish red acrylic, and each letter is dripping down the canvas in ghoulishly thick rivulets. The bloodlike drips and bright letters emerge from a crusty, granular brown background made of garnet crystals, looking like a cry for help echoing out of an ancient cave. It reads like a phantasmagoric horror poster, with someone, somewhere, desperately yearning for another. The words themselves are a variation on the first phrase Alexander Graham Bell spoke through the first prototype telephone. Regardless of the immediate practical necessity of the words for either Bell or his assistant Thomas Watson, it is no coincidence that the first words spoken over the telephone convey the desire to erase the distance between two people, a distance that the telephone was ostensibly designed to overcome. Instead, the distance becomes emphasized by the new technology, not transcended.

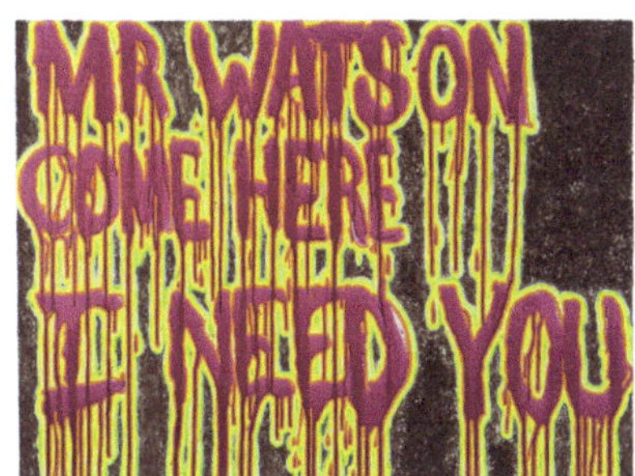

Figure 4, Plate 4, 2011.

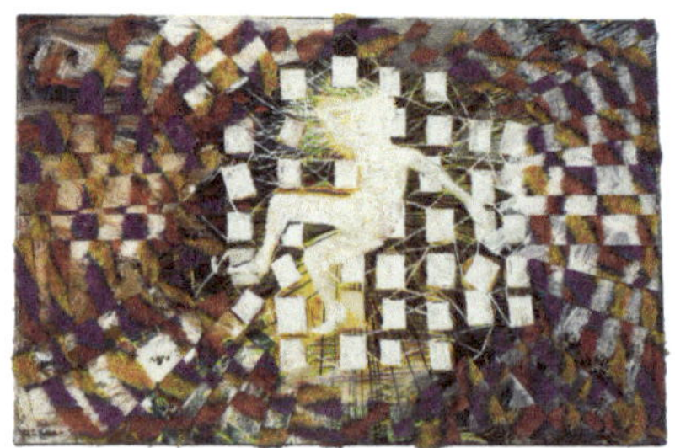

Figure 7, Plate 29, 2009.

Katie Herzog makes images that address the process of data and information entering bodies and coming back out. *Information Entropy* (Figure 7) depicts a woman's body, painted in short white strokes, in a seeming freefall through a vortex of white rectangles painted in the same shade of white as her body. These white rectangles reappear throughout her oeuvre and can be read as documents/chips of data, but in this picture the person at the literal center of this vortex is made of the same substance as the documents. A sense of swirling movement is created by the pattern of cut canvas that is circularly arranged around the body, yet there is also a sense that the body has stopped falling, and remains in the position that will later be carved in chalk as at a crime scene—legs akimbo, neck awkwardly craned, one arm outstretched and limp, the other reaching for the heart.

All living things end in death—the ultimate (ostensible) equilibrium. The urge to actively seek the inevitable homeostasis of the matter from which we are made was dubbed Thanatos, or the Death Instinct, by Freud, and appears in inextricable opposition to Eros, the drive toward creativity and procreation. It is a fight that Eros unfortunately always loses. (We can never have enough sex to overpower death, but we will die trying.) The question that Herzog's *Information Entropy* asks is what role outside stimuli—images, information—play in our immediate response to the fact of our own death. Stimuli, by their definition, are supposed to give us a spark and engage and excite our nervous system into reactions. But we're conscious of more stimuli than we can react to, so they can also overwhelm our bodies into catatonias wherein we don't have the resources to process the onslaught of information. Something has to give, and that something is often within us. *Status Update: Art is a form of gift-giving.*

The iconography of objects representing information, stimulus and communication from a distance permeate Herzog's work. Exhibiting her work within the context of XEROX, "The Document Company," makes perfect, tense sense. For the installation of her show at XEROX PARC (Palo Alto Research Center), she hung the dark painting *Documents (Heads You Lose)* (Figure 10) in the reception area. A sky of white rectangles dominates the upper half of the painting, and this time the documents have the addition of straight black drips that mimic the look of text on a page. They are hovering above a row of ten skulls smoking cigarettes that are perched on top of a curtain holding more documents, though these are diagonally oriented. Another circular swirl of small brushstrokes, this time in orangish yellow over a field of brown, forms the background at the top. In the center of that background is a red circle like a setting sun. A hazy, ghostlike and smokelike blue wafts around the skulls and their curtain at the bottom of the picture, inverting the typical landscape relationship of blue sky at top and earthtoned ground at the bottom. The documents are more menacing than the skulls, similarly inverting the power relationship of people to information. It is the documents that appear to be casting a spell, or at least a pall, over the skulls, and could be seen to have taken part in the skulls' separation from their respective bodies: the heads are literally lost. Welcome to XEROX.

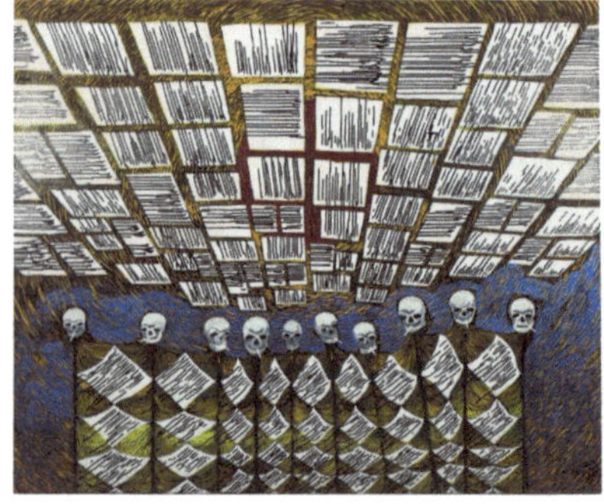

Figure 10, Plate 2, 2011.

Libraries also feature prominently in Herzog's iconography, naturally, as they are the places that hold and contain books and other assorted information deemed valuable. How the body relates to the landscape of information is always fraught. In *Today The Library Was Ripped A New Asshole* (Figure 11) over twenty bodies—most of them children, some of them ghosts—cavort inside an explosively colorful children's area. A couple kids are crouched in the fetal position against a shelf, some are flying through the air, several are climbing the shelves, one is practicing kung fu, another has his head buried in an adult's stomach—seemingly desperate for a hug—one is crawling on the floor like a dog, an older man appears to be hitting on a coy woman and one adult has given up and is lying supine on top of a shelf of books. And then there are the ghosts: three figures emerging from the bottom right corner, painted in thickly abbreviated brownish grey. The books in this library display the dense, bright colors of their spines on the shelf, but the floor is also littered with them open and no longer colorful or attractive, just piles of lightly glowing green that hint at toxicity. Not a single body is reading a book, despite the letters on the wall that command "READ," and even these letters are surrounded by a mixed-up alphabetic jumble. It is as if the open books have unleashed something in the air that makes everyone avoid the documents themselves. The closest a book gets to a person is one that looks like it has just been thrown at one of the flying children, and whose cover is lodged against his forehead. This is the place of knowledge: where the vast variety of printed wisdom is in the air, literally and figuratively, and the people within the space are unable to directly absorb it, unless you count the blow to the head.

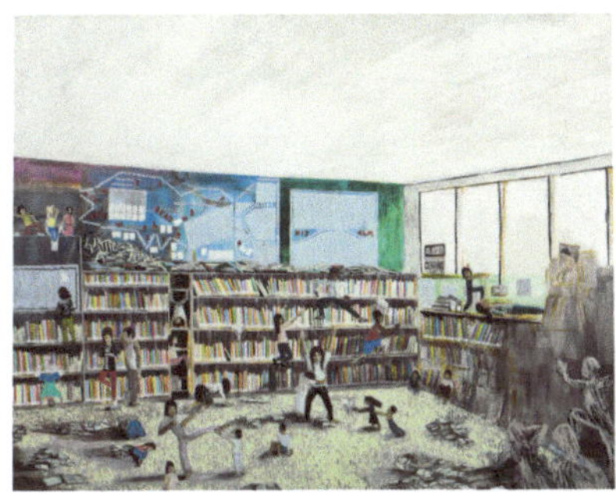

Figure 11, Plate 38, 2007.

The library scene in *Library Wedding* (Figure 9) presents the ultimate conflict between information and knowledge, and colors the library as a place of confusion. Four rows of books recede from foreground to background on the right side of the canvas, while a brown-skinned couple with downcast eyes lock their arms in the middle distance on the left: he in a blue suit, she in a wedding dress. One adult stands upright watching them, and a couple of kids pay semi-attention, one of them pretending to spy on the couple behind a row of books. Whereas libraries are about recognizing that we don't know something and are looking for it, weddings are about lovers committing to what they think they know about their spouses. The people who attend are people who also already know the people in the wedding. Documents emphasize their distance and distinctness from you: they don't change after you experience them, regardless of what happens to you. But a wedding is about the formation of a union: two people coming together to form a single entity, recognized by the state. Herzog's wedding couple have their eyes lowered: they are not taking in any new information from the library. *They know what they know.* This piece presents the confusion between how a library is supposed to function—we arrive, we get our information, we retreat—versus how we actually experience it: we arrive, we are affected, we become committed to what we know, we can't escape without a great big hassle.

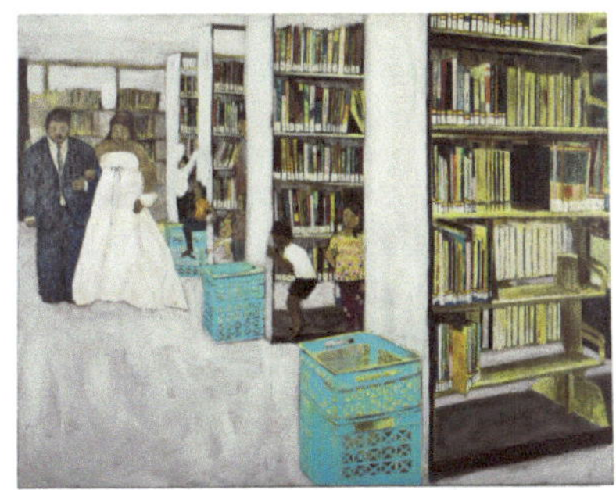

Figure 9, Plate 39, 2006.

Because libraries are containers of knowledge and not knowledge itself, they have been culturally coded as feminine, conjuring images of spectacled

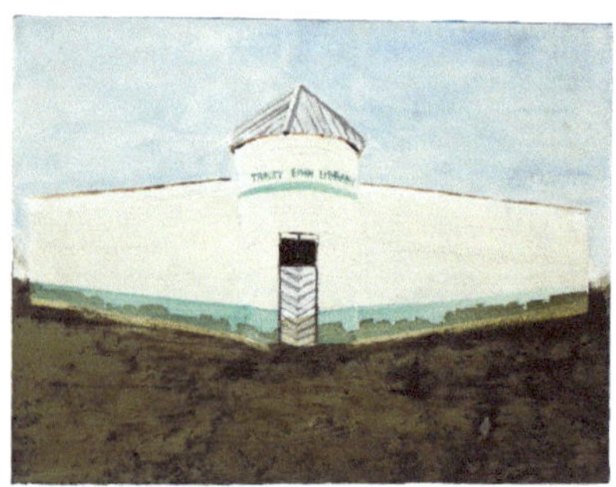

Figure 12, Plate 27, 2009.

female librarians and quiet corridors: users hope to enter them and come out enlightened. Herzog's painting *Tracey Emin Library, Uganda* (Figure 12) is a straightforward landscape of the windowless building, unpeopled and without any other surrounding architecture. It stands alone. Emin, the YBA most often associated with deeply autobiographical work dealing with her sex life, is often criticized as being unintellectual. So what does Emin do with her fame and notoriety and "unintellectuality"? She builds a library, a literal erection of—and tribute to—knowledge, in Africa. In a column for *The Independent* about the library, Emin wrote, "I often feel dissatisfied or dislocated in my life, like I am not complete. I tire of seeing the spoils of my hard work constantly pouring into a vat of myself."[1] This tiredness with the self is how she frames the desire to build the library: it is something for others. In Herzog's depiction, the library is empty of people on the outside, and we are left to imagine that it is teeming with learning on the inside. But we know better: the emptiness on the outside hides the chaos within. Because once we enter the library, it is the vat of information and documentation that pours into the self, and mixes and mingles with the vat of self already astir. The calm exterior betrays the internal conflict.

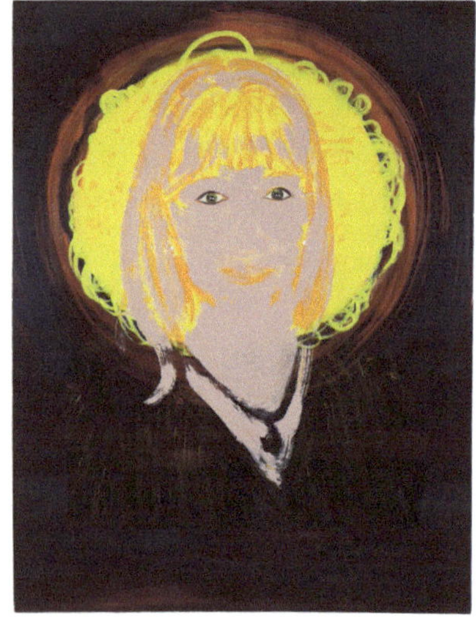

Figure 13, Plate 27, 2009.

Women and technology
Bumblebees and a shoestring tease
Such a rote rope-a-dope
That women aren't adept at technology.

At XEROX PARC Lynn Conway broke that stereotype. As a designer of the microchip, her engineering prowess was renown. Almost as equally renown after she left PARC was her story as a transexual. Herzog painted her portrait, *Lynn Conway* (Figure 13), and hung it at the end of a long hallway at PARC. Behind her head are golden swirls that resemble a halo from a distance. The background is black and dark orangey, and her torso is faintly outlined across this background in the same golden hue. She floats like mist. Current employees walked toward her portrait in long purposeful strides during Herzog's show, allowing her presence to gradually get larger and larger. Herzog's *Digital Gender Divide* (Figure 14) offers another glimpse into the swarm of technology and gender. It started life as a portrait of ladies at IBM working with punchcards, but, in a moment of aggression, Herzog struck the canvas with her brush and swooped through the typing women. The shape of that gestural line resembled a snake that she fleshed out and that we now see arcing around the picture and bending its neck to rear back, open its mouth and spew poisonous white venom. The snake has recently eaten, as evidenced by its lump, and within the arc formed by the snake's body are an assortment of poisonous plants. The snake makes sense: don't touch. The issue is volatile and dangerous and touchy and the closer you get to revealing the biological stereotyping, the closer you get to inadvertently poisoning yourself.

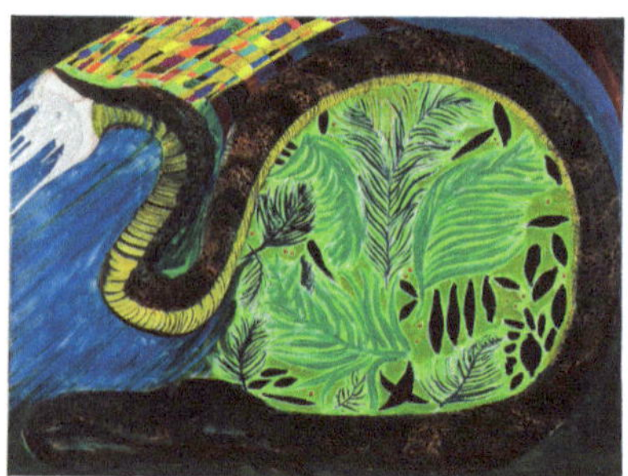

Figure 14, Plate 9, 2011.

Issues of documentation and femininity coalesce in Herzog's *Head Scarf* (Figure 15). Using a found white scarf printed with red roses, yellow daisies and small bits of ambiguous green vegetation, Herzog diffused black ink throughout the scarf, distancing the brightness of the white and the vivacity of the floral design. Four brain scans have been painted in ink onto the patterned floral print in the pattern of two rows of two that is used in medical brain scan documentation. Nebulous shapes of negative, unpainted space—simultaneously brain-like and vegetal—appear in the middle of each head: the light ink that has diffused throughout the rest of the scarf and the dark ink that forms the shape of the head make this exposed territory inside the head stand in relief. The layering and application of black to the material ultimately reveals and highlights a specific portion of the scarf that was already there, and remains untouched in the final work: the bottom layer becomes the foreground. The interior of the body has not only been made external, but has been relocated to a fashion accessory, an item explicitly designed to accentuate the body by covering a portion of it. The tension between an image as data (the way an x-ray is read) versus its literal status as a picture of a human (this is, after all, what an x-ray is) is further complicated by the idea embodied in this work: we can use information to hide ourselves, even information as deeply about ourselves as glimpses of our (supposed) internal being.

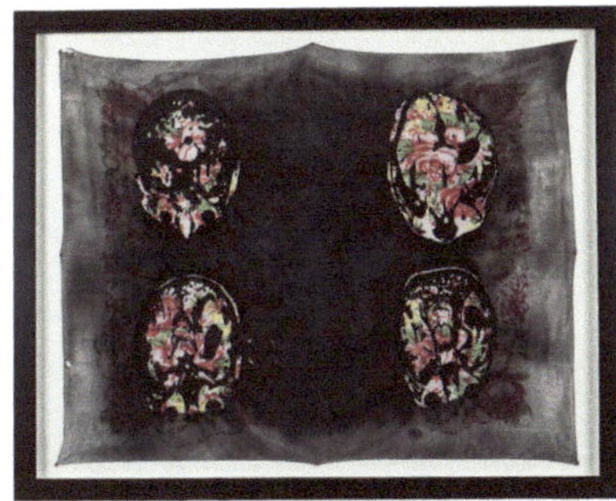

Figure 15, Plate 46, 2001.

This line of investigation continues in Herzog's series of "Cycling for Libraries Jerseys," in which she paints phrases from Norman D. Stevens' *Archives of Library Research from the Molesworth Institute* on t-shirts worn by her during a librarians' "think tank on wheels" nine-day bicycle ride from Copenhagen to Berlin. One of these shirts simply states *Freedom From Information* (Figure 16) diagonally over the back in dark red letters that are outlined with a layer of greenish blue tracing and then pink on a white t-shirt. The phrase emphasizes the need to escape the burden of information, and also the fact that another kind of freedom—a moral, spiritual and attitudinal freedom—unfolds when the body is able to resist and push back against the onslaught of information imposed on it from without. Putting this slogan and the others in this series on clothing to both wear and broadcast while pedaling from city to city twists them into advertisements for the ability to escape the psychological affects of advertising. The shirt offers literal and symbolic protection from the onslaught of elements both physical and informational. The fact that the shirt and phrase combine to become a moving document of ideational information—while explicitly expressing the need to be free of information—appears as a necessary evil equal in its phantasmagoricality to Bell's first tele-communicated phrase. Thus, it's no surprise that Herzog uses a toxic and glowing pink around these letters similar to the one she used in *Mr. Watson Come Here I Need You* (Figure 4). The convolutions and tensions that emerge from all communication—and every act is a piece of communication—mean that there is no escape from adding to the stimulus overload, even if what you add is a critique to the over stimulus. *Thank you, Wikipedia: "[T]here are many books published to encourage awareness of information overload."*[2]

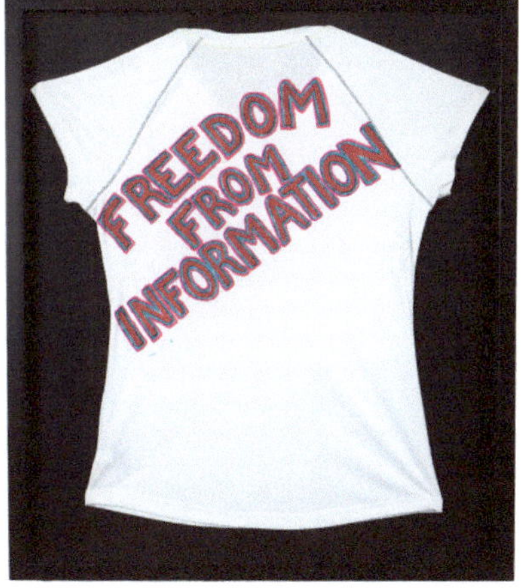

Figure 16, Plate 16, 2001.

The focus on clothing in Herzog's work can also be read as an extension of her material emphasis on the fact that a canvas is a canvas and not a pictorial plane. When she cuts it up or weaves the shards of canvas together or blends painted fibers and embroidery and burlap sacks together with canvas, we see that these objects are not just paintings attempting to represent reality, but

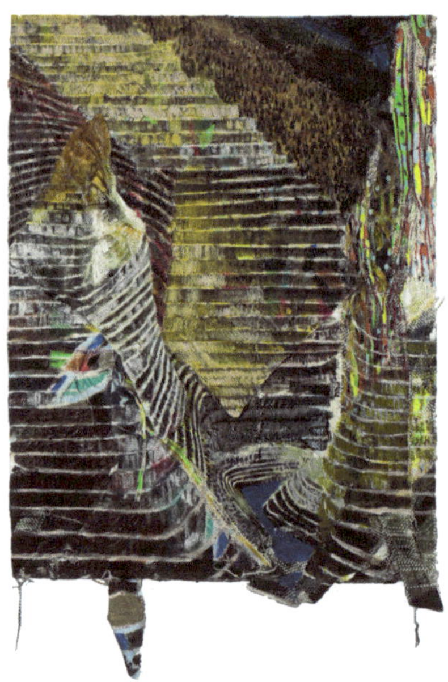

Figure 17, Plate 30, 2009.

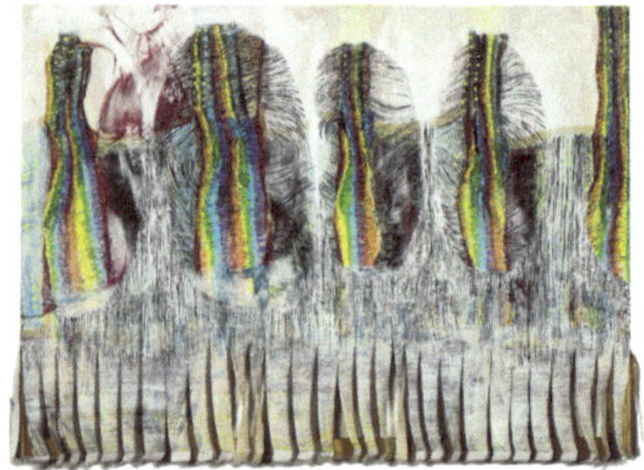

Figure 18, Plate 32, 2008.

material things that are a part of reality on their own. Extending the nuances of this idea even further, several works—*Phone Books, Quarry* (Figure 17), *Urinalysis* (Figure 18), *You Are Here* (Figure 19), etc.—feature strips of canvas that hang from the bottom, evoking flyers posted on telephone poles and in coffee shops and community centers that advertise local services, sales and band members needed by individuals in the neighborhood, and which include relevant contact information in small, evenly cut strips of paper at the bottom: take one and get in touch later.

In the center of *Urinalysis* (Figure 17) are three large fingerprints in black ink, with vertical rainbows flowing through their centers. These fingerprints are surrounded by vertical black lines of the same thickness that flow down into the tops of the cut portion of the canvas. A vague discoloration, like the canvas itself has been soaked in an unidentified liquid, permeates the background. While both urinalysis and fingerprinting are used to test someone—did you do drugs? are you pregnant? were you at the crime scene? are you who you say you are?—the hanging strips function like an offering: would you like to take a part of me home with you? do you want to touch me? can I help you? do you need something? The fingerprints themselves are the traces of a touch, enlarged and playfully rainbow-accented. Instead of taking the fingerprints and urine away for cloistered laboratory analysis, they are put on display. The combination of the inviting strips with the uniquely personal and identity-defining fingerprints in the center enhance the artwork's effort to not only communicate at a distance, but extend the effort into an attempt to touch another, both physically and metaphorically. This pursuit of touch, in all its metaphorical glory, is what separates the creative impulse from the fixing of identity in the conscious, technological drive toward resolution and the ultimate homeostasis of equilibrium. "[I] put all of my emotion into my pieces and hope there is some human contact," Herzog said of her method and state of mind while working.[3] Data and testing can only get us so far, especially when what we're ultimately after is the thriving and writhing of a generative connection.

C is for Cookie (Figure 2) also features little things hanging beseechingly from the bottom: fringed tassels belonging to a wool blanket that evoke the body and the tactile experience of covering up for warmth and protection. The piece is a grey blanket that already had patterned vertical striations of white, green, yellow, orange, red, black and brown across it. Herzog slightly shifted the pattern and perspective by selectively repainting portions of the stripes and background greys, and then adding two eyeballs and a black mouth, forming the shape of the Cookie Monster holding up both the letter "C" and a cookie. This image is a direct reference to the first image to be sent from one computer to another in 1973, and it happened at PARC. Journalist Michael Hiltzik, in *Dealers of Lightning: XEROX PARC and the Dawn of the Computer Age*[4] described the scene of how this image moved from one computer (the Nova) to another (the Alto), and the revolutionary feel it had at the time:

The Alto's operating software hadn't yet been written, so its brains resided temporarily in a commercial minicomputer called a Nova[...] A few members of the lab had crafted a sort of animated test pattern by converting several drawings of Sesame Street's Cookie Monster into sequences of digital ones and zeros. Thacker switched a flip or two and the bitstream flowed over the cables from the Nova into the Alto's own processor and memory. There it was reordered into machine instructions that governed which of the display screen's half-million dots, or "pixels," were to be turned on and which were to be left dark. If it worked properly, this process would produce the series of test images in black outline against a glowing white background.

Everyone's eyes focused on the screen as it flickered to life. Suddenly the pattern appeared. As the group watched, transfixed, Cookie Monster stared back at them, shaggy and bug-eyed and brandishing its goofy grin, flashing upon the screen while holding the letter C in one hand and a cookie in the other.

That the image itself stood in absurd counterpoint to the sheer power of the technology didn't matter. The message was not in the content, any more than the world-altering significance of the telephone could have been found one century earlier within the literal meaning of the words, "Mr. Watson, come here, I want you." (p. xxii - xxiii)

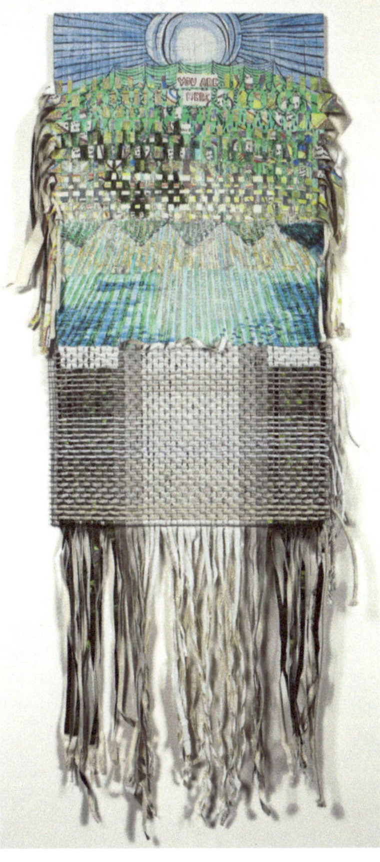

Figure 19, Plate 37, 2008.

An incredible, indelible scene, to be sure. Herzog's image recreates this scene as a static image by painting it on a woven blanket that has thousands of individual threads that form a field of cushiony dots, mirroring the original pixels, while the pre-existing striations—and her altering of them—amplify the sense of low-bandwidth image-loading: one line at a time. The Cookie Monster's defining speech is broken English and non-linguistic phonemes—"Me want cookie!" and "Om nom nom nom"—a characteristic that couldn't have been lost on Herzog, who said "a lot of the work in this show is the result of not having words for things."[5]

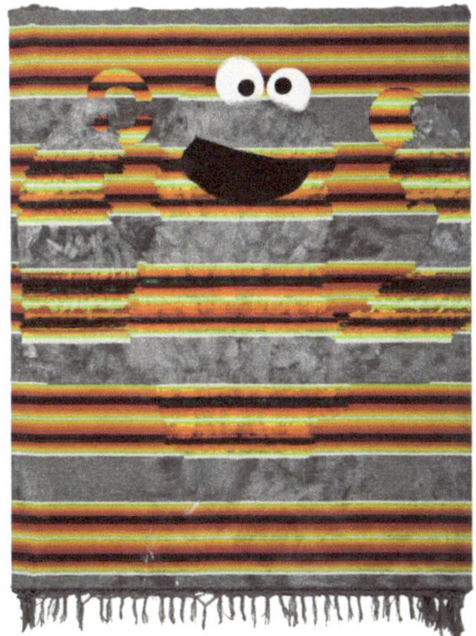

Figure 2, Plate 1, 2011.

Despite Hiltzik's claim to the contrary, the fact that the Cookie Monster was the first image broadcast from one computer to another using solely digital coding as communication is significant. The Cookie Monster's character is defined by his voraciousness: he not only eats cookies, but also inedible objects. The Cookie Monster, as first representative of the computer age, is an entity whose only function is to perpetuate itself by means of appropriating and incorporating into himself everything that is other than himself, continually widening his circle of consumption to consume even the indigestible. Nothing is unsusceptible to his appetite. "[H]is primary craving is cookies, but he can (and often does) consume anything and everything, from apples and pie to letters, flatware and hubcaps."[6] Hiltzik's contention that "the message was not in the content" reveals a misunderstanding of Marshall McLuhan, a misreading of who the Cookie Monster is, and a lack of critical foresight about the cultural shape of things to come that were set in motion by this event: the computer age we're currently living in and from which perspective Hiltzik is ostensibly writing from. The Cookie Monster *is* the message: he is a preternaturally prescient representation of the voraciousness and effectiveness of the computer's infestation into every facet of our lives, the primordial ur-document of the computer age. Herzog's decision to hang her version of it in the welcome area of PARC, and with only a doorway separating it from *Documents (Heads You Lose)* (Figure 9), reflects a complex ambivalence mixed with a fear of the power of the digitization of

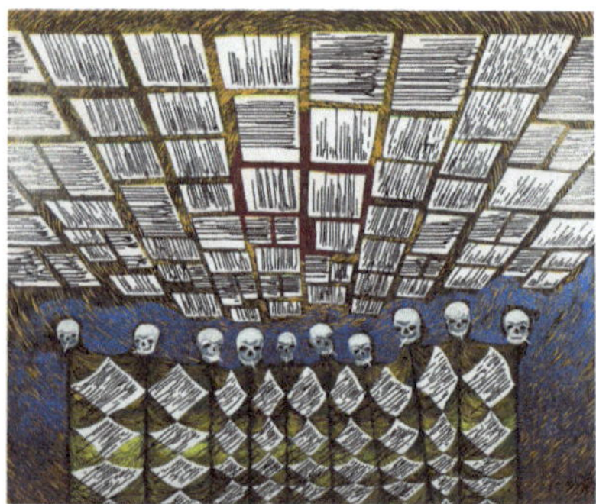

Figure 10, Plate 2, 2011.

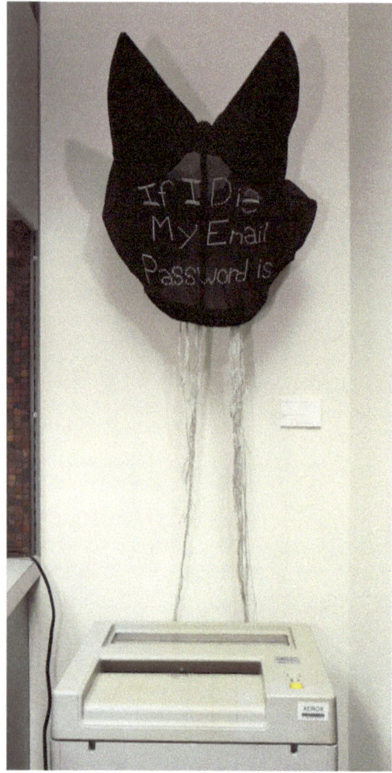

Figure 20, Plate 11, 2011.

information: the supposedly benign influence and attractive image of the Cookie Monster is literally juxtaposed with disembodied skulls smoking in a claustrophobic dungeon of documents.

I've touched a little bit on the power of the placement of work in Herzog's show, but a couple additional pieces deserve attention in this context as well. Her sculpture *If I Die My Email Password Is* (Figure 20) was hung over the scanner in the copy room. The sculpture is a horse fly mask (used for protecting a horse's face from flies), with white embroidery spelling out the text of the title. Several dozen white strings (again) hang loosely from the sculpture and disappear behind the scanner, hinting that the sculpture may be plugged in, or at least connected to the machine underneath. The mask itself is a large, ominous black shape with big pointy ears. The absent horse's head haunts the shape like a memento mori, yet the "If" of the title calls into question the inevitability of death. A belief in the power of technology is coupled with the possibility of escaping death, and also, importantly, with the more quotidian matter of preserving and archiving, or at least accessing the contents of an old email account. There is also an undeniable humor in this piece—in the idea that a horse may have an email account—yet we all recognize that Mr. Ed would surely have a Twitter feed if he were on the air today. In a grim and perverse way, *If I Die My Email Password Is* also alludes to the relatively routine steps required for enacting a post mortem correspondence. The ultimate desire underlying the generation of technology for its own sake becomes a refraction of the artist's desire to make art for art's sake: immortality. The sculpture also hangs over a scanner, a piece of technology that reads a document but does not give you one back, like a copier. Instead, it holds the document in the purely digital realm, and awaits instructions about modification or transference rather than manufacturing an object: it takes documents and transforms them into another virtual state, not unlike the movement from life to death.

On another wall in the same copy room, Herzog hung *Freedom (Richard Stallman Folk Dancing)* (Figure 21). Stallman, who is revered now for his advocacy and design of free software and open-course coding, clashed with XEROX in the early 1980s over their unwillingness to share the source code for the copy machine they donated to the AI lab where he worked at MIT. That clash between the potential he recognized in the machine versus the proprietary coding of what made the machine function became the impetus for his creation of the Free Software Movement. He is shown in the painting flying across a rainbow and a light blue sky while wearing a traditional Greek folk dancing outfit, with his feet together, arms outstretched and long hair gloriously adrift. He is not shown with machines or codes, but instead engaged in one of his hobbies: folk dancing. And in the sky, to boot. Freedom and joy are his modus operandi. Installing an image of him in between two copy machines at XEROX is the perfect tribute, as he appears to bless the multiplication of documents, and perhaps even slyly hope that what is being copied is in violation of copyrights (which he deems overbearing and in opposition to the formation of community) and will instead now be widely and freely distributed.

Let's talk about drugs, baby, psychedelics and shrooms, yummy, the counterculture in silicon valley, whoopee! The influence of 1960s counterculture on the rise of silicon valley is recounted in detail in journalist John Markoff's *What The Dormouse Said: How the Sixties Counterculture Shaped the Personal Computer Industry.*[7] On Steve Jobs and dropping acid, Markoff writes "[Jobs] still believed that taking LSD was one of the two or three most important things he had done in his life" (Ibid, xix). The West Coast, and the Bay Area in particular, was the locus of significant psychedelic experimentation, whether with or without Owsley, Ken Kesey and the Merry Pranksters. The International Foundation for Advanced Study (IFAS) in Menlo Park was specifically set up to explore "the therapeutic uses of LSD" (Markoff, p. 59), but it was "[e]ngineers rather than medical professionals [who] led the project" (Ibid, p. 59). Doug Engelbart, inventor of the mouse, was one of the more than 350 scientists, researchers, engineers and architects to take acid under the guidance of IFAS, whose research objective was to discover if LSD could improve rational cognitive abilities in addition to providing colorful mind-expanding hallucinations (Ibid, p. 65). This era and this area weren't just about the psychedelic drugs, though. Anti-war activism was rampant. In the 1960s Robert Taylor was an employee in the Department of Defense and a central figure working on the ARPANET (Advanced Research Projects Agency Network), the core network of which became the internet. As an engineer in the Department of Defense, he made several trips to Vietnam to "straighten out the information systems that were being used to report the progress of the military effort to Lyndon Johnson in the White House[...] Critics subsequently argued that the American failure in Vietnam was due in large part to the over-reliance on a body-count algorithm, which ignored the real world policies of the civil war. It fell to Taylor to rationalize the body count[...]By the end of his second trip, he was convinced the U.S. military had no business being in Southeast Asia" (Ibid, pp. 74-75). This man became a co-founder of XEROX PARC.

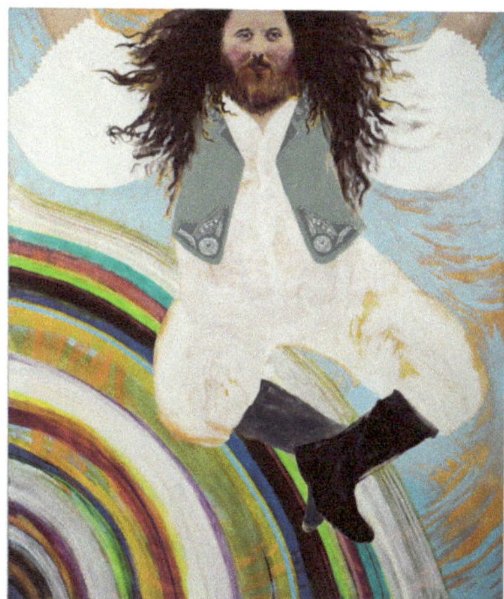

Figure 21, Plate 31, 2008.

Herzog's work in the show at PARC primarily references this history and the influence of the counterculture through the use of color. I've already discussed several pieces containing rainbows, but she also incorporates a motif of prismatic grids of bright colors that counterbalance and make polyvalent the grave and dire consequences of information and documentation I've covered. Directly behind the venomous snake's head in *Digital Gender Divide*, which I discussed above in the context of gender and technology, lurks a kaleidoscopic slab of colors. The pleasantness of the colorful array contrasts with the viciousness of the snake's open mouth and the whiteness of the venom dripping from its jaw. The free love and psychedelic color in the background of the counterculture may be kept 'in the back of the mind'—just as this grid seems to be emanating from the back of the snake's head—but the reality for women is that they were often neglected and excluded from engaging in active roles in the formation of the technologies appearing at the time. The rhetoric and surface of the counterculture was really just a background compared to the foreground reality of precariousness for women, especially single women attempting to singlehandedly support their families and gain employment in this field. Rapidly rising divorce rates in the early 60s meant that not every mother was free to bliss out and make the expansion of her consciousness a priority. Free love in the bedroom, sure; equality in the meeting room or laboratory, nah. Additionally, there is a dark side to psychedelics, just as there is to the omnipresent accessibility and imposition of information made possible with computer technology, as this spray of color associated with the dangerous snake reveals. *Warning*.

The issue of pleasantness and the pleasure taken in looking at a work of art vitally informs Herzog's aesthetic. The pieces in this catalog are a sensual pleasure to look at. Color abounds, light bounces playfully in Herzog's spaces and soars off the page. The physical joy she takes in the act of painting is apparent. Just because her subjects are complex doesn't mean the works aren't a pleasure to look at. She loves color, and in the series of works she made for this show, she found multiple subjects that warranted an engagement with color, even if that engagement was done under the guise of problematizing commonplace yet volatile issues and notions. Regarding the place of beauty in her work, she said, "the debate started long ago when I was a girl becoming conscious of gender. I remember throwing a penny into a wishing well and hoping to be ugly when I grow up. I think I was terrified of the implications of femininity in our society and possibly men in general, although I was too young to really understand that and articulate it. I may have been using painting as a platform to reject 'beauty' (through awkward figuration, ripped surfaces, and garish palette for example)."[8] Her large acrylic painting on burlap and canvas *On Denoting (stat rosa pristina nomine nomina nuda tenemus)* (Figure 22) explicitly addresses 'the ugly': the book on the table in the center of the painting is open to a page that reads only "Le Laid" (The Ugly) across the pages. A color rendition of a Paul Delvaux engraving, Herzog's layered work in acrylic is painted in the drabbiest of drab colors (lots of browns) and even the interesting colors like pastel green and navy blue and garnet are juxtaposed with so many varieties of sloppy orange and crummy brown that they lose their luster. Wax strings in a multiplicity of colors are glued in a tangled mess down each side of the main canvas, but the arrangement of these colors makes them look like detritus from a failed sewing project, especially compared with the vibrant patterning with which Herzog uses these exact colors in her more psychedelic paintings. Hanging off of this main canvas and folding out over the floor is a long flap of burlap onto which Herzog has sewn "stat rosa pristina nomine nomina nuda tenemus" in mirrored letters. These Latin words are the last lines of Umberto Eco's 1980 novel *The Name of the Rose*. They can be translated as "Yesterday's rose endures only in name/ we hold only empty names". Herzog's own title for this piece, *On Denoting*, emphasizes the crux of the problem: giving something a name both changes the thing named and has the potential to last longer than the thing named. Even if the thing changes over time (the ugly becomes beautiful or vice versa), the name or label lingers. Willfully calling something ugly and painting the name-calling into a picture inverts the role of artist and critic while also freeing the image to live another life outside of the name-calling. The text is sewn into the burlap in fiery pink, yellow and orange, with various threads squiggling like live worms, giving the sense that the words themselves are a decomposing corpse, and therefore have the possibility of decomposing just like matter.

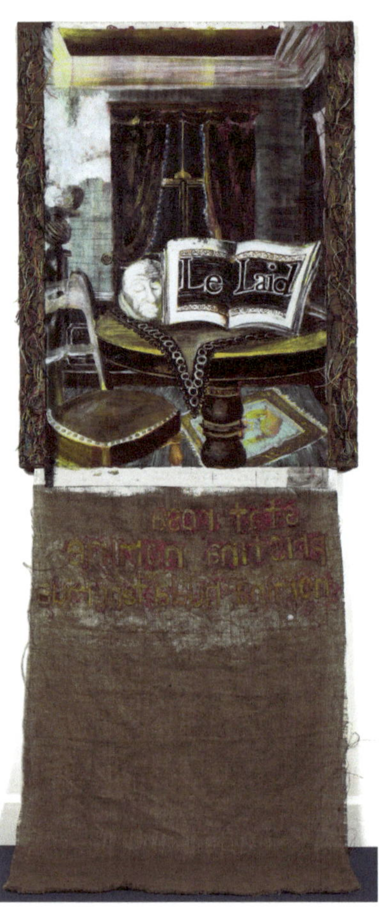

Figure 22, Plate 25, 2010.

Language as painted, sewn and embroidered text proliferates in Herzog's work: they become things. In my interview with her, she mentioned how in the past she was "an extremely intuitive worker who processed emotion by working through stuff in the studio. But for [this series] I started a lot of works coming from thinking about language and not having words for things." So she made words into things. Her painting *California Substance Abuser* (Figure 23) brings her recurrent motifs of drugs, California culture, information and language together in a hilarious and poignant image. The background canvas is painted a smooth white, and in the middle is another rectangle of thicker white in the shape of a license plate. Consistent with the California license plate, "California" is painted in a cursive red at the top, and the letters "*SBSTNCABSR*" are painted in wrinkly blue. Language is made into an object on license plates, especially personalized plates, which are both self-advertising and government-identifying. Painting a personalized license plate onto a canvas turns language into an object twice over. The fact that there are too many letters to practically fit on this particular plate if it was manufactured in the real world underscores the nature of what it communicates: this person is either on drugs or regularly abusing them, so what fits in practical reality is not their concern. To request this license plate from the state is to hope to advertise what is usually private and hidden: drug addiction. To amplify the point, she installed this painting next to the restroom at PARC. The office restroom is the ultimate place where the essence of private acts become semi-public (who is that in the stall next to me? who left that piece of pizza floating in the toilet? what is wrong with that woman? what's that on my face?). Vowels are the melismatic liquid that make speech possible, and the dearth of vowels—except "A", the first letter of the alphabet—makes the phrase "*SBSTNCABSR*" literally unspeakable in its current form, despite the fact that it's meaning can be grasped. Appropriately enough, since the experience of drug abuse does not translate into language: try explaining an acid trip. *California Substance Abuser* represents another facet of the gaps that open up in that act of communication.

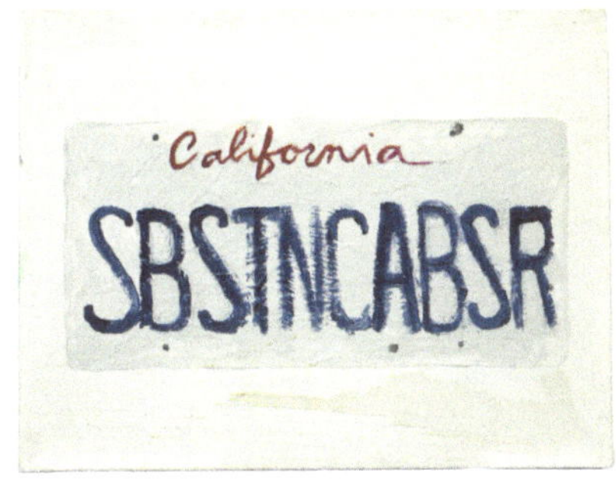

Figure 23, Plate 42, 2005.

The title of Herzog's show at PARC, "Object-Oriented Programming", refers to modularly built information systems that allow relatively independent pieces or strings or lines of code to communicate with each other: they become movable, reproducible objects. From phenomenology to psychoanalysis to neuroscience to computer programming, the relationship between two objects coming together is what forms knowledge and fosters higher cognition. In our computer age, after the impact of mechanical reproduction has been absorbed into our bodies and psyches, Herzog manufactures unique paintings that communicate with each other and with the Other of technology. These pieces address the power of words and information to be things that physically affect us. Replicating/ doubling/ embodying/ one-step-furthuring that power, she makes them into things, with the effect that the viewer is put into the position of both experiencing the thing and becoming enlightened as to the process of how the information becomes a thing. The struggle of that experience—wading through information and unrequested stimulus—is a process that cannot be escaped. Learning to cope is learning how to touch and be touched.

Endnotes

[1] Emin, Tracey. "Tracey Emin: My Life In A Column." The Independent. (January 25, 2008) http://www.independent.co.uk/news/world/africa/tracey-emin-my-life-in-a-column-773709.html
[2] Wikipedia. "Information Overload." http://en.wikipedia.org/wiki/Information_overload.
[3] Interview with the author, April 20, 2012.
[4] Hiltzik, Michael A. Dealers of Lightning: Xerox PARC and the Dawn of the Computer Age. HarperBusiness, 2000.
[5] Interview with the author, April 20, 2012.
[6] Muppet Wiki. "Cookie Monster." http://muppet.wikia.com/wiki/Cookie_Monster
[7] Markoff, John. What The Dormouse Said: How the Sixties Counterculture Shaped the Personal Computer Industry. Penguin Books, 2005.
[8] Interview with the author, April 20, 2012.

Plates

Plate 1
(opposite page)
C is for Cookie (PARC)
2011

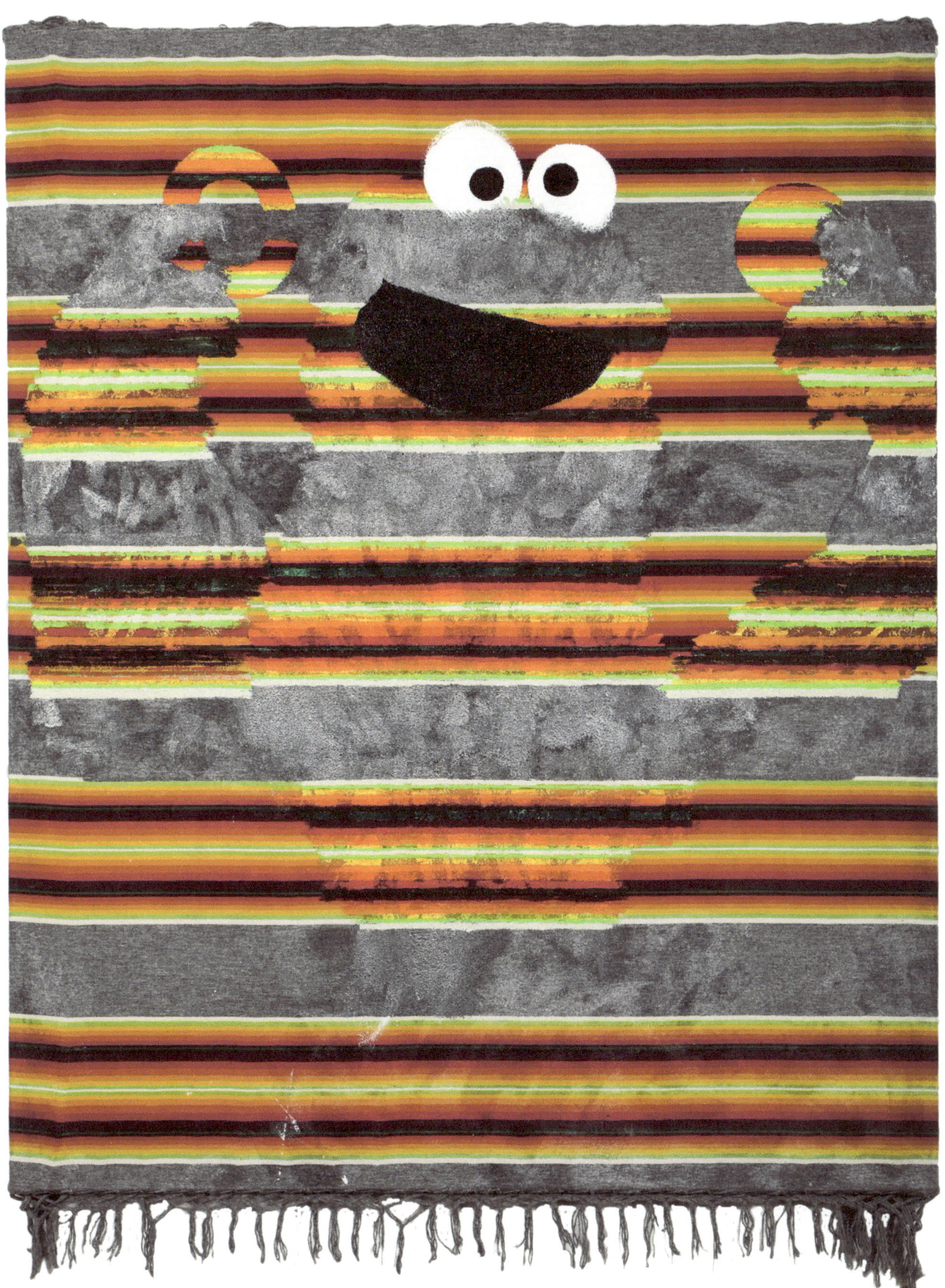

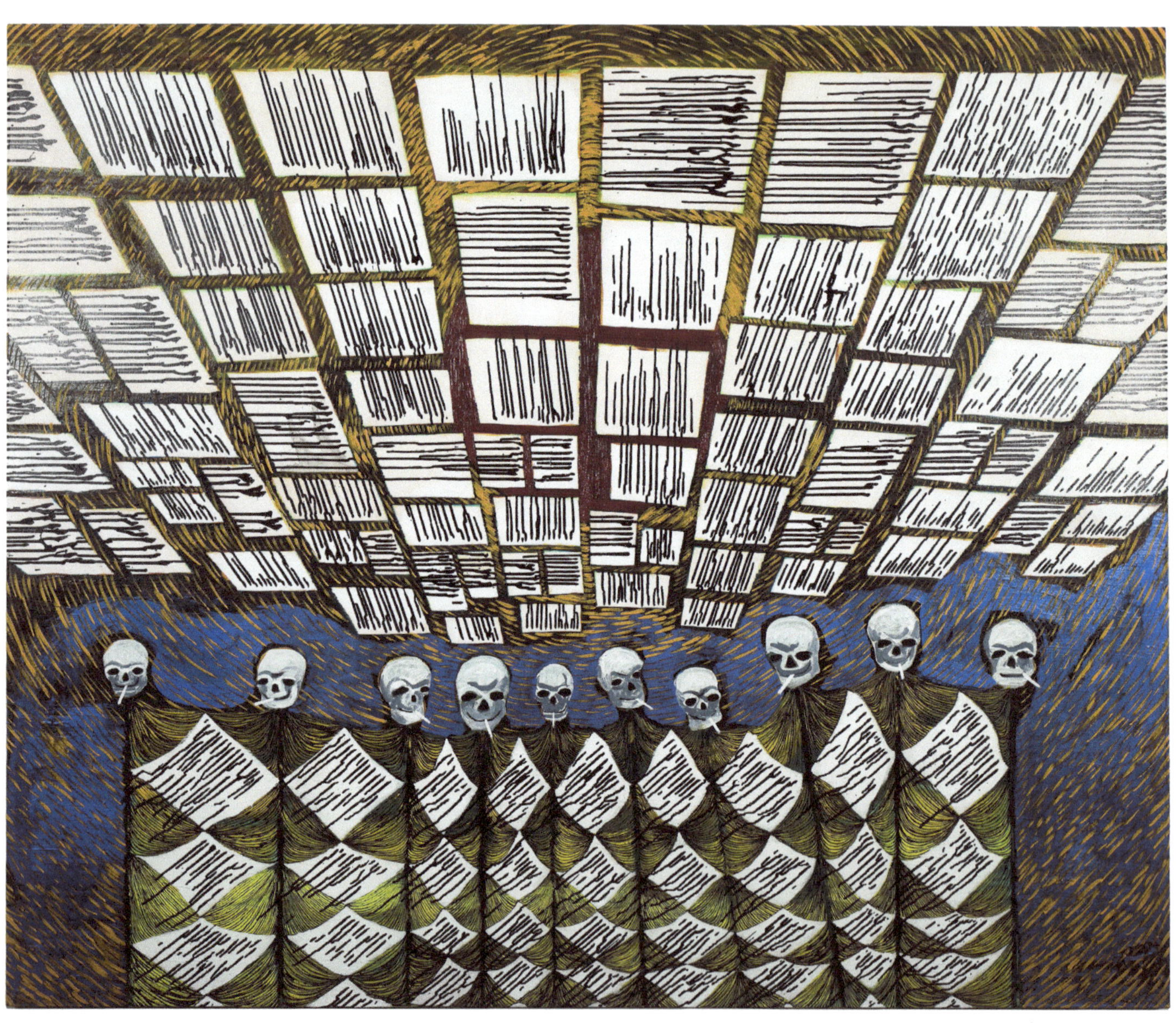

Plate 2
Documents (Heads You Lose)
2011

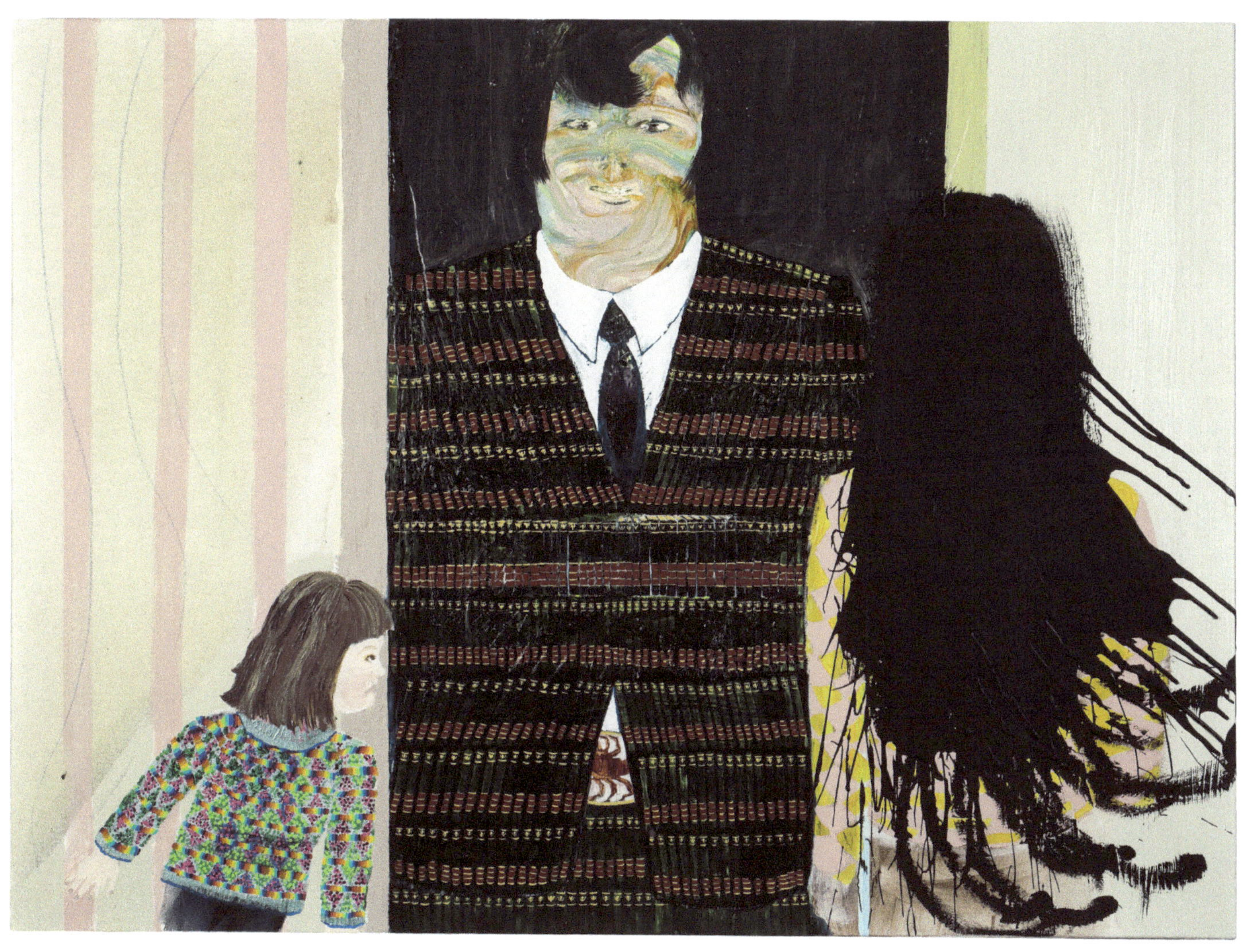

Plate 3
Door to Door Encyclopedia Salesman
2011

Plate 4
Mr. Watson Come Here I Need You
2011

Plate 5
(opposite page)
Pío Pico
2011

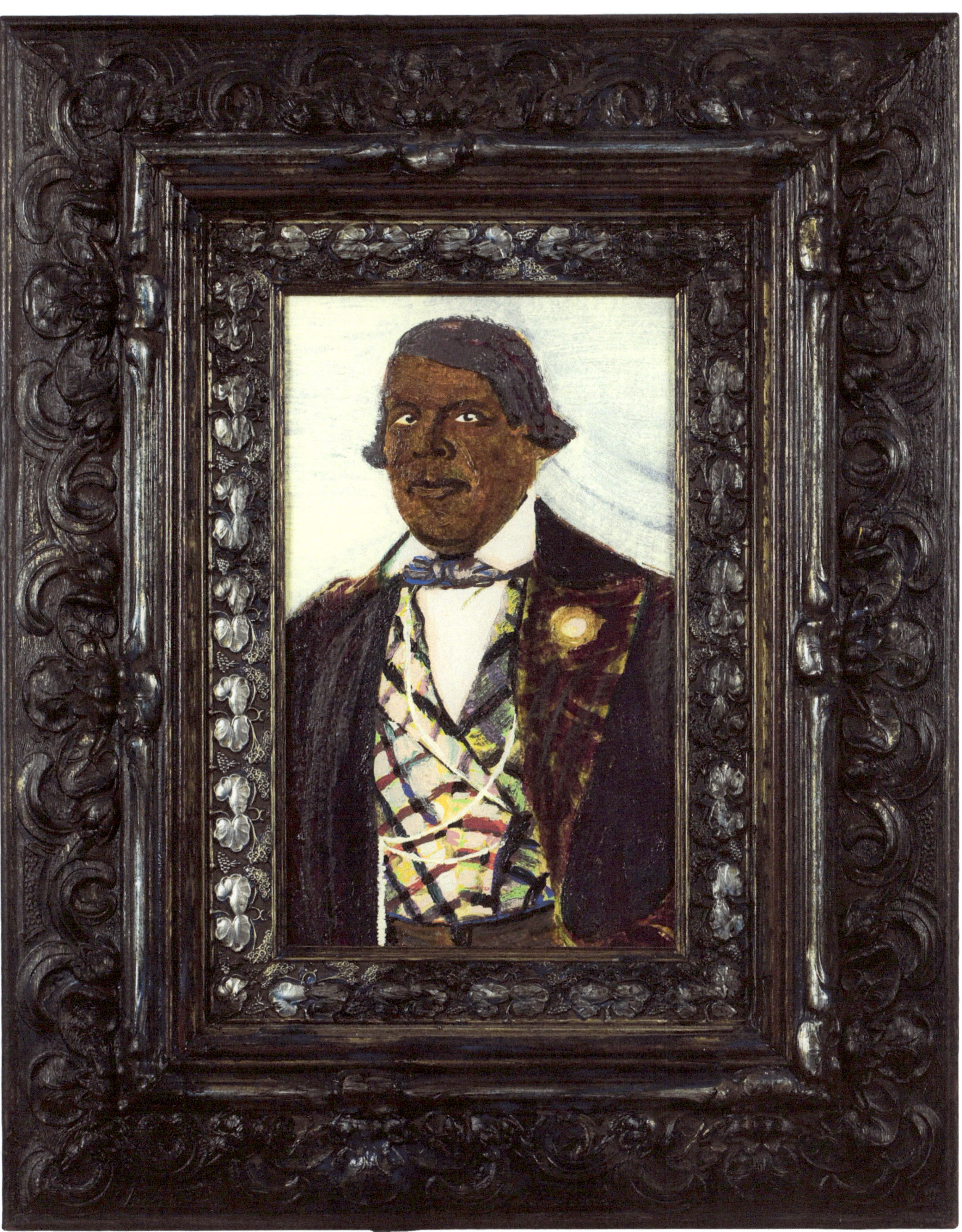

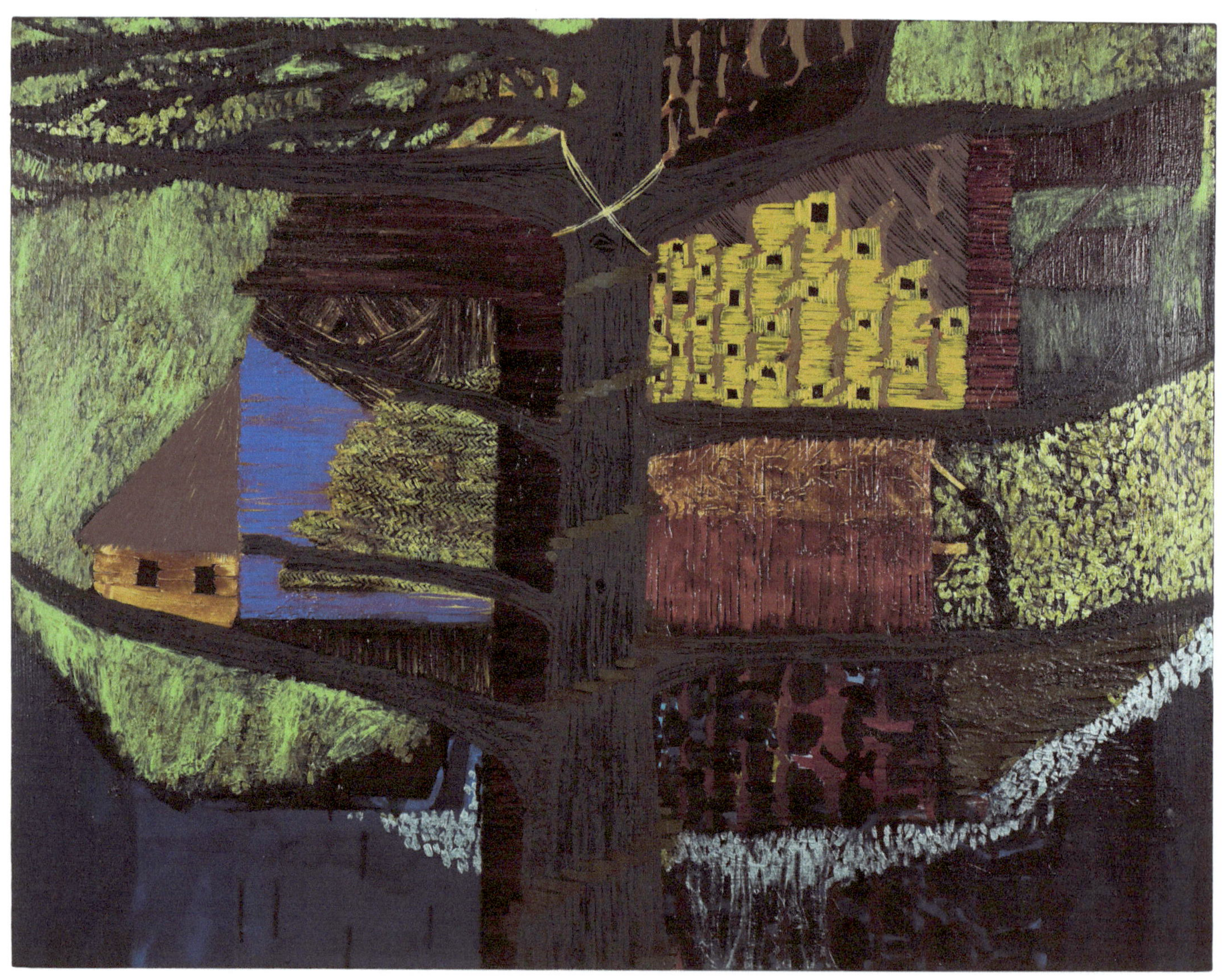

Plate 6
Doug Engelbart, Red Cross Library, The Philippines
2011

Plate 7
(opposite page)
Lynn Conway
2011

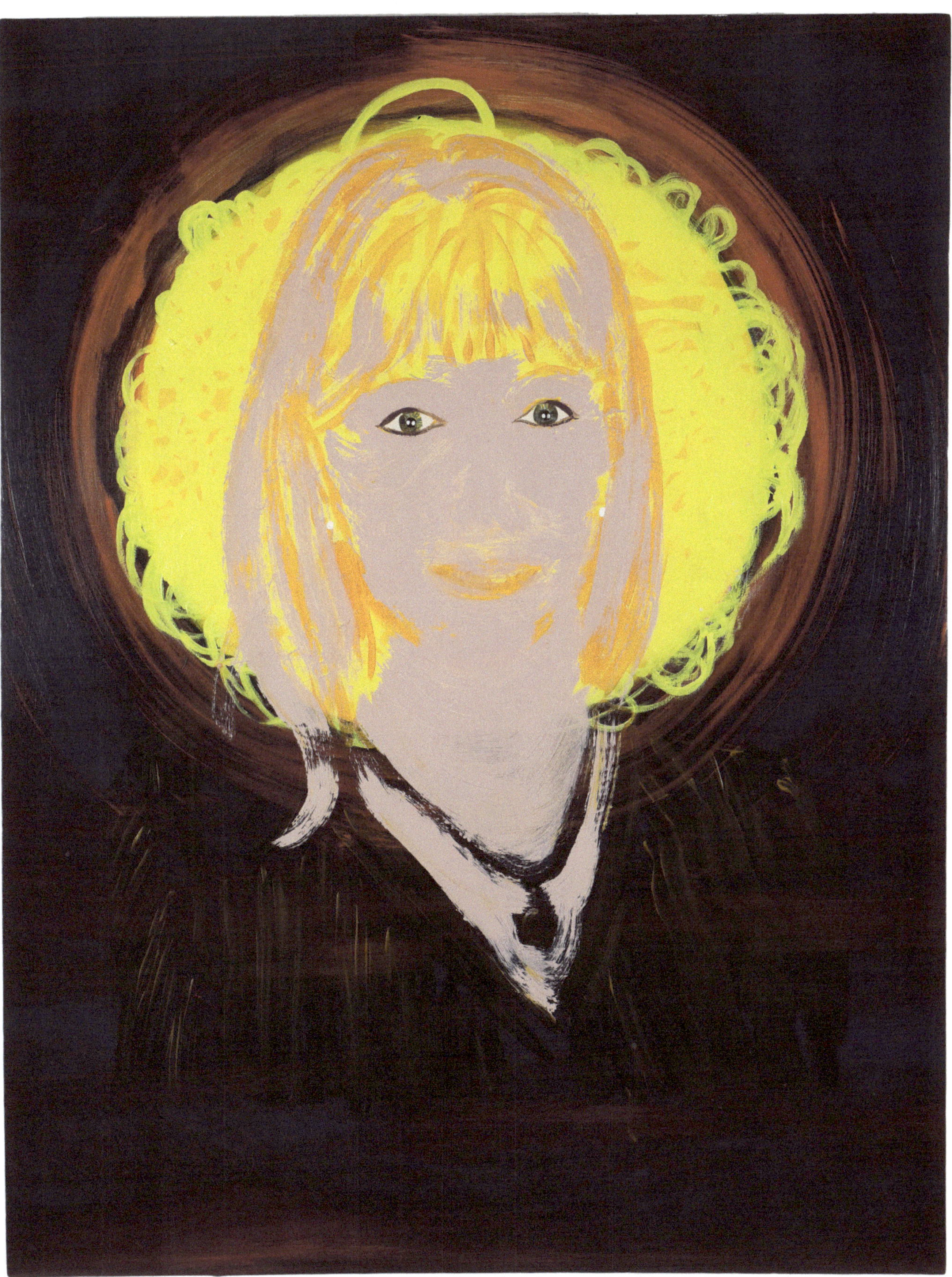

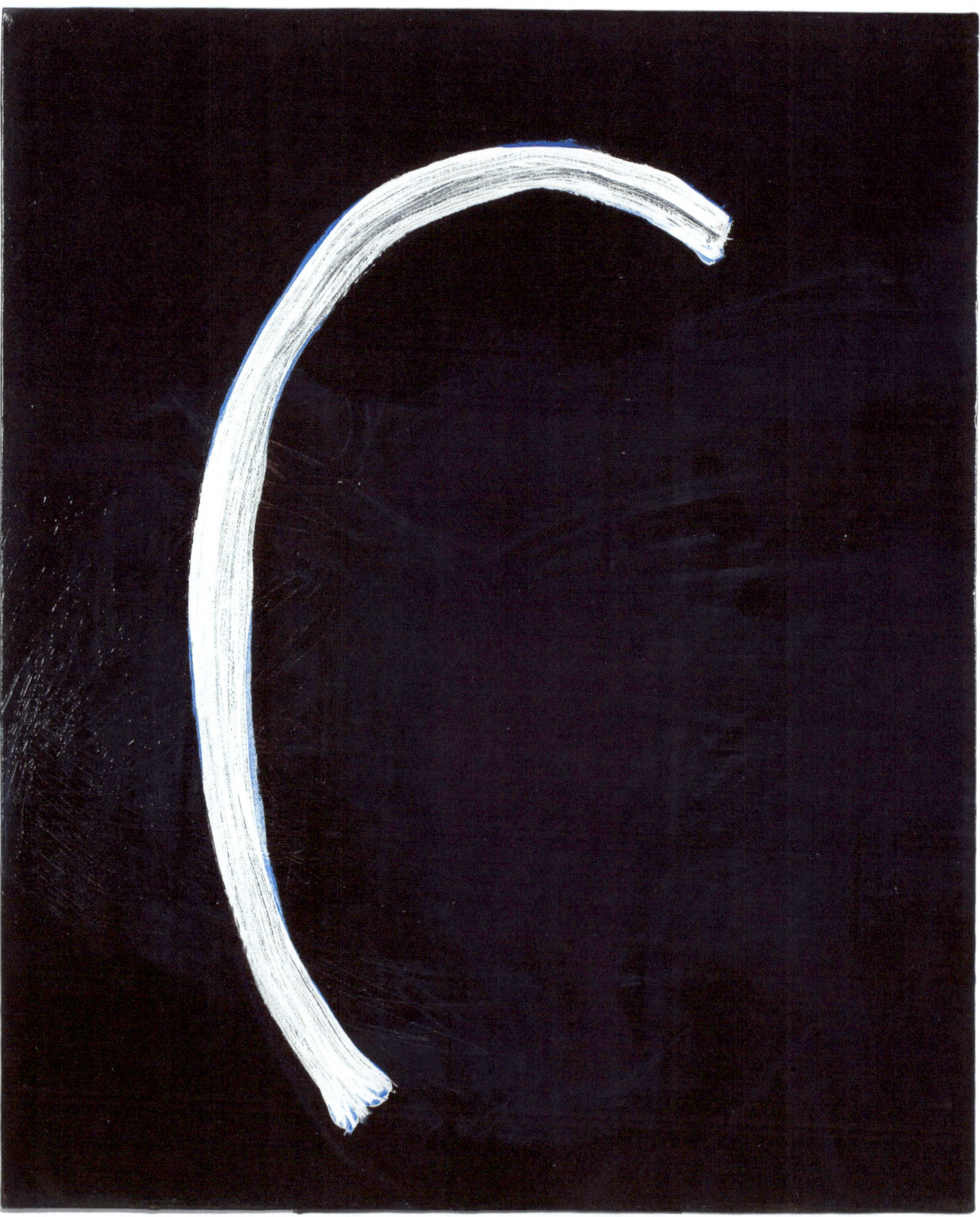

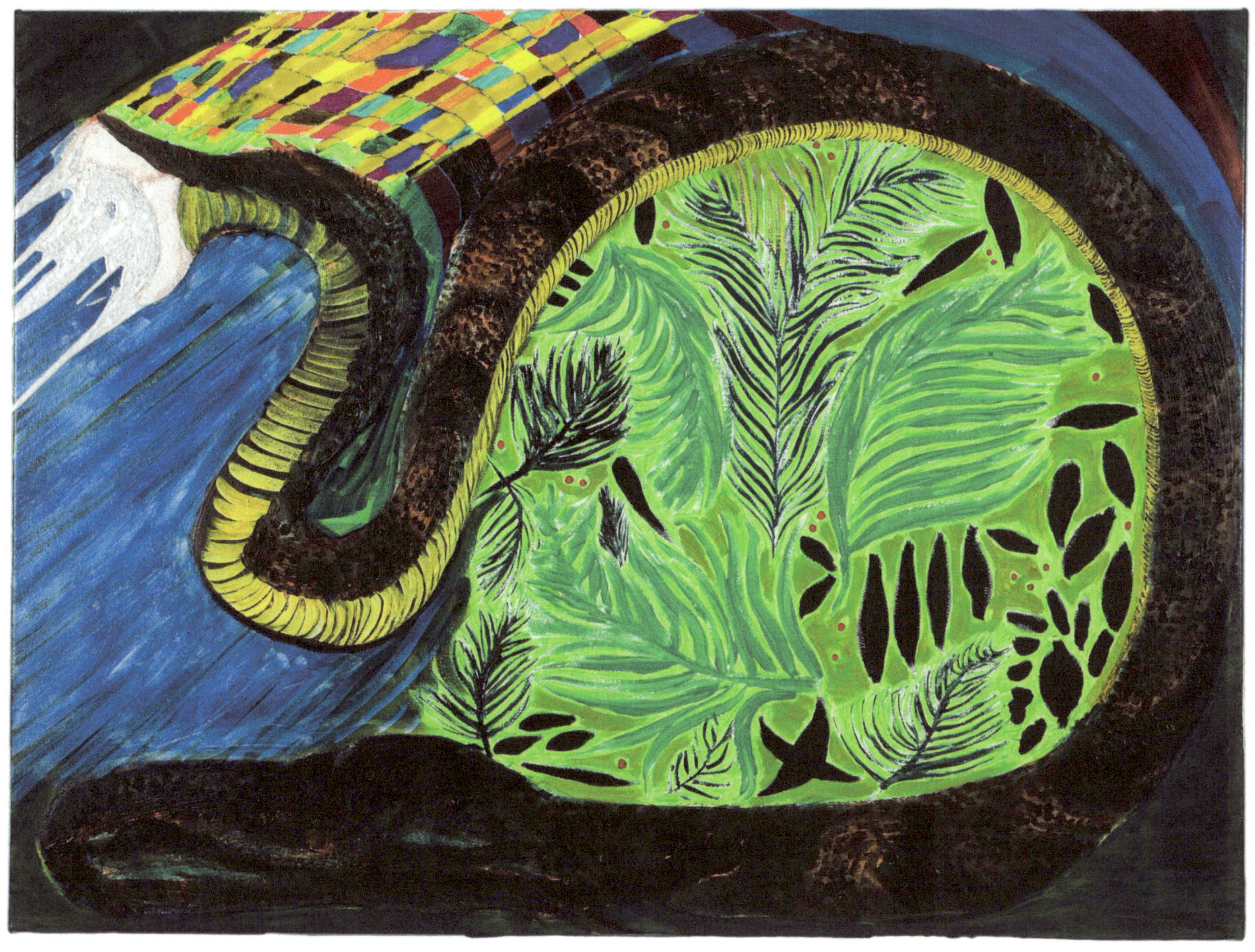

Plate 8
(opposite page)
Melvil's Rib (Dewey)
2011

Plate 9
Digital Gender Divide
2011

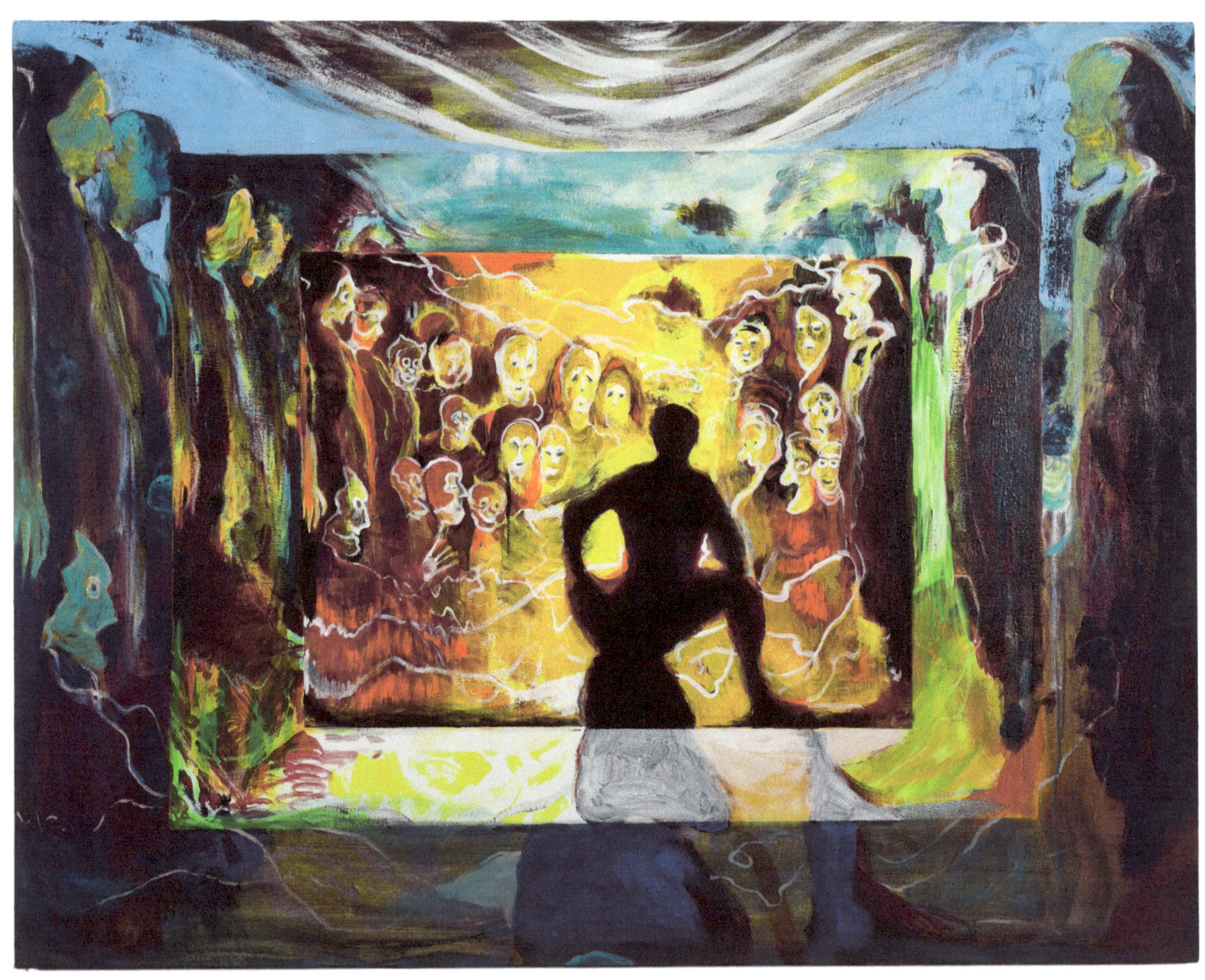

Plate 10
The Owners Historic Lesson
(Flag 1954 - 1955)
2011

Plate 11
(opposite page)
If I Die My Email Password Is
2011

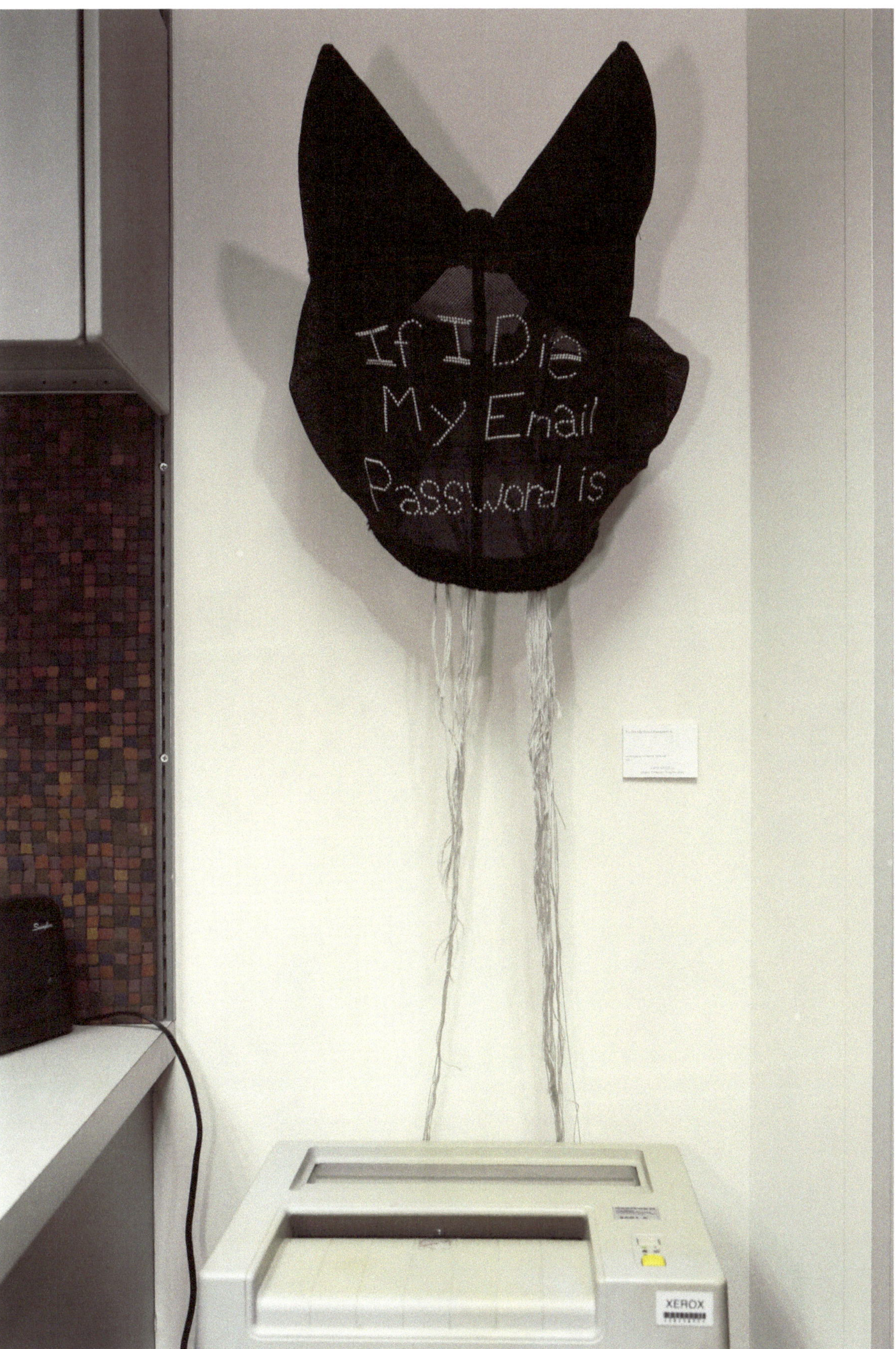
If I Die
My Email
Password is
XEROX

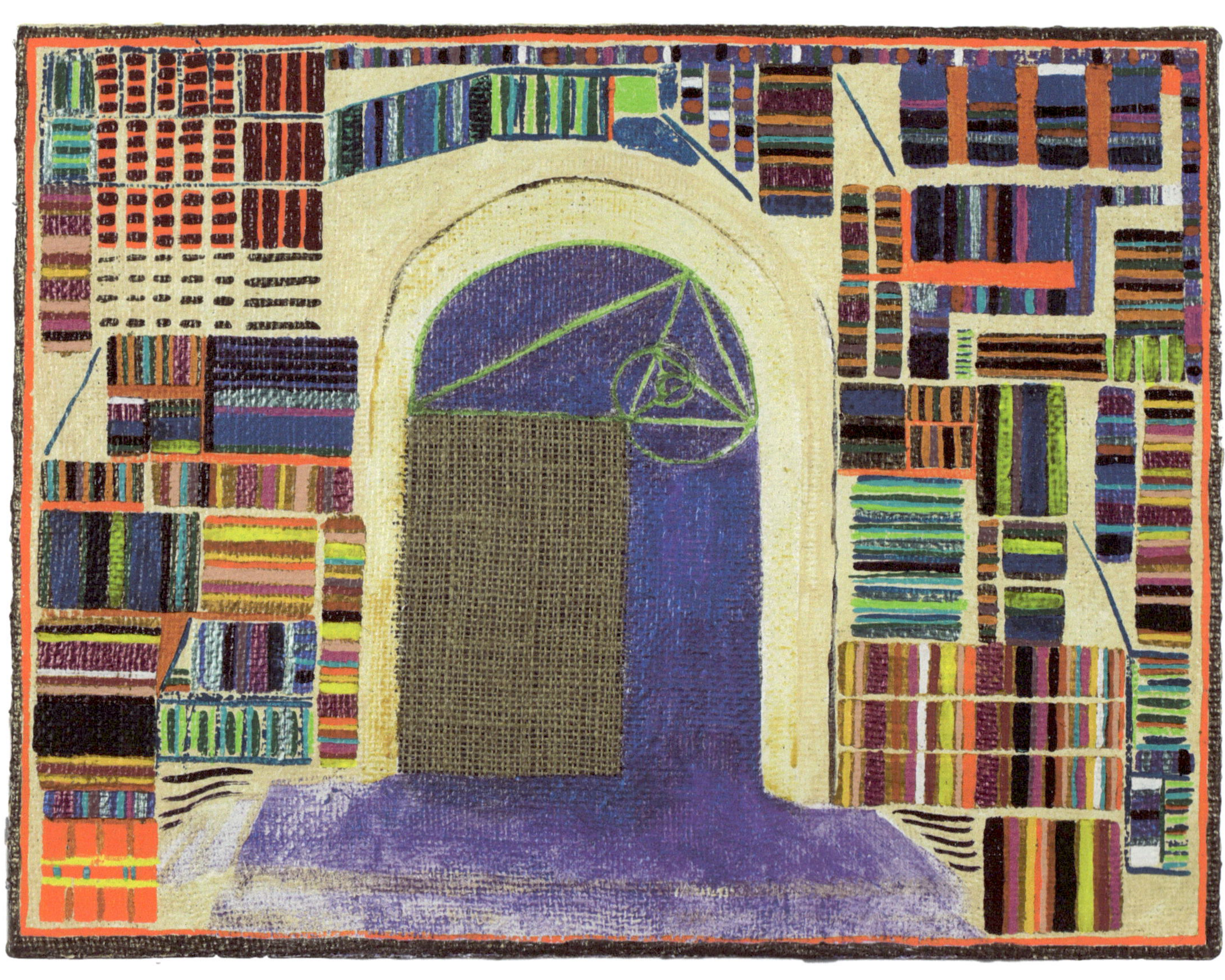

Plate 12
Golden Ratio Microprocessor
2011

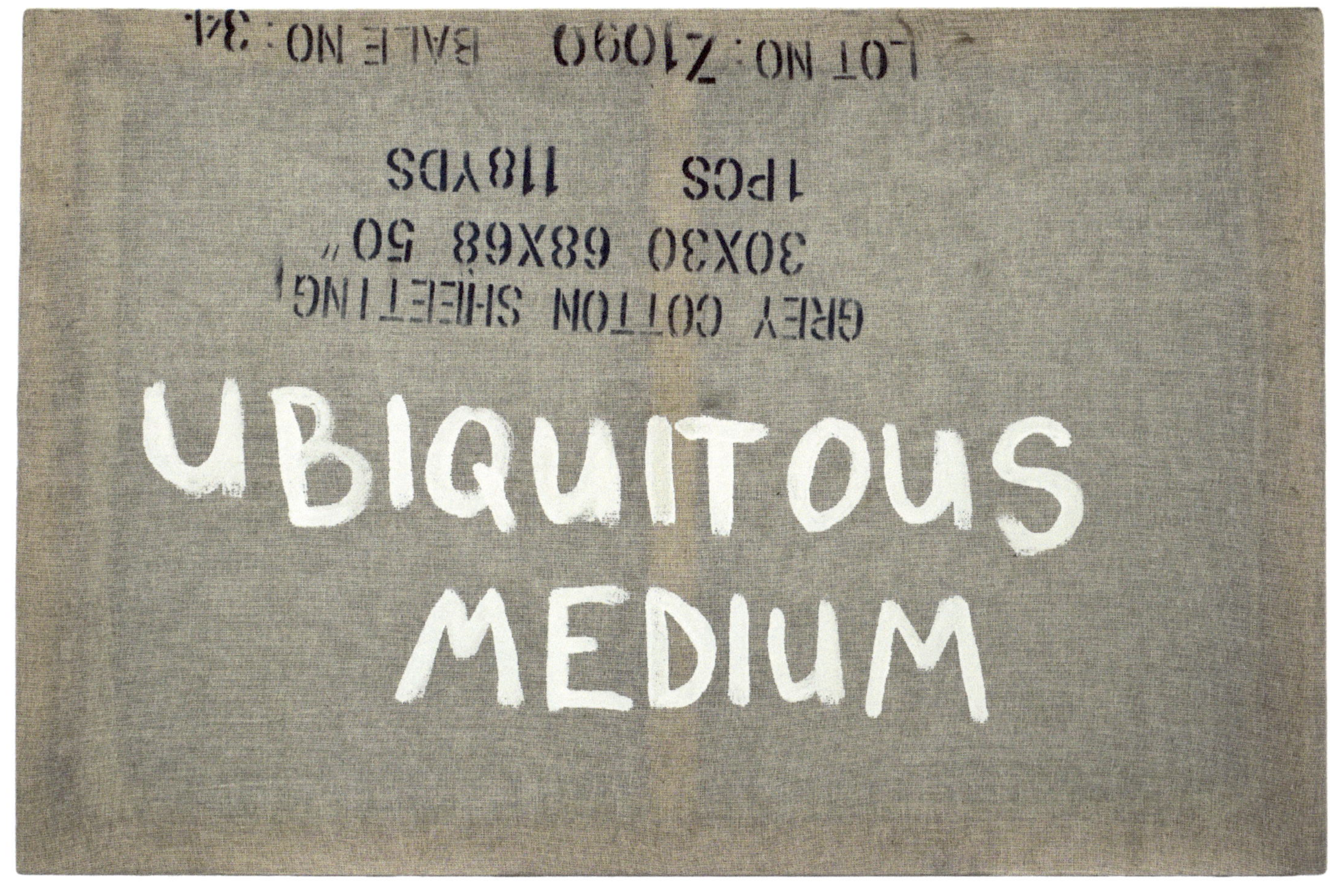

Plate 13
Ubiquitous Medium
2011

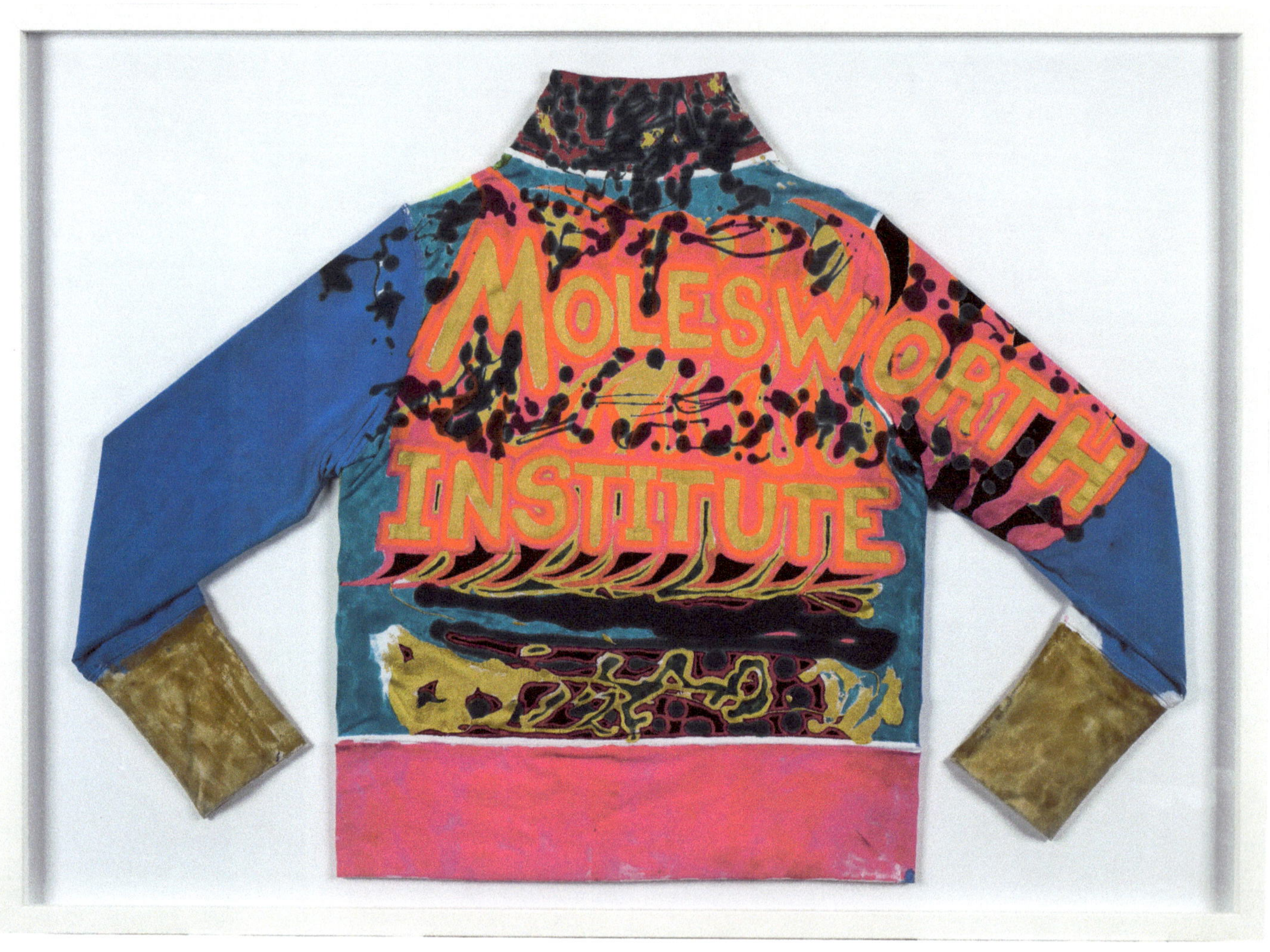

Plate 14
Cycling for Libraries
Molesworth Institute Jacket
2011

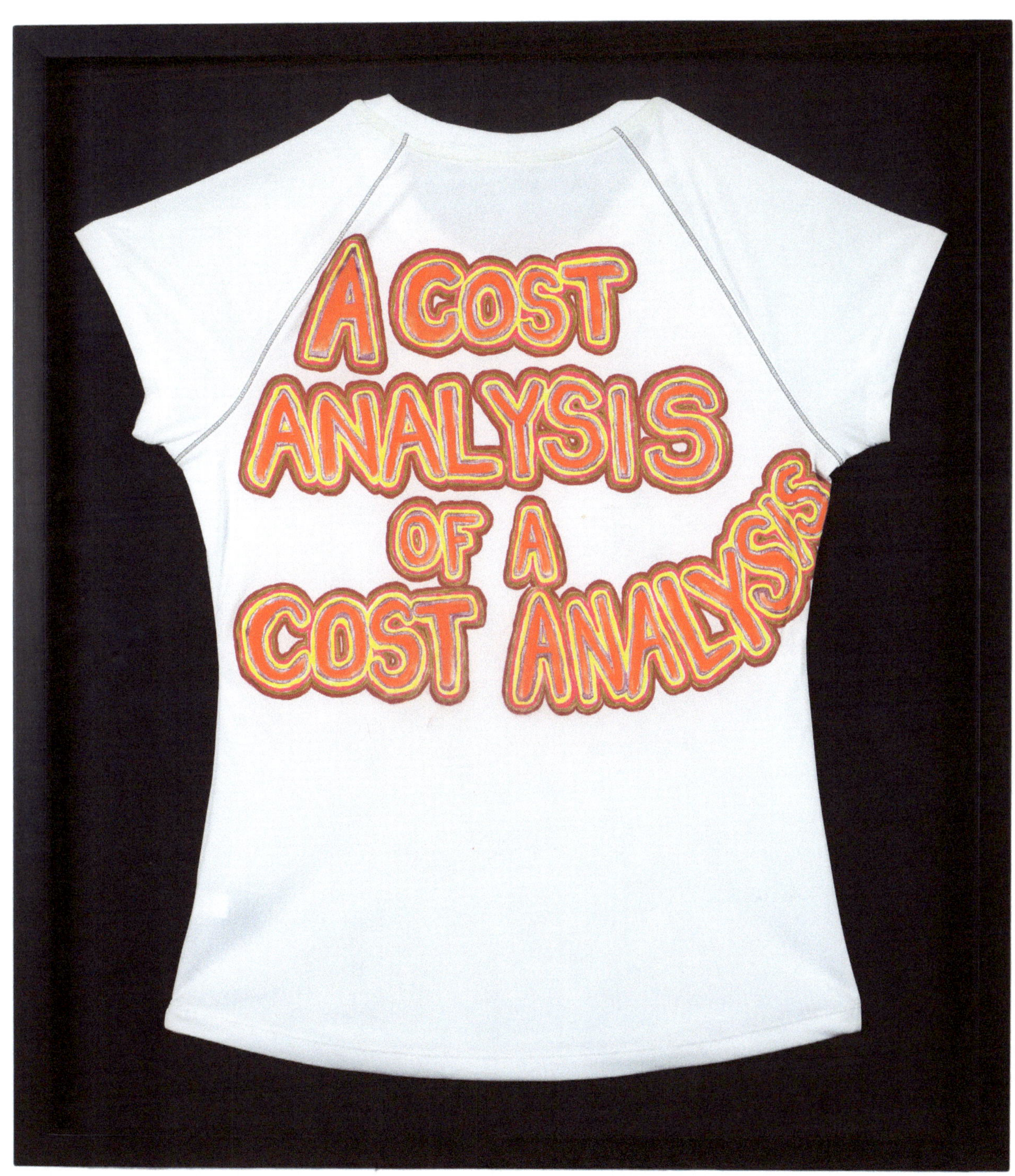

Plate 15
Cycling for Libraries Jersey:
"A Cost Analysis Of A Cost Analysis"
2011

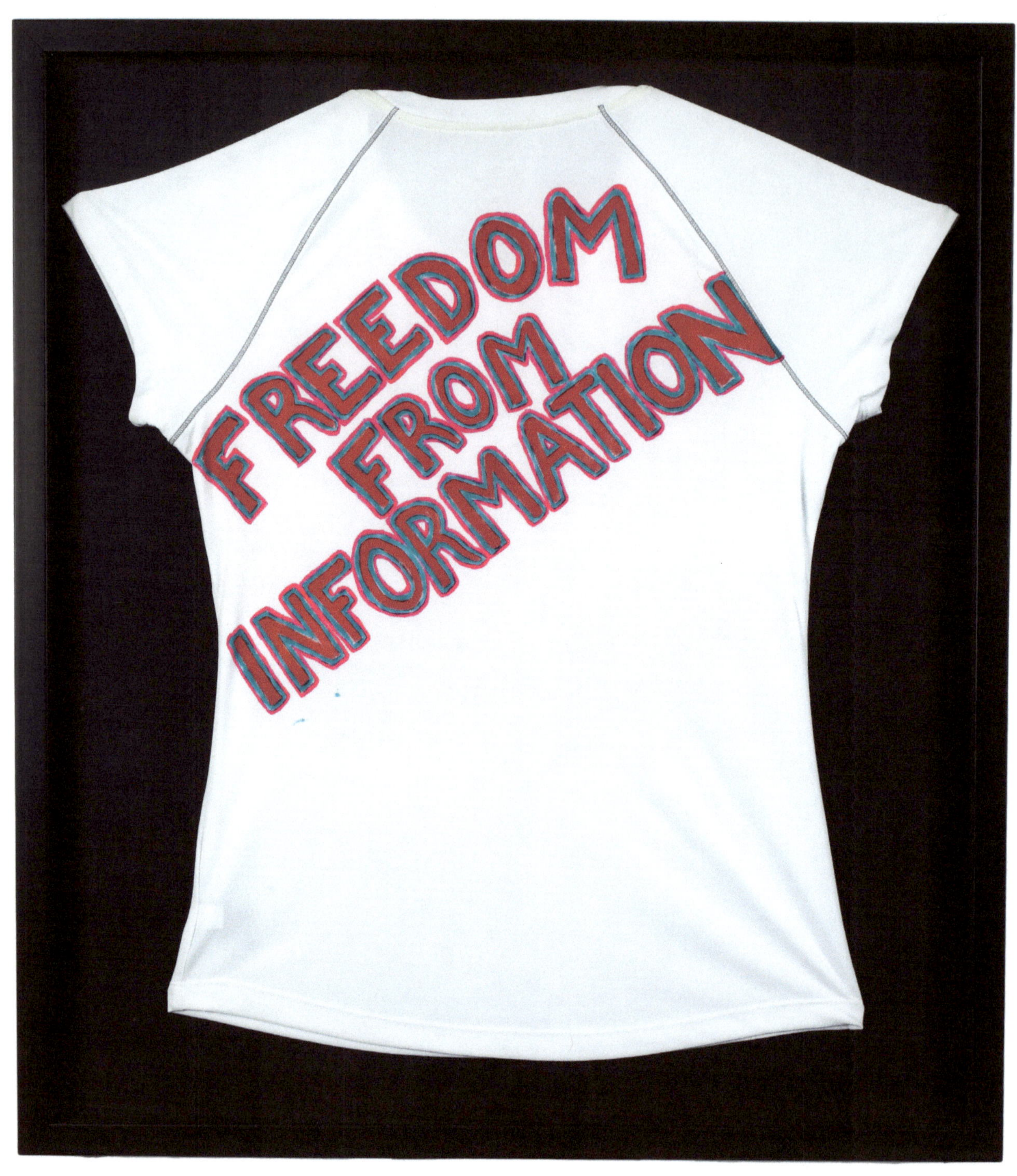

Plate 16
Cycling for Libraries Jersey:
"Freedom From Information"
2011

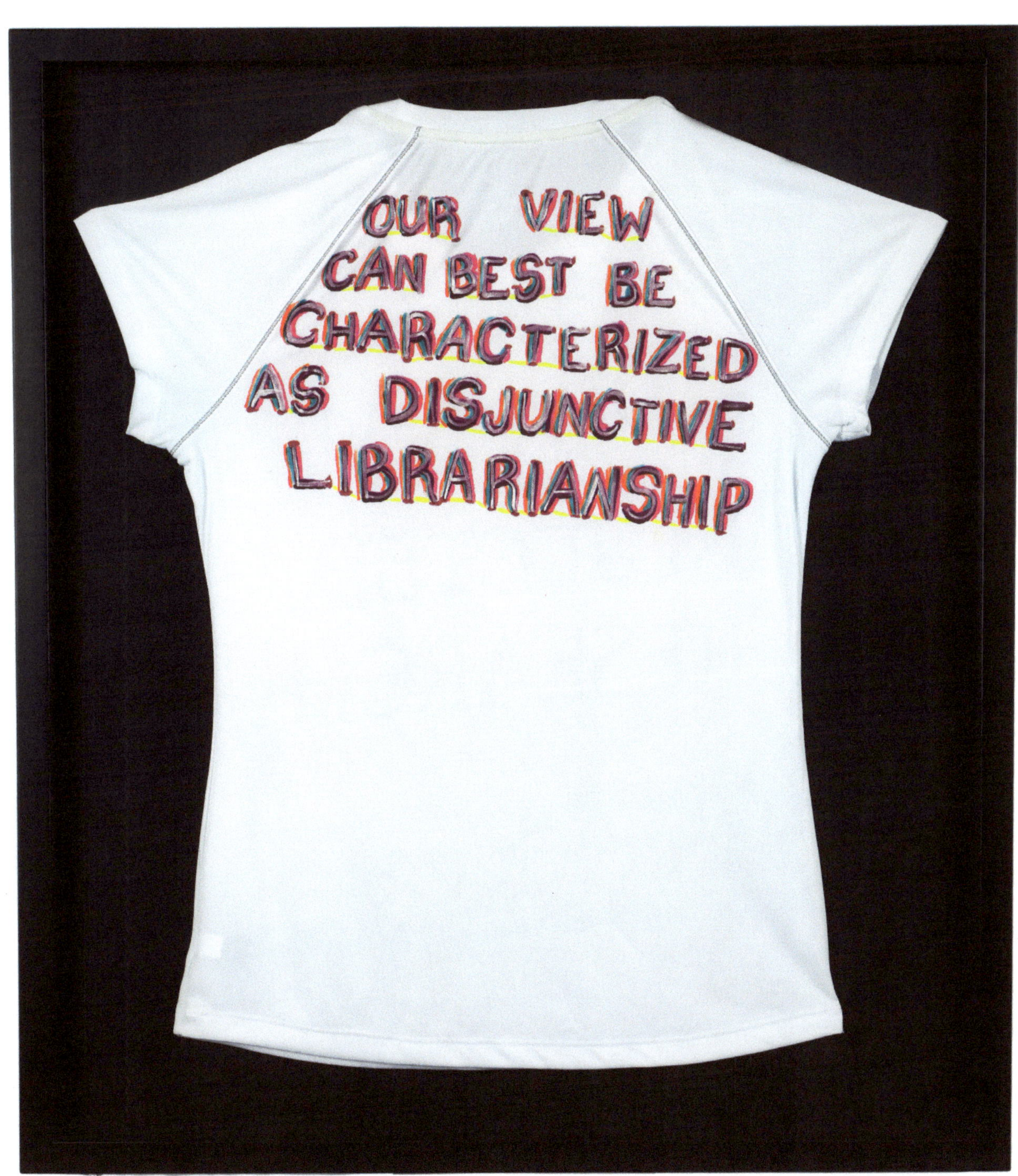

Plate 17
Cycling for Libraries Jersey:
"Our view can best be characterized as disjunctive librarianship"
2011

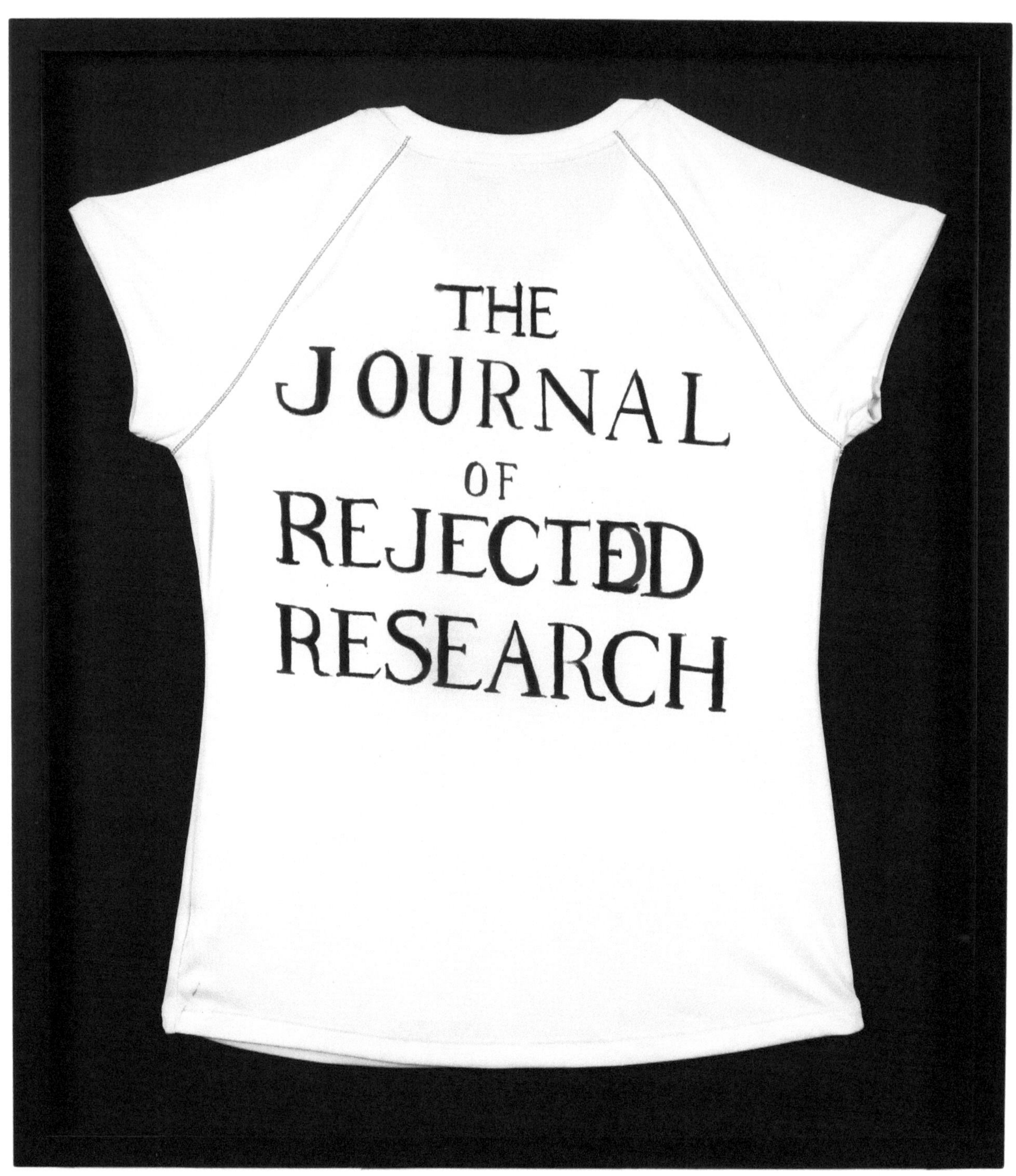

Plate 18
Cycling for Libraries Jersey:
"The Journal of Rejected Research"
2011

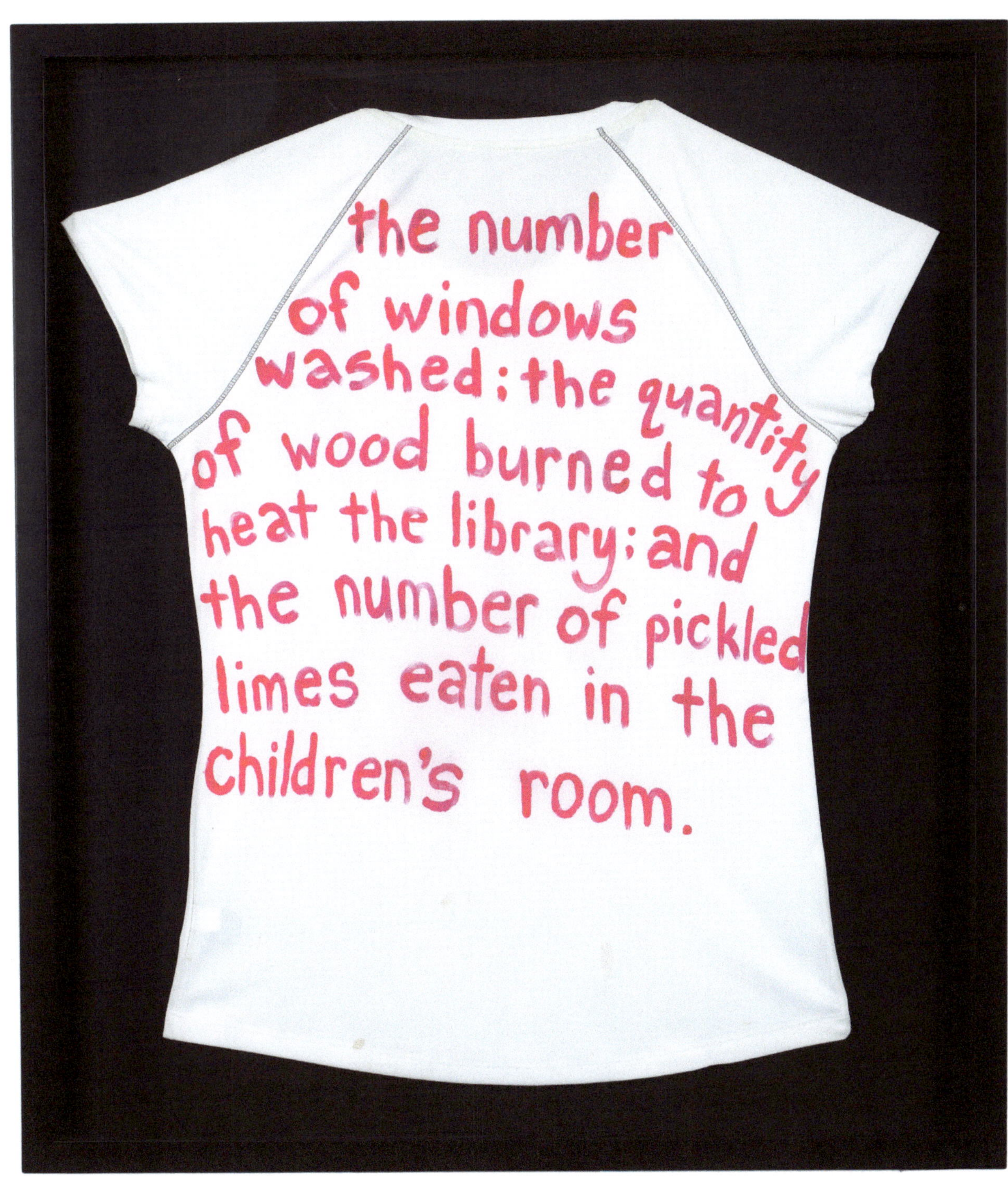

Plate 19
Cycling for Libraries Jersey:
"The number of windows washed; the quantity of wood burned to heat the library; and the number of pickled limes eaten in the children's room."
2011

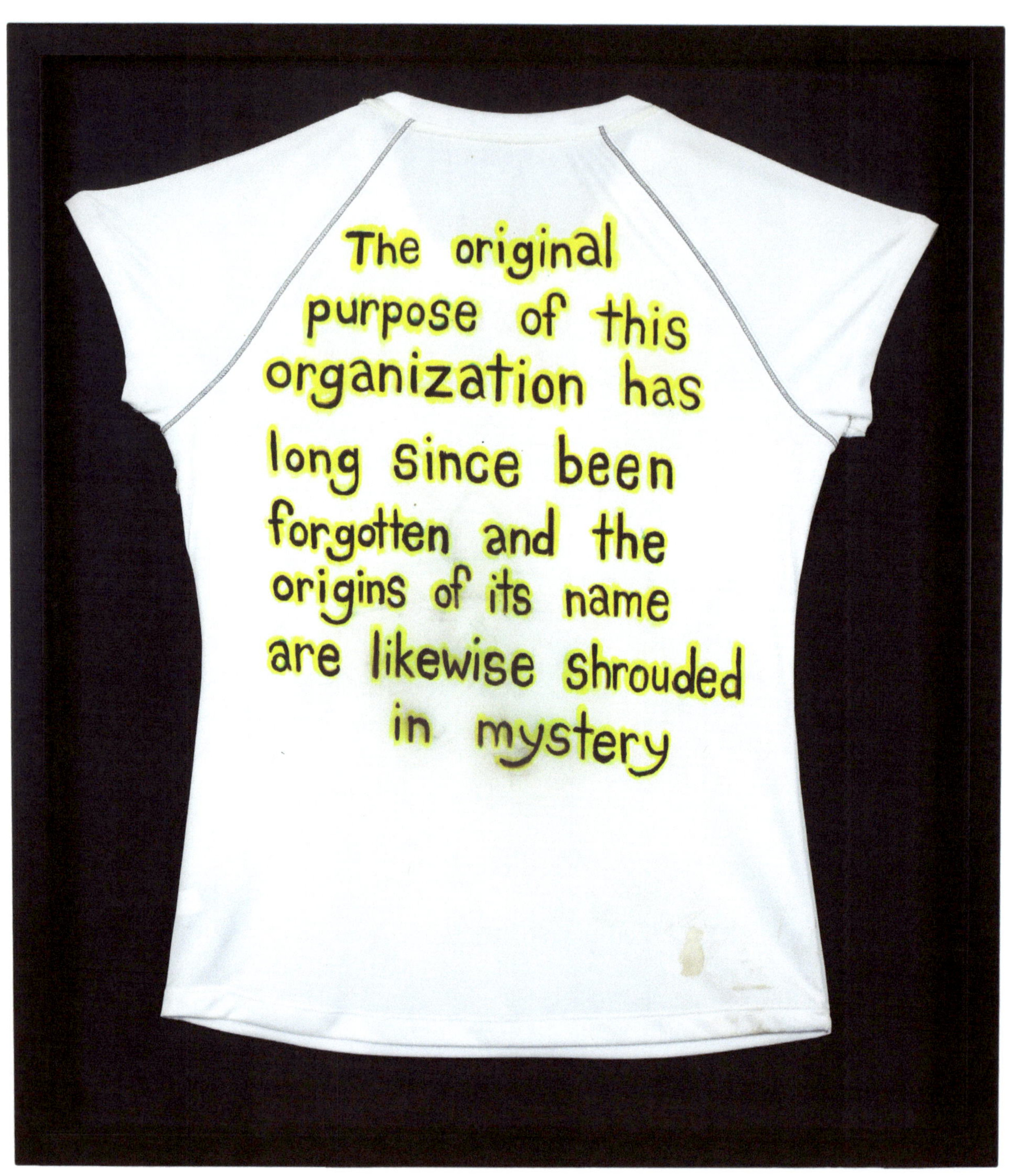

Plate 20
Cycling for Libraries Jersey:
"The original purpose of this organization has long since been forgotten and the origins of its name are likewise shrouded in mystery"
2011

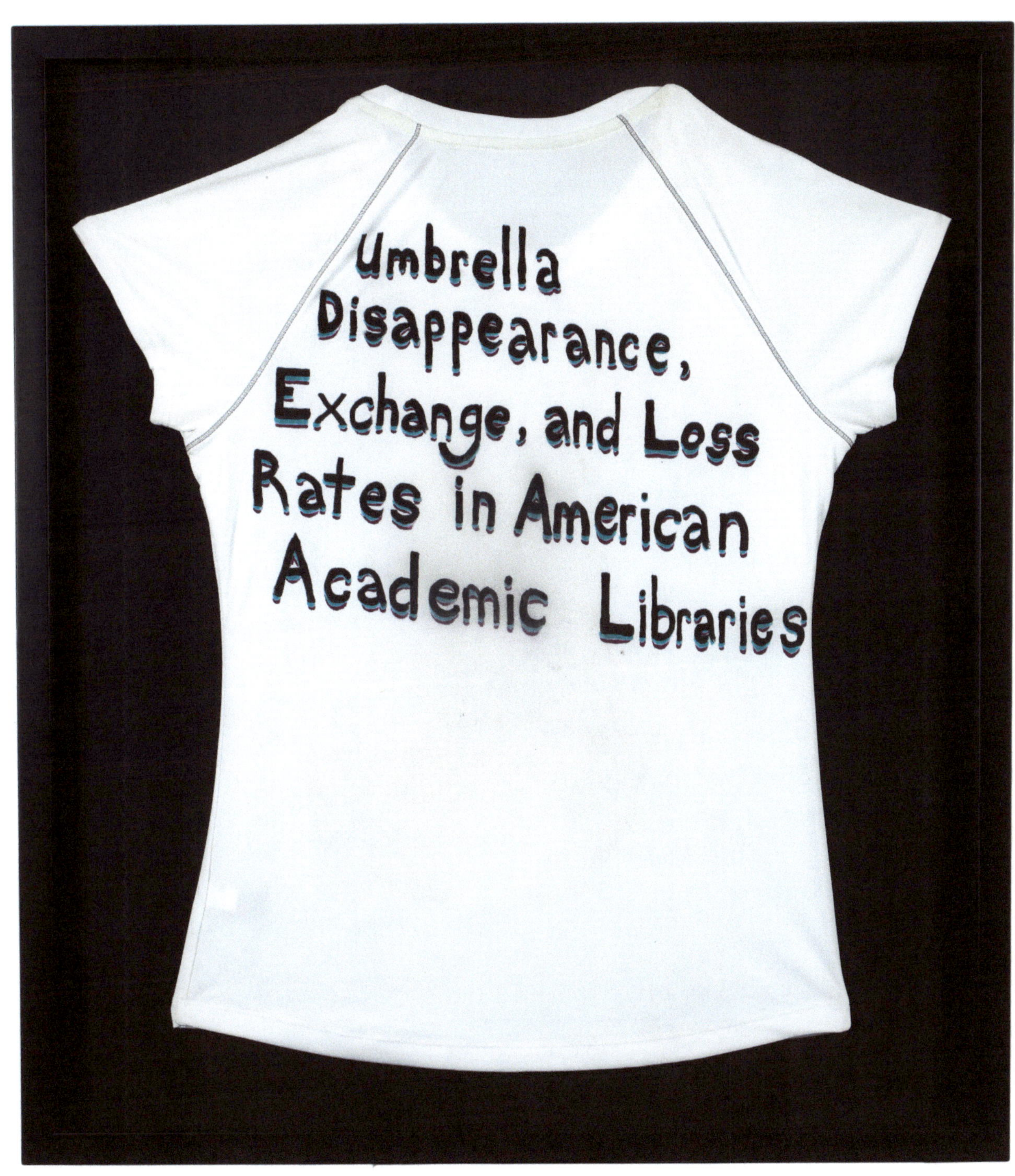

Plate 21
Cycling for Libraries Jersey:
"Umbrella Disappearance, Echange, and Loss
Rates in American Academic Libraries"
2011

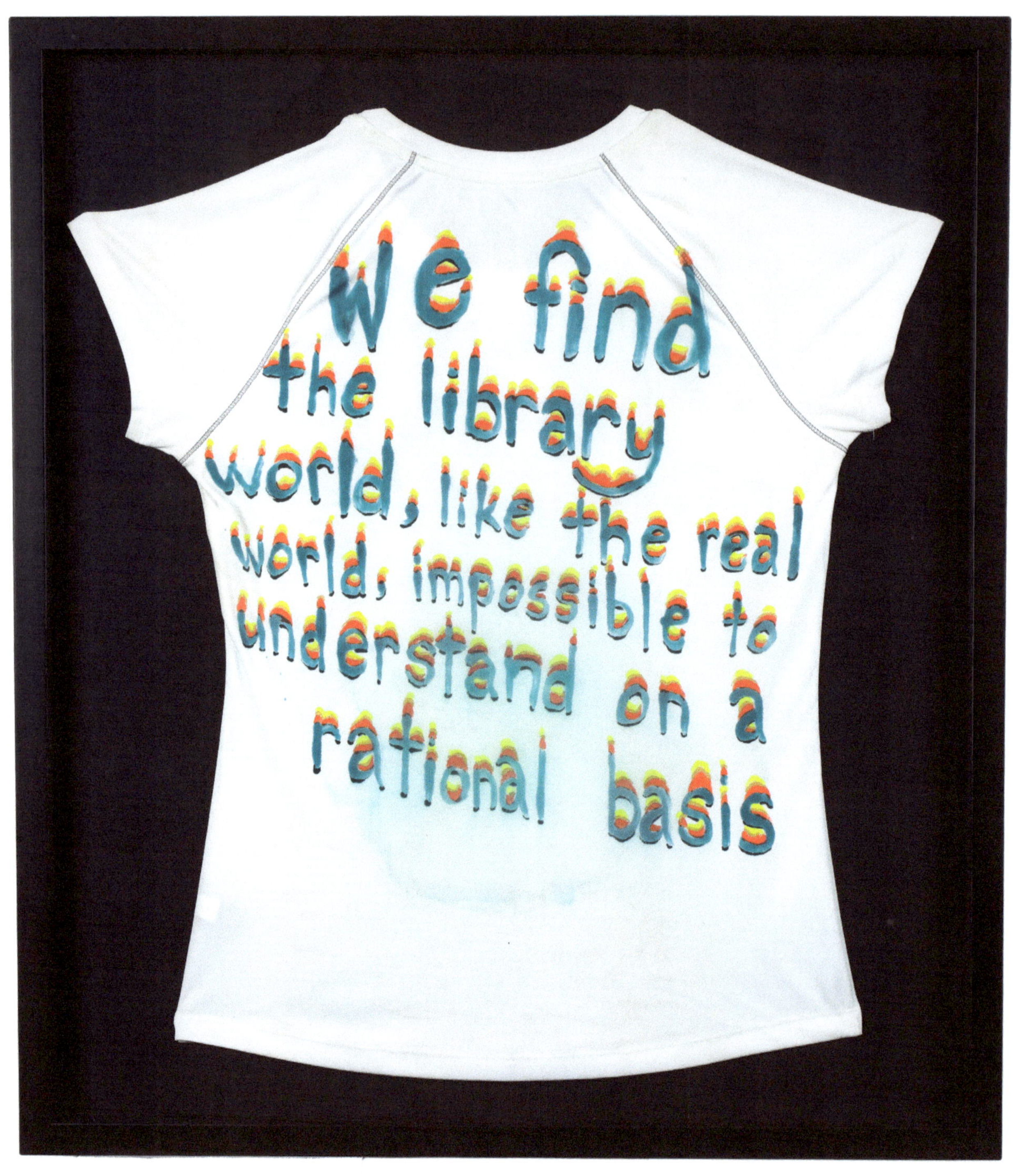

Plate 22
Cycling for Libraries Jersey:
"We find the library world, like the real world,
impossible to understand on a rational basis"
2011

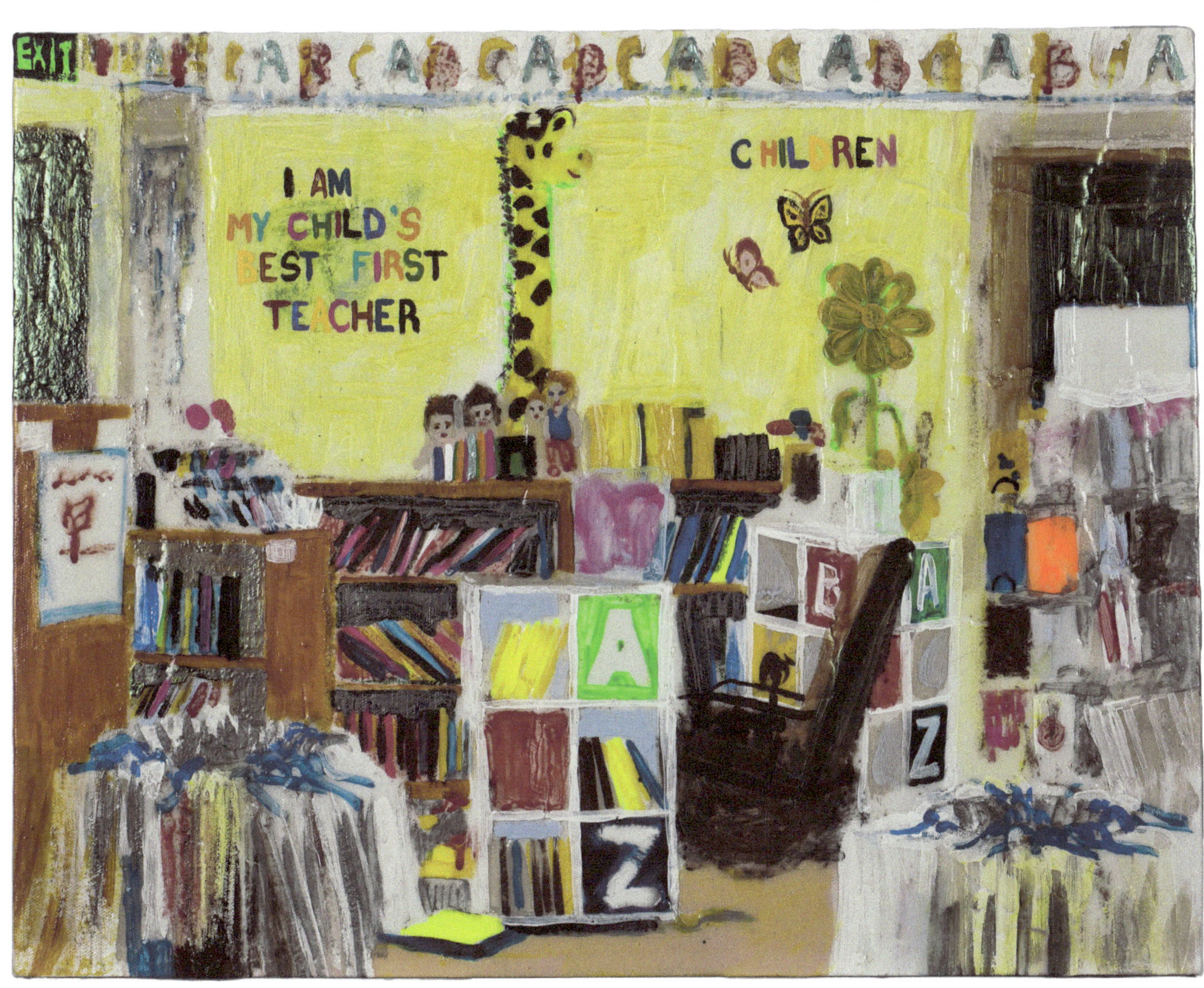

Plate 23
I Am My Child's Best First Teacher
2010

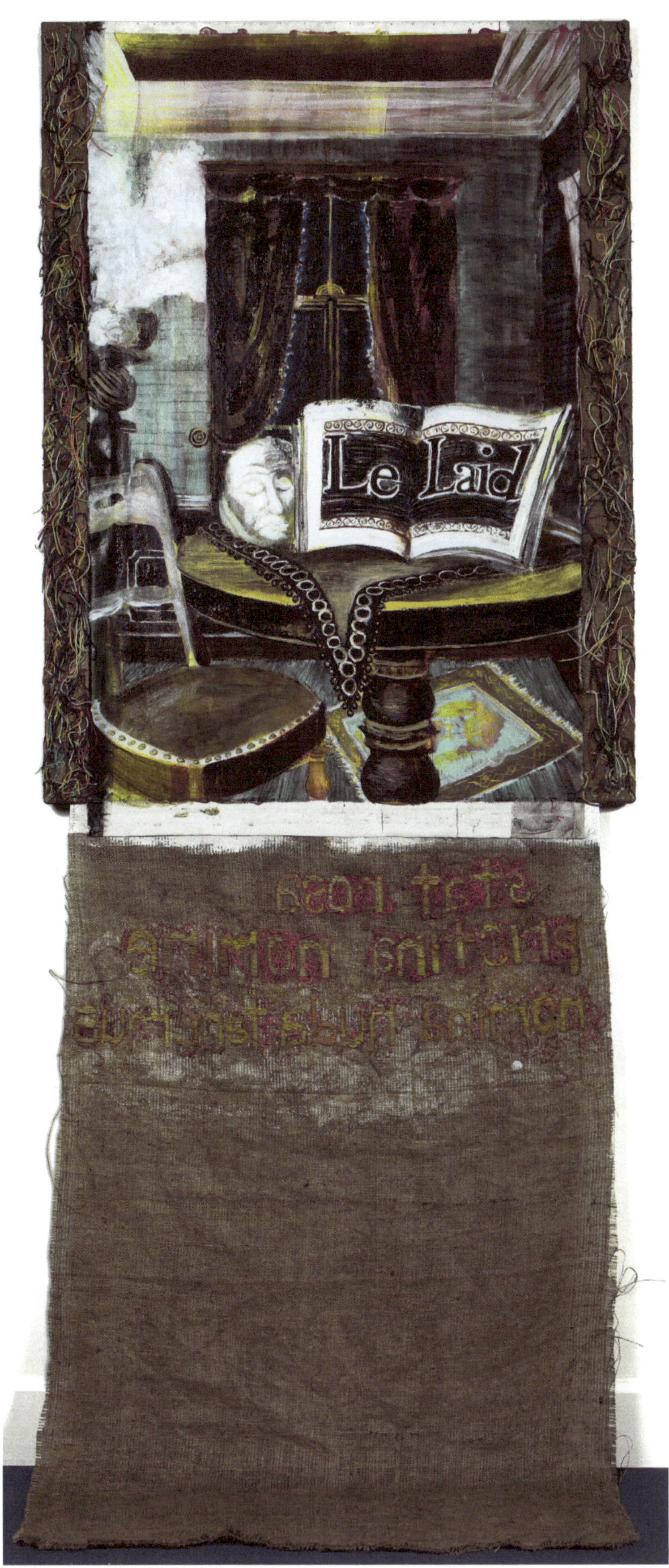

Plate 24
(opposite page)
Memory School Dropout
2010

Plate 25
On Denoting (stat rosa pristina nomine nomina nuda tenemus)
2010

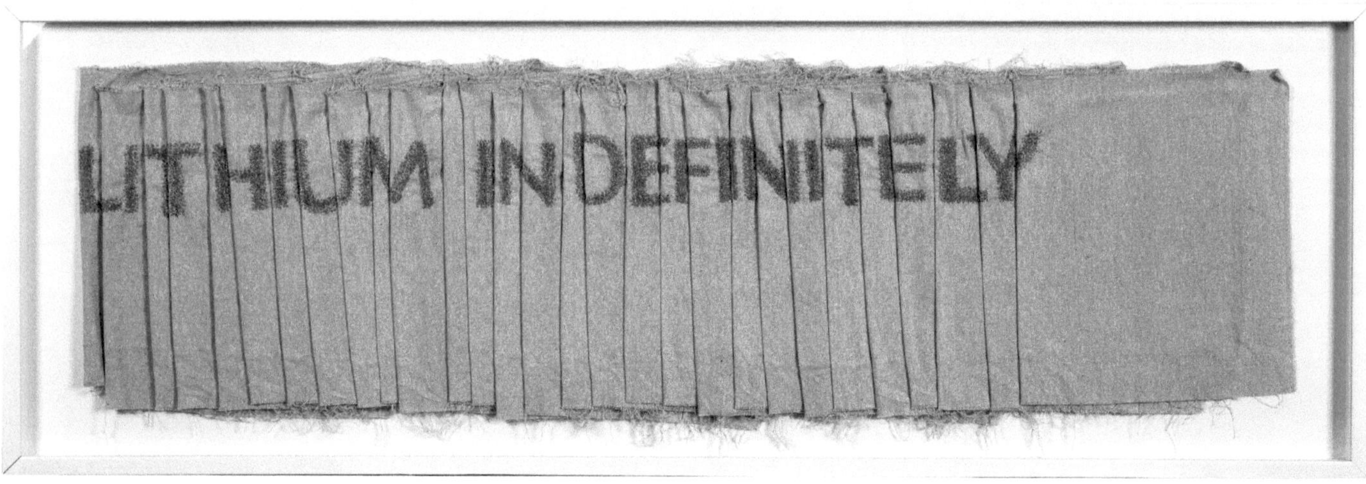

Plate 26
Encyclopedia Book Cover Set (Lithium Indefinitely)
2009

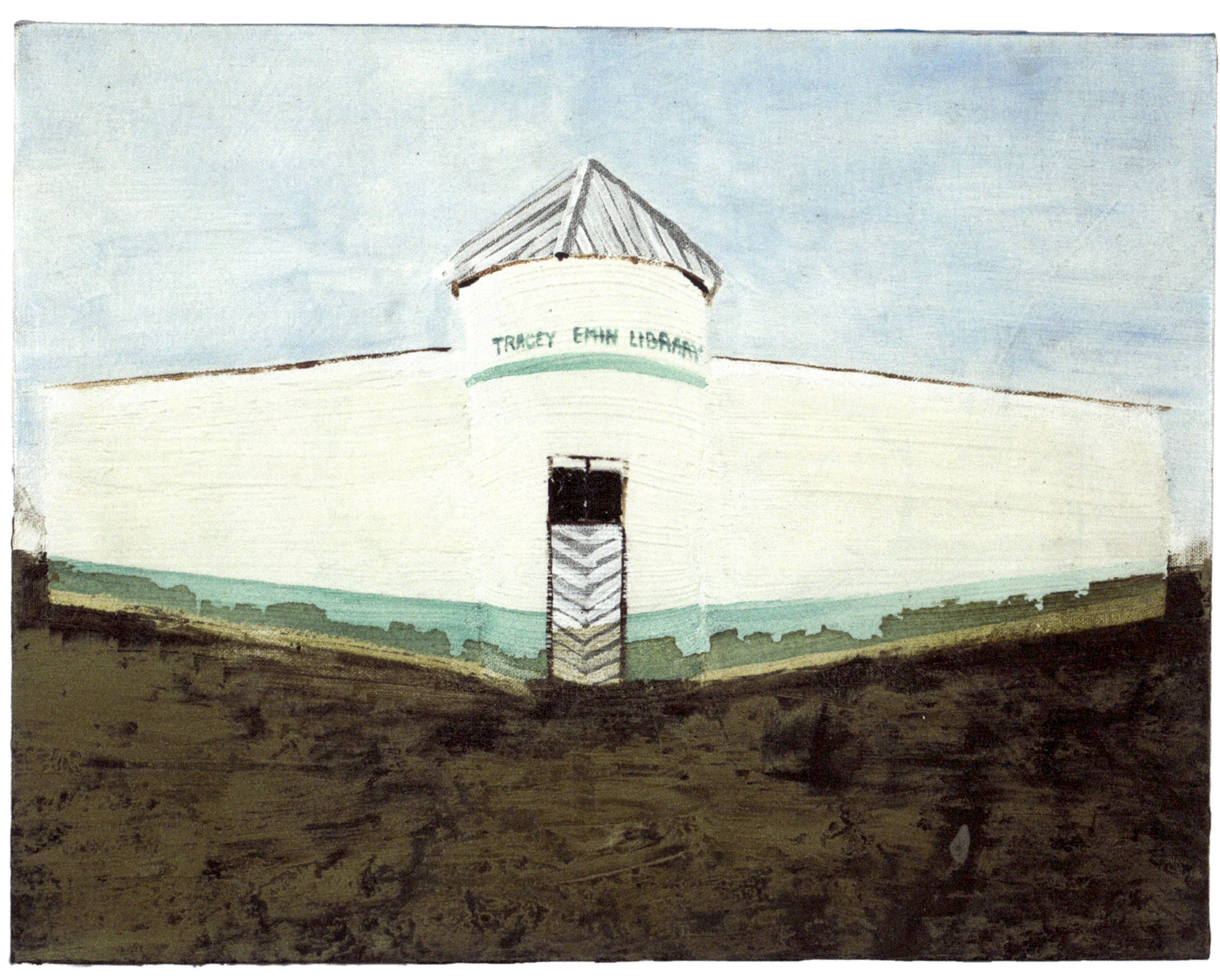

Plate 27
Tracey Emin Library, Uganda
2009

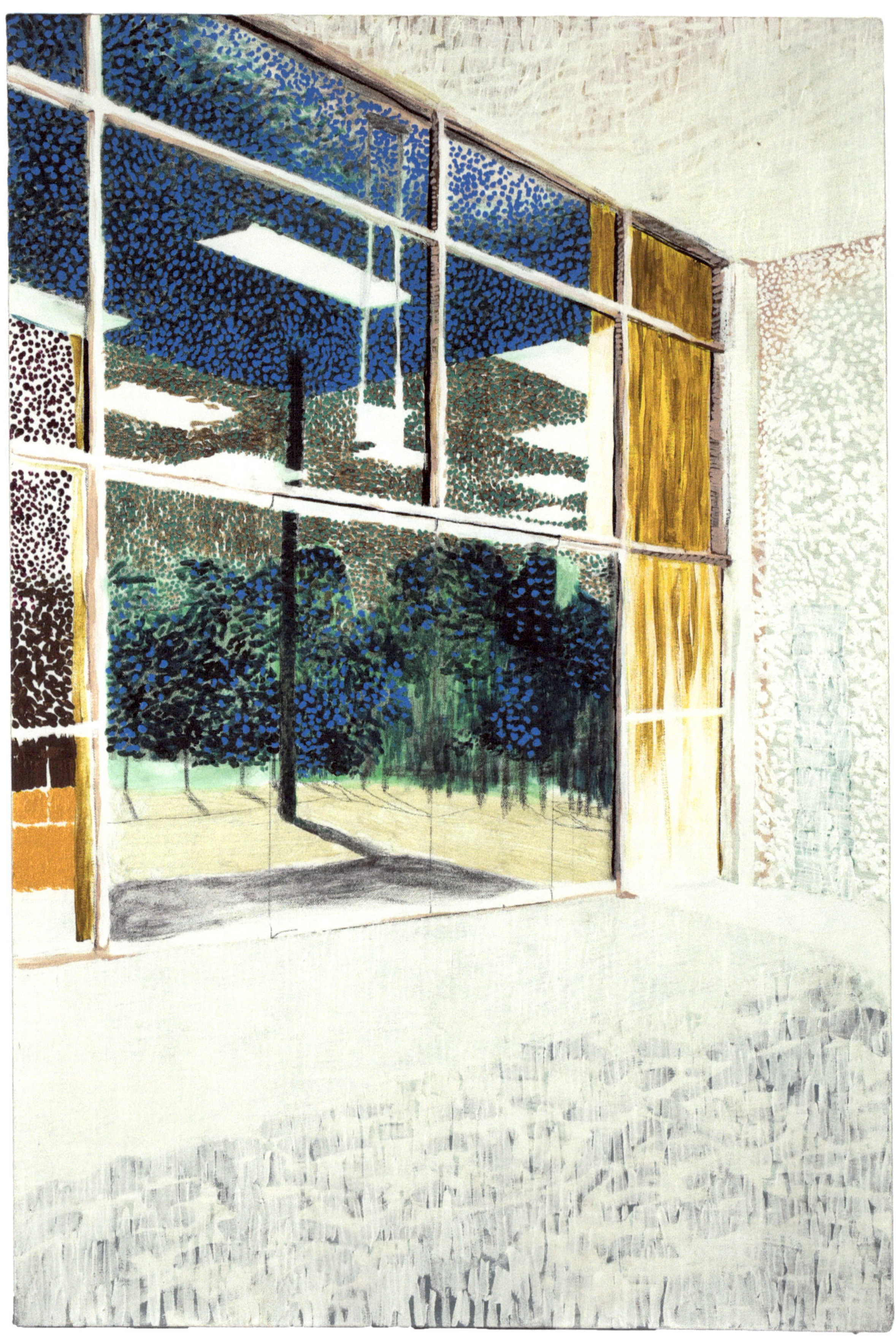

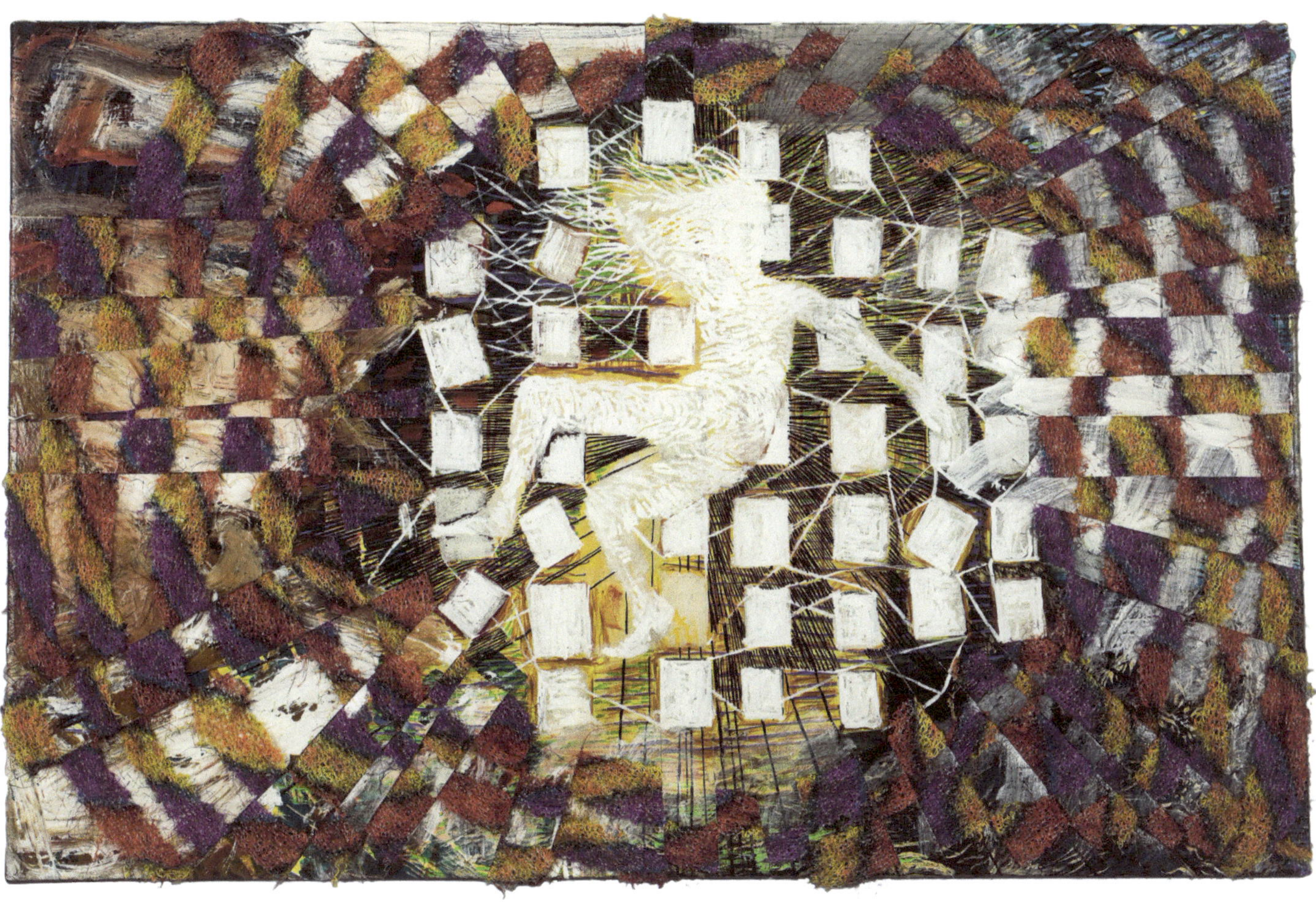

Plate 28
(opposite page)
Whittier Public Library (entrance)
2009

Plate 29
Information Entropy
2009

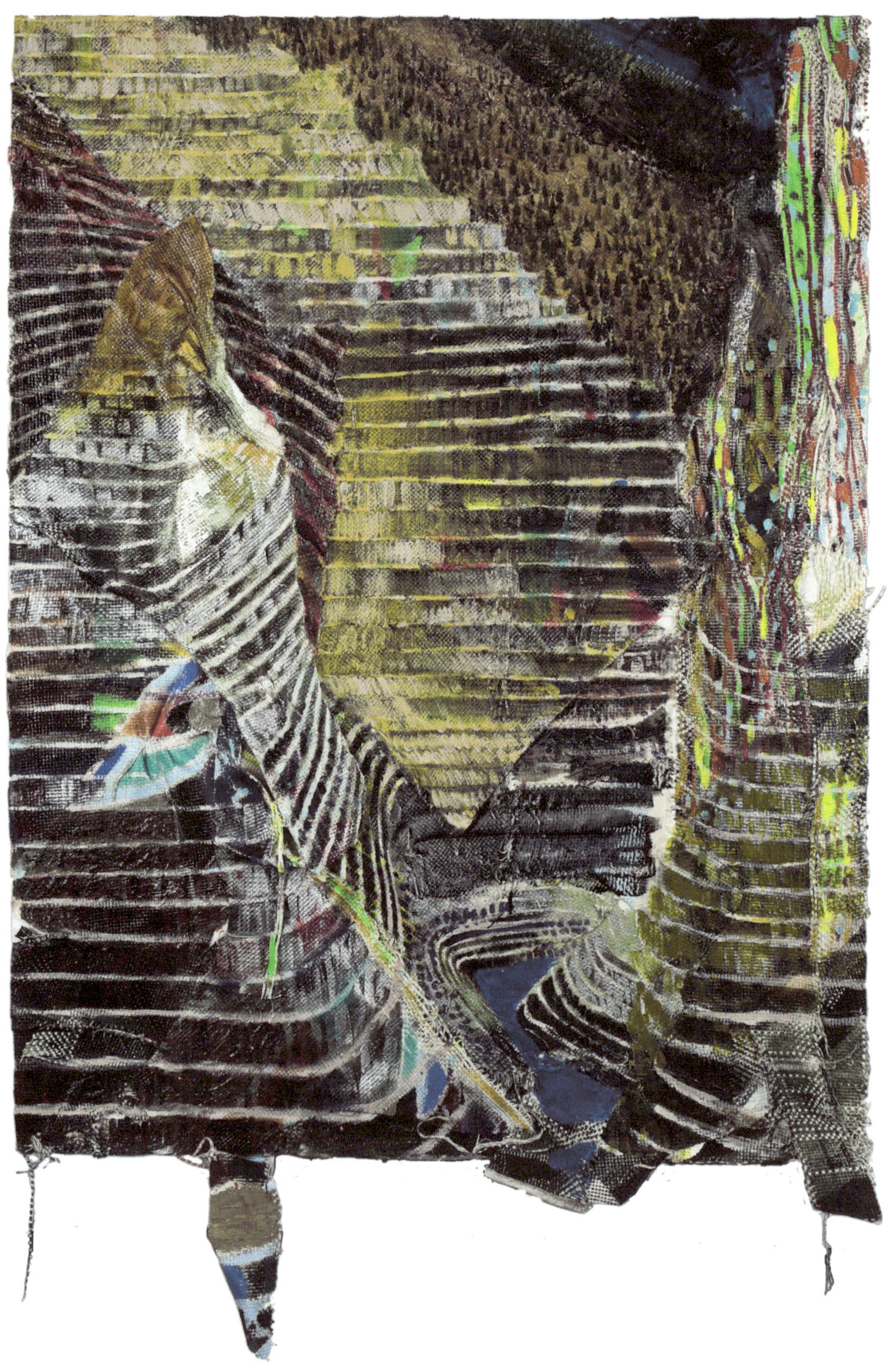

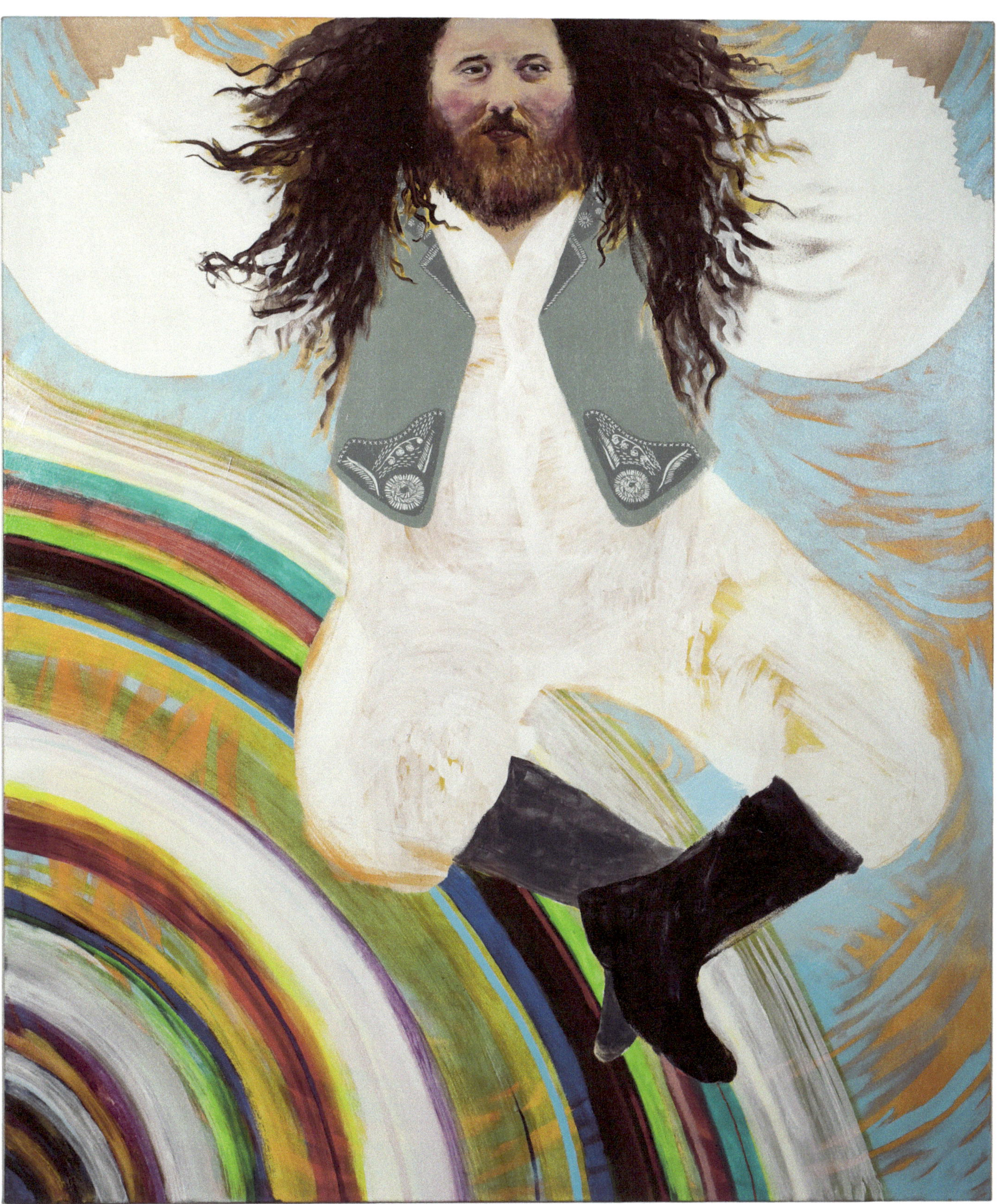

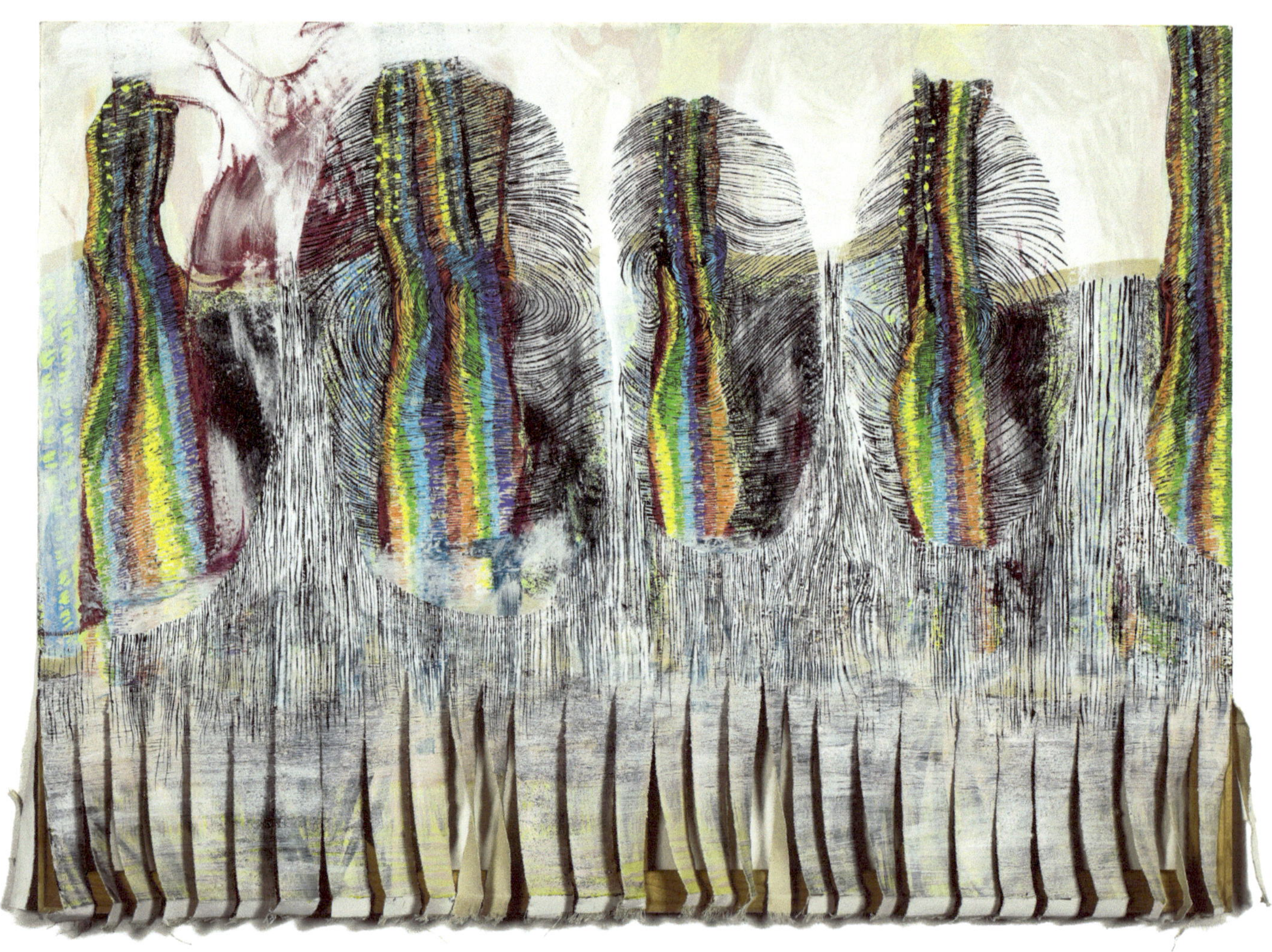

Plate 30
(previous spread, left side)
Quarry
2009

Plate 31
(previous spread, right side)
Freedom (Richard Stallman Folk Dancing)
2008

Plate 32
Urinalysis
2008

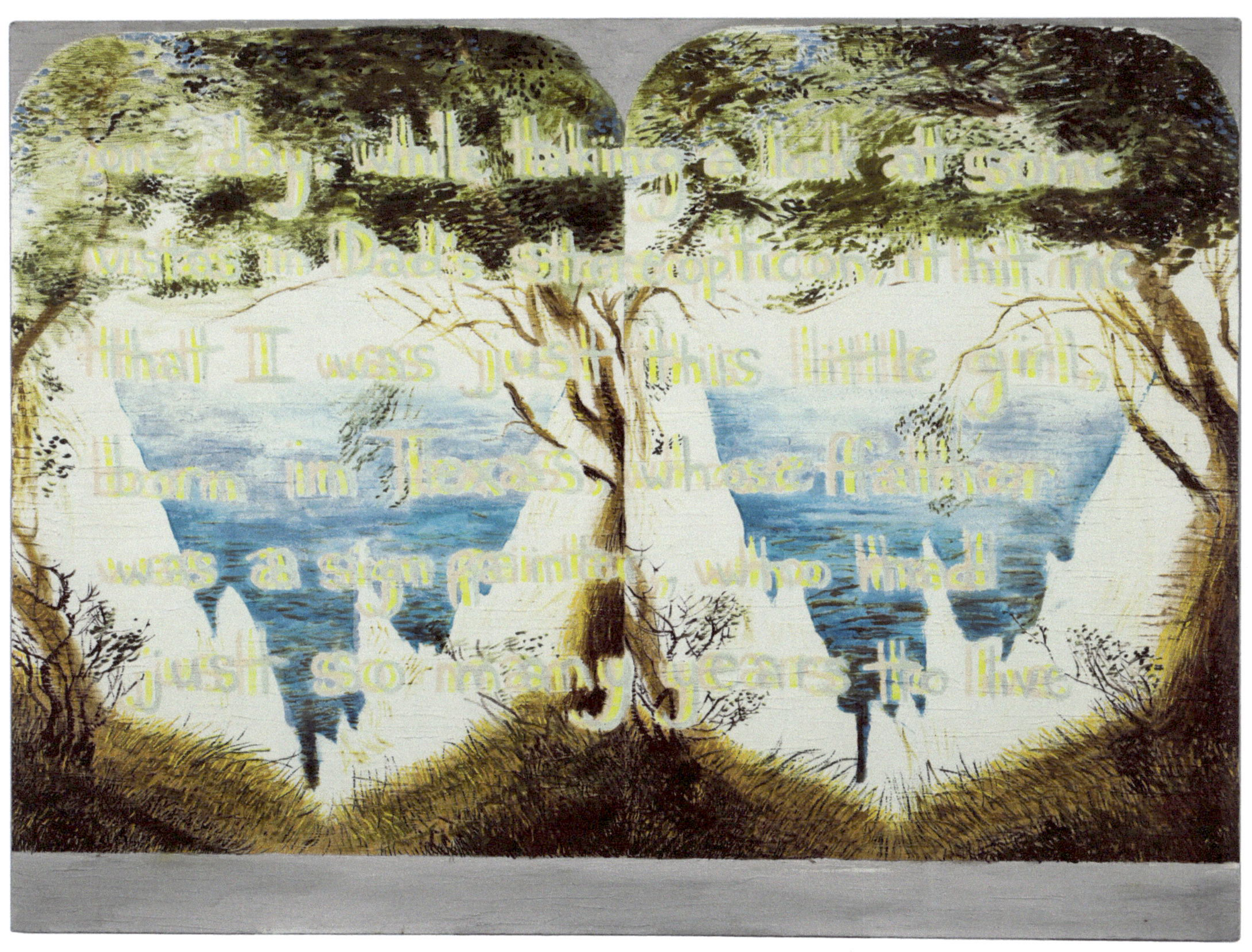

Plate 33
Stereopticon (One day, while taking a look at some vistas in Dad's stereopticon, it hit me that I was just this little girl, born in Texas, whose father was a sign painter, who had just so many years to live)
2008

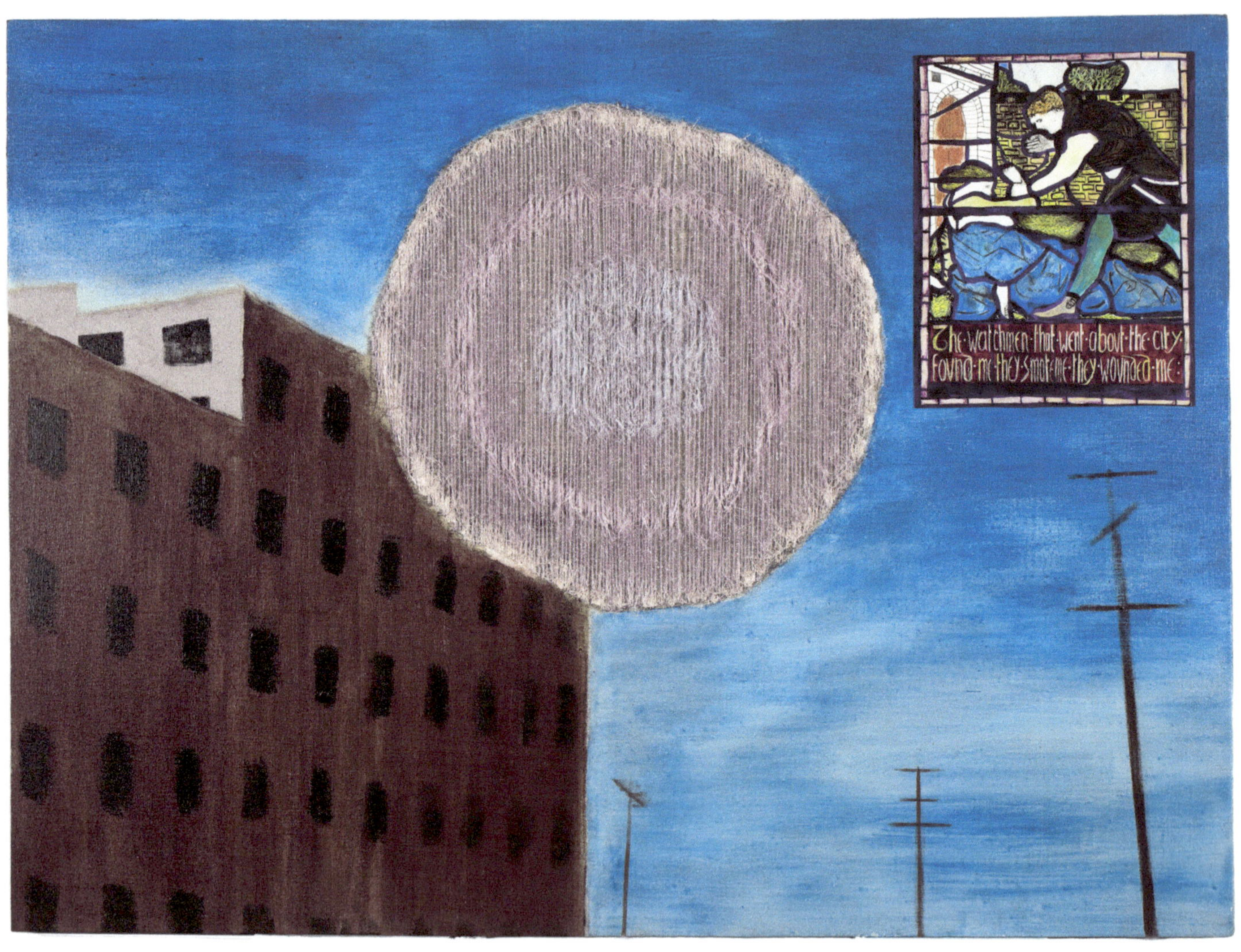

Plate 34
Don't Turn Away From Love, Sailor
2008

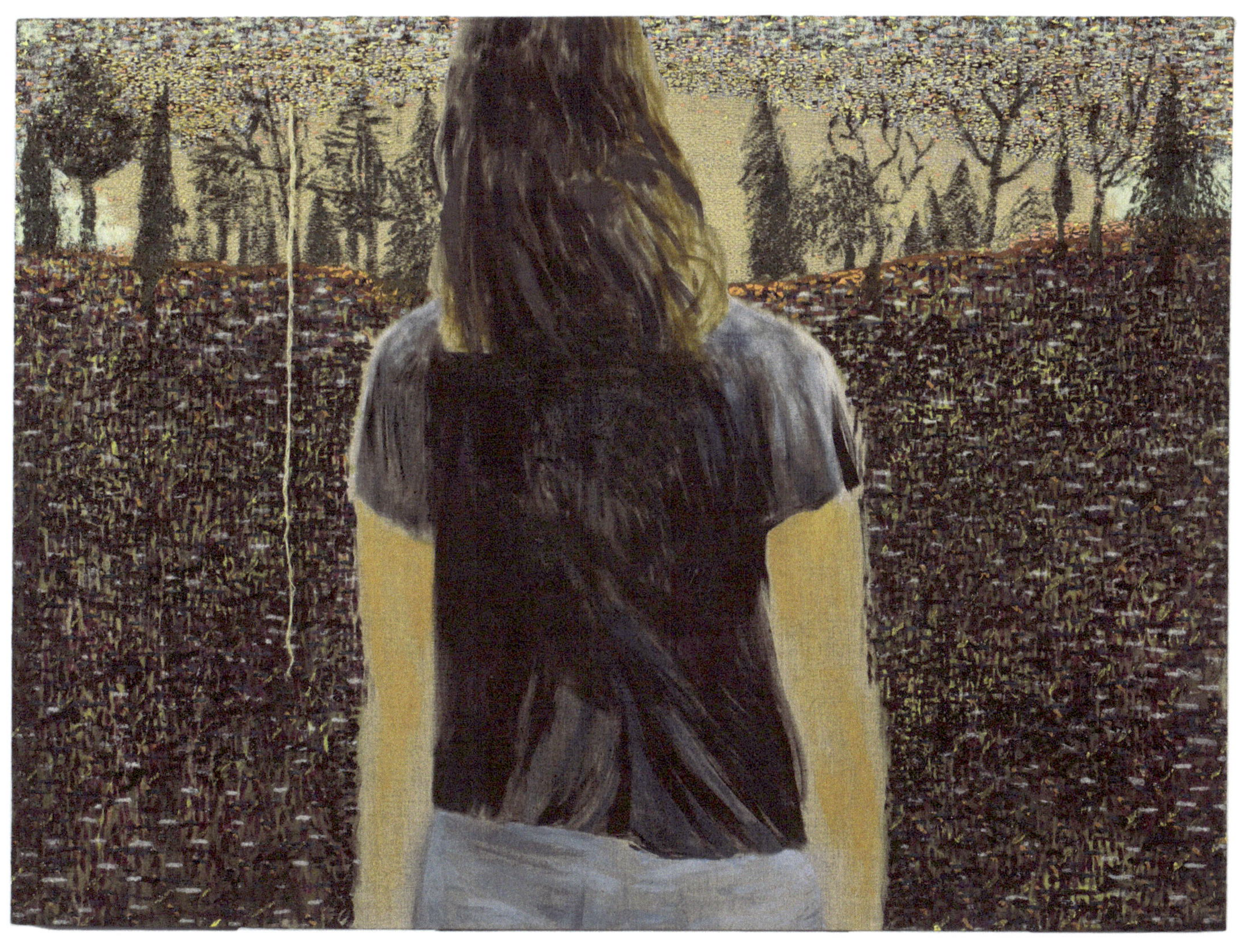

Plate 35
Lux Aeterna
2008

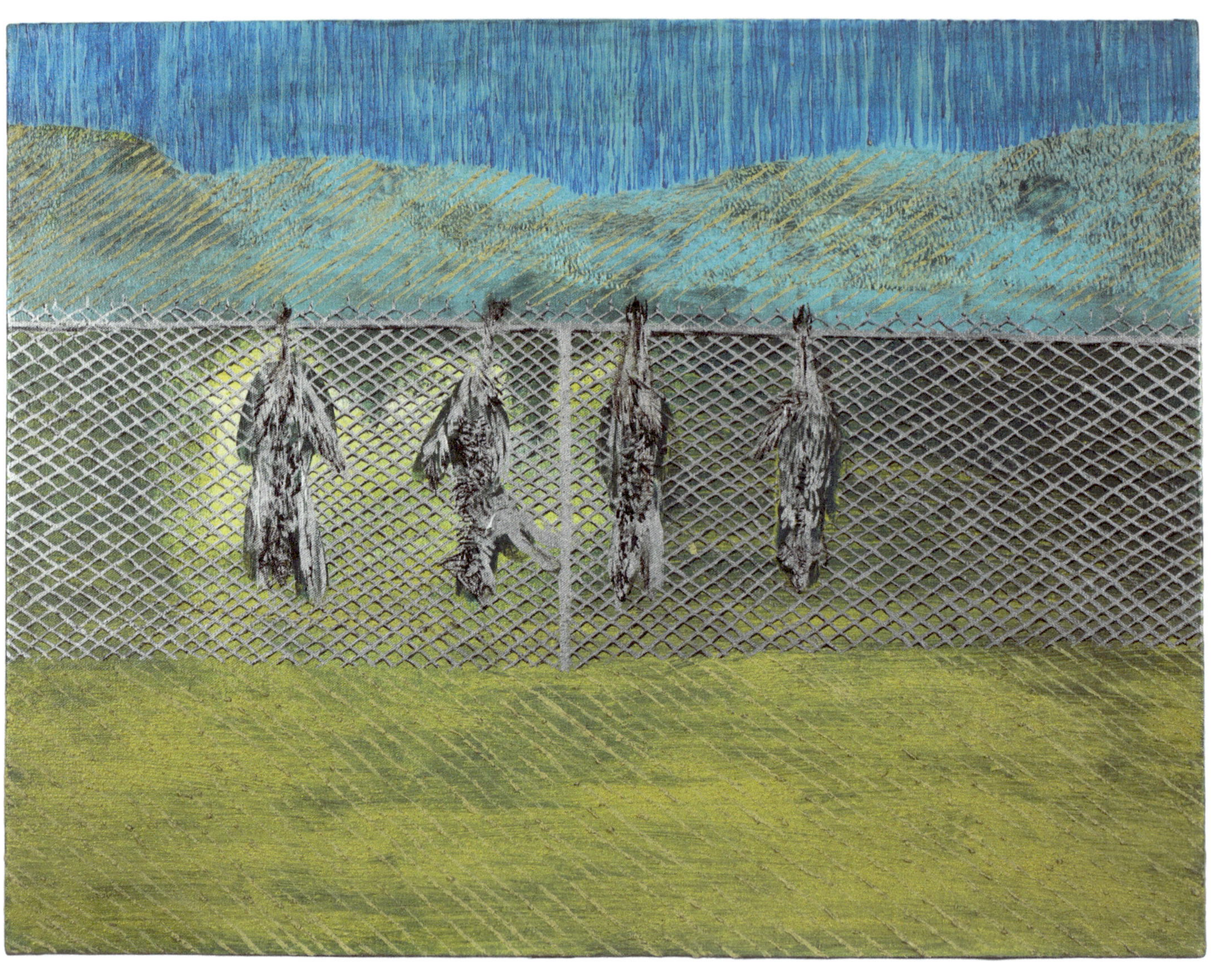

Plate 36
Dead Coyotes on a Fence
2008

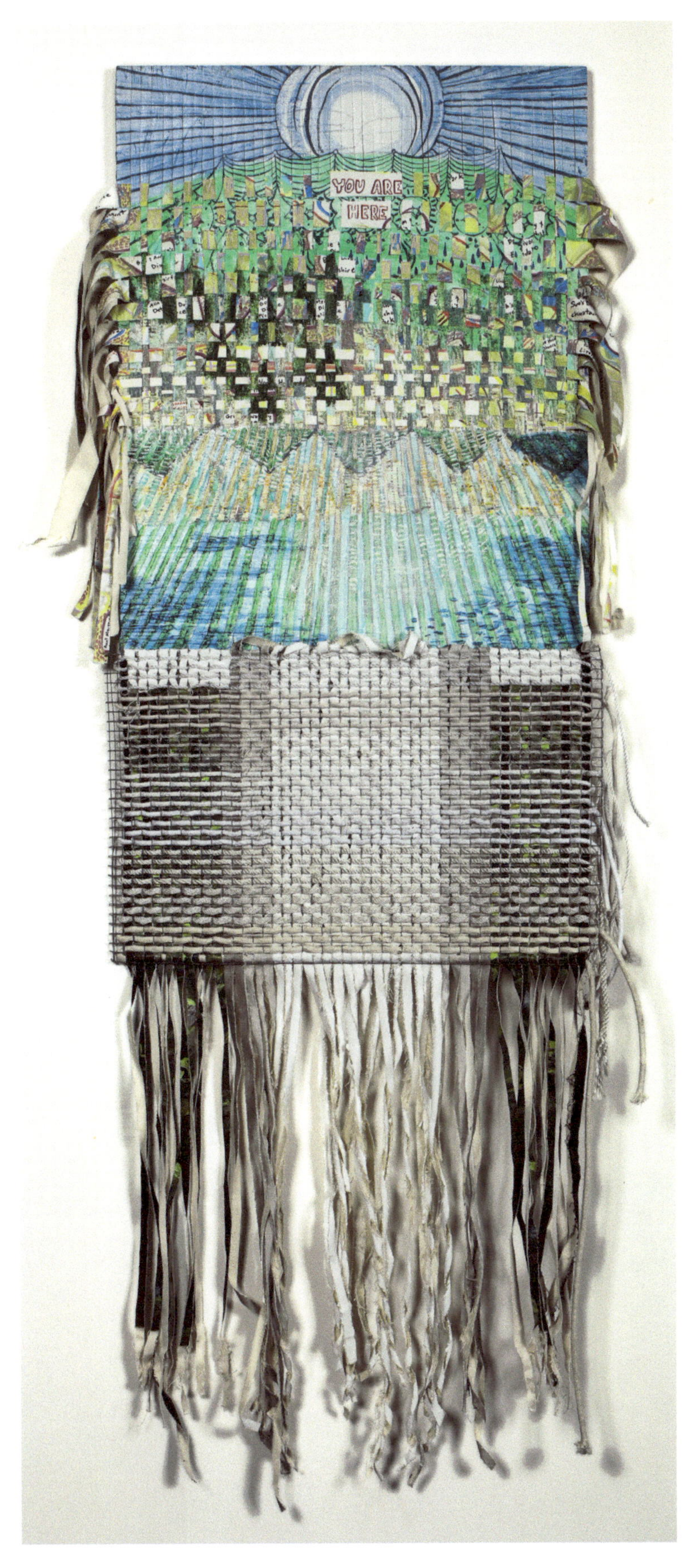

Plate 37
You Are Here
2008

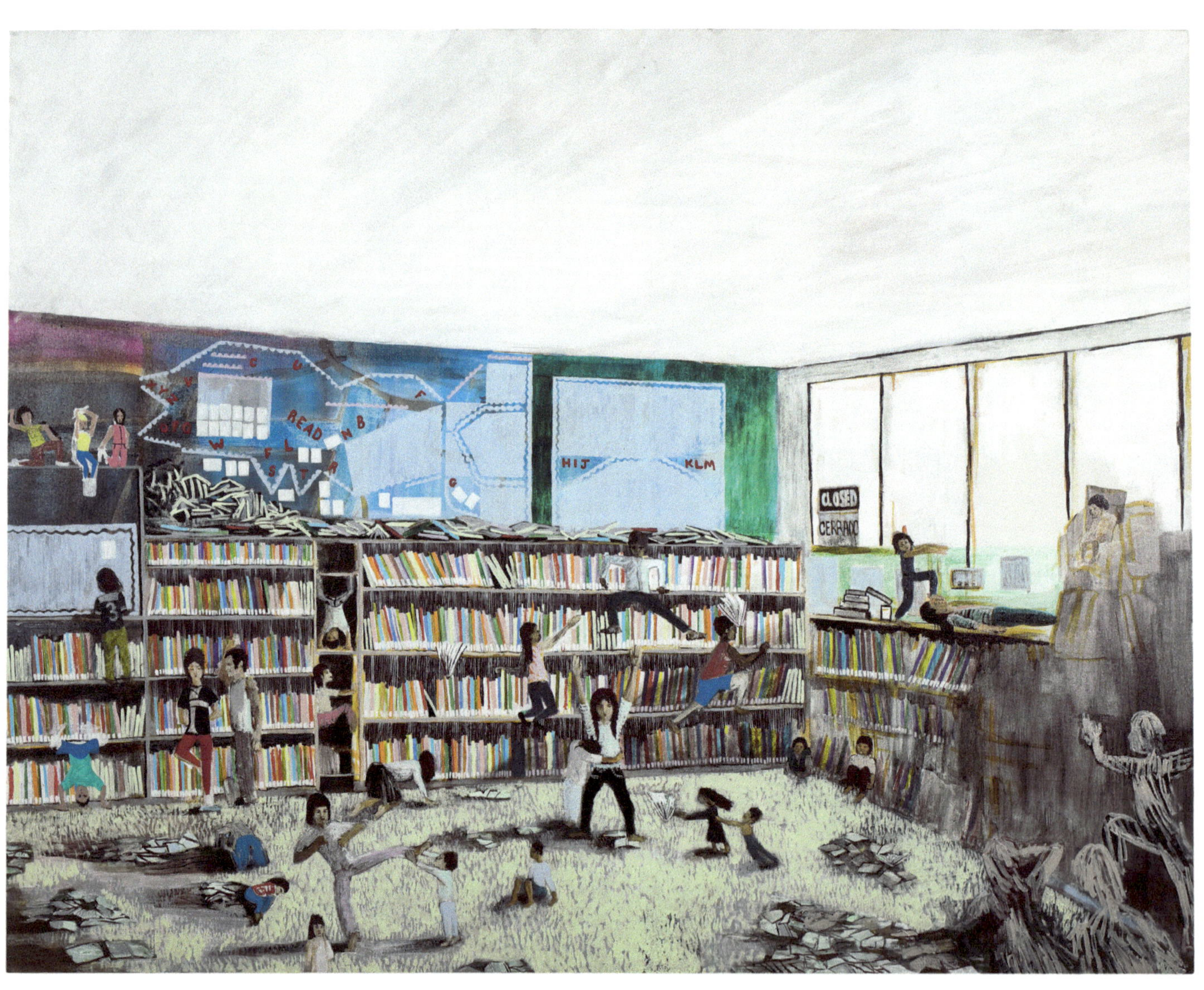

Plate 38
Today The Library Was Ripped A New Asshole
2007

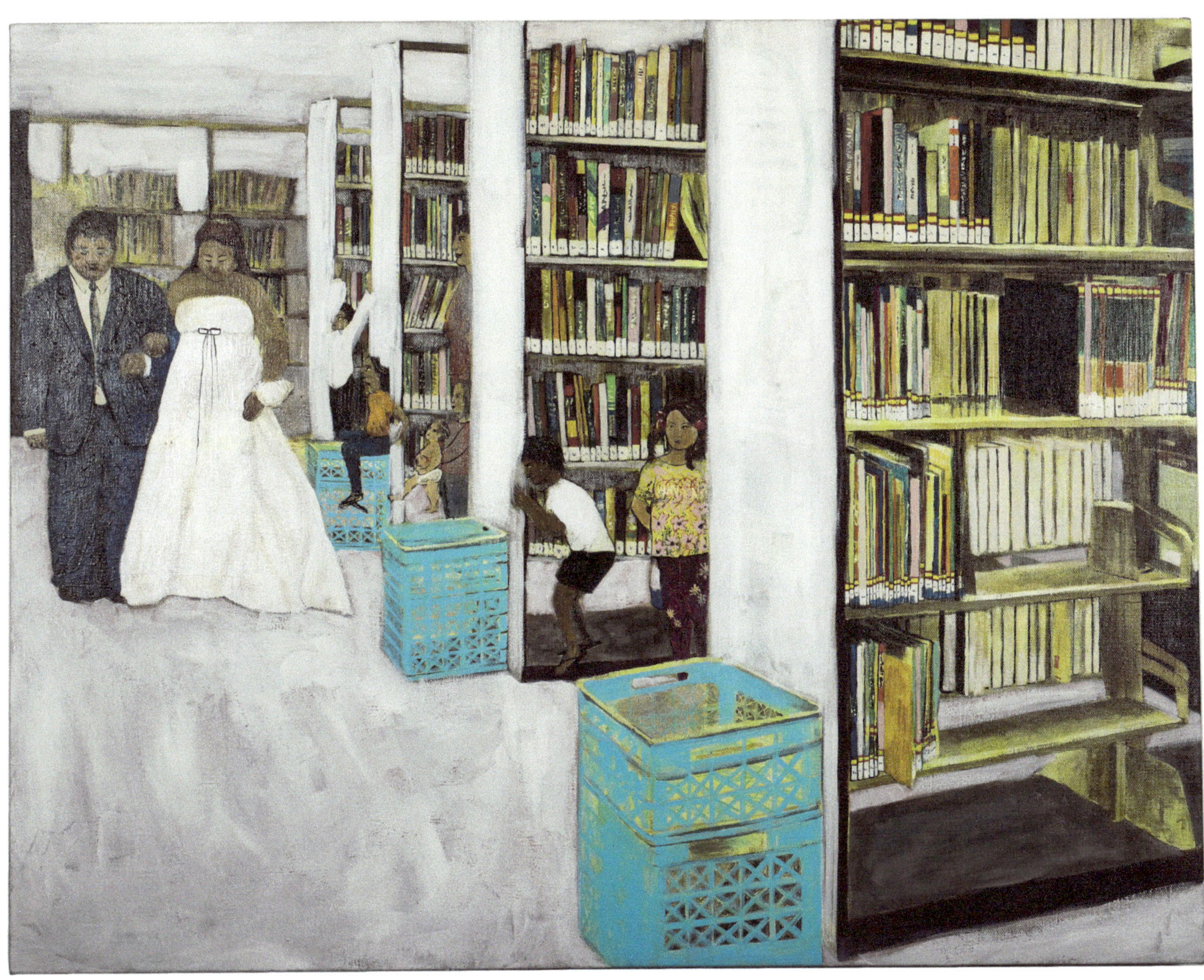

Plate 39
Library Wedding
2006

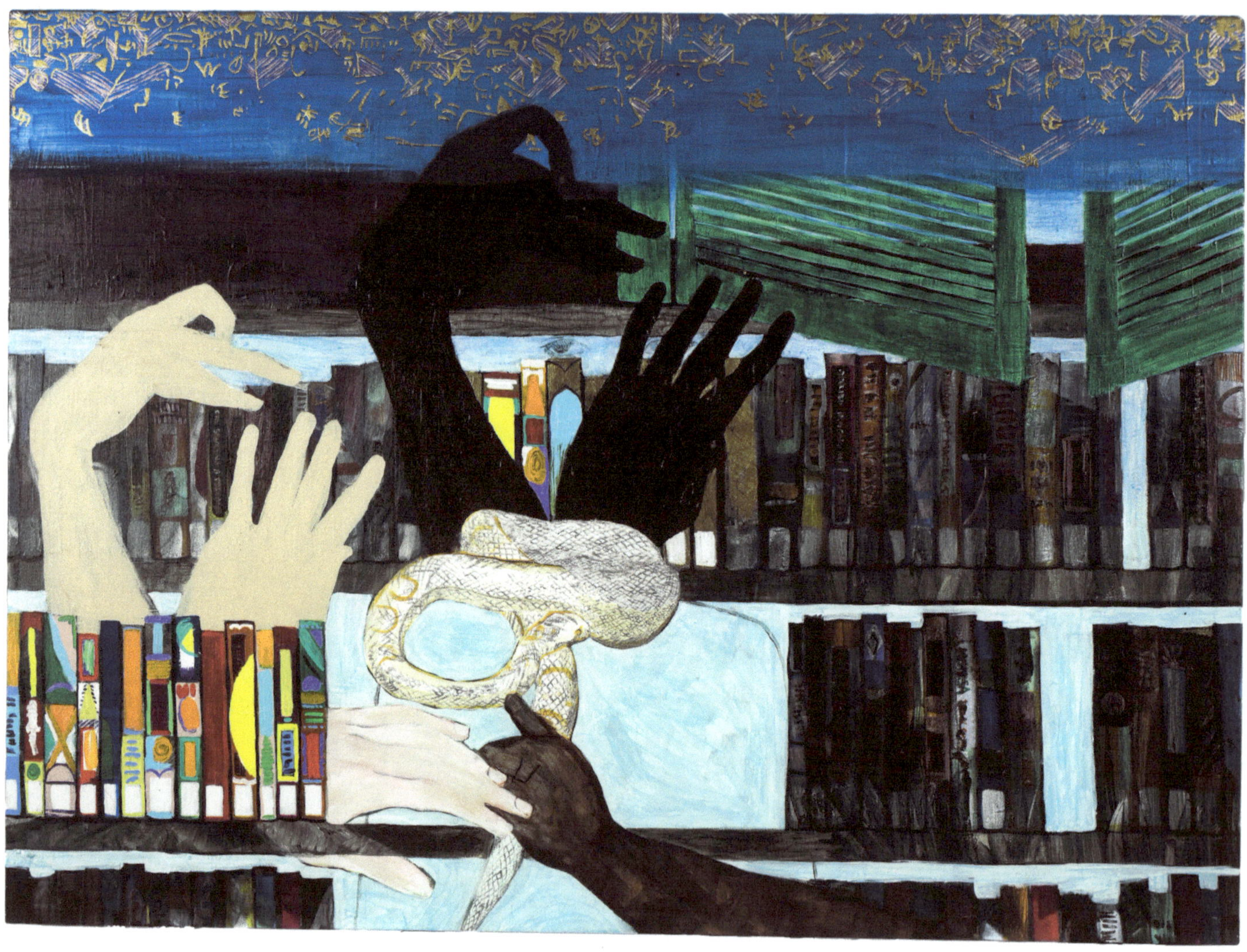

Plate 40
Swan Shadow
2006

Plate 41
(opposite page)
United States Mint
2006

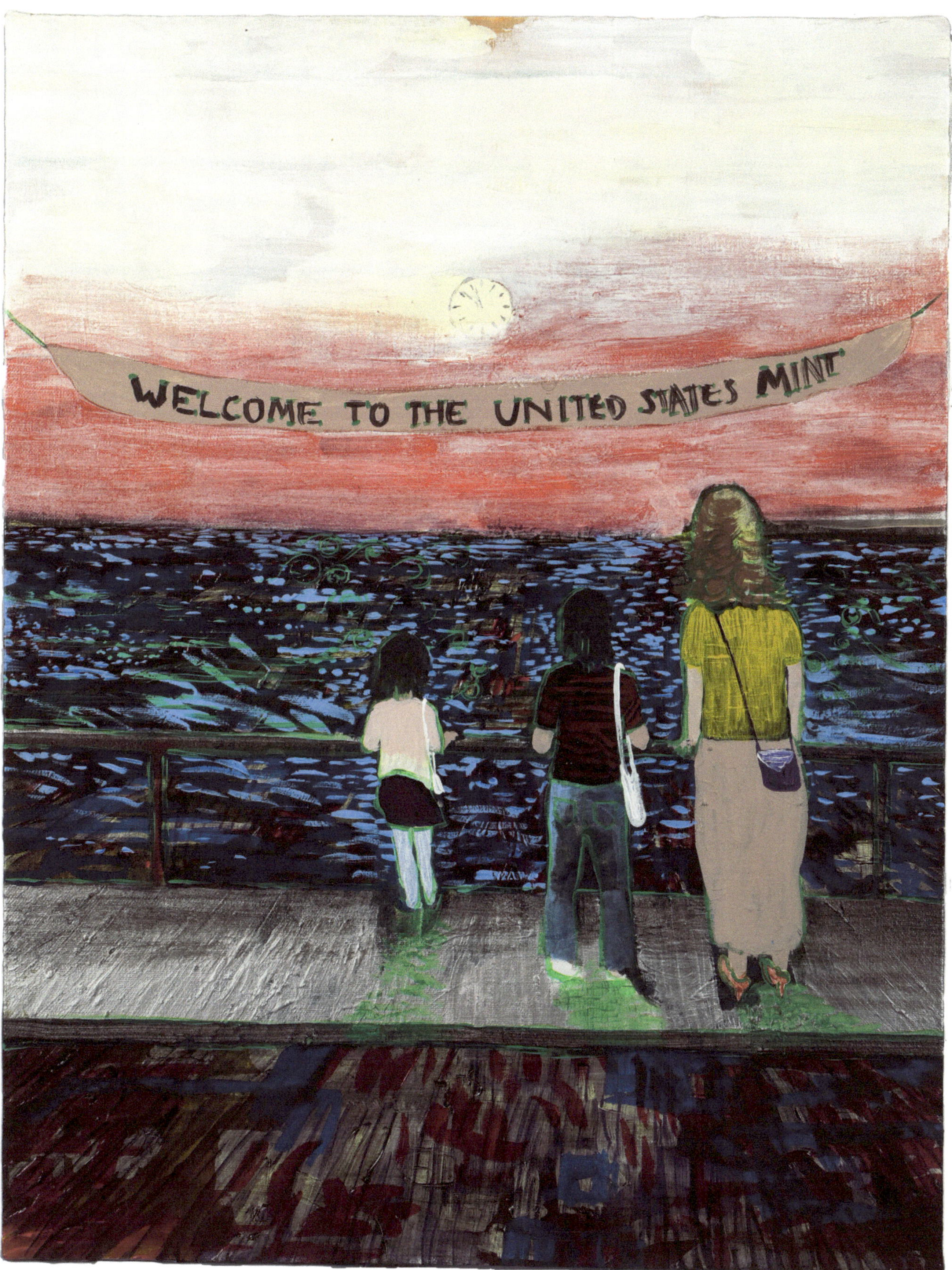
WELCOME TO THE UNITED STATES MINT

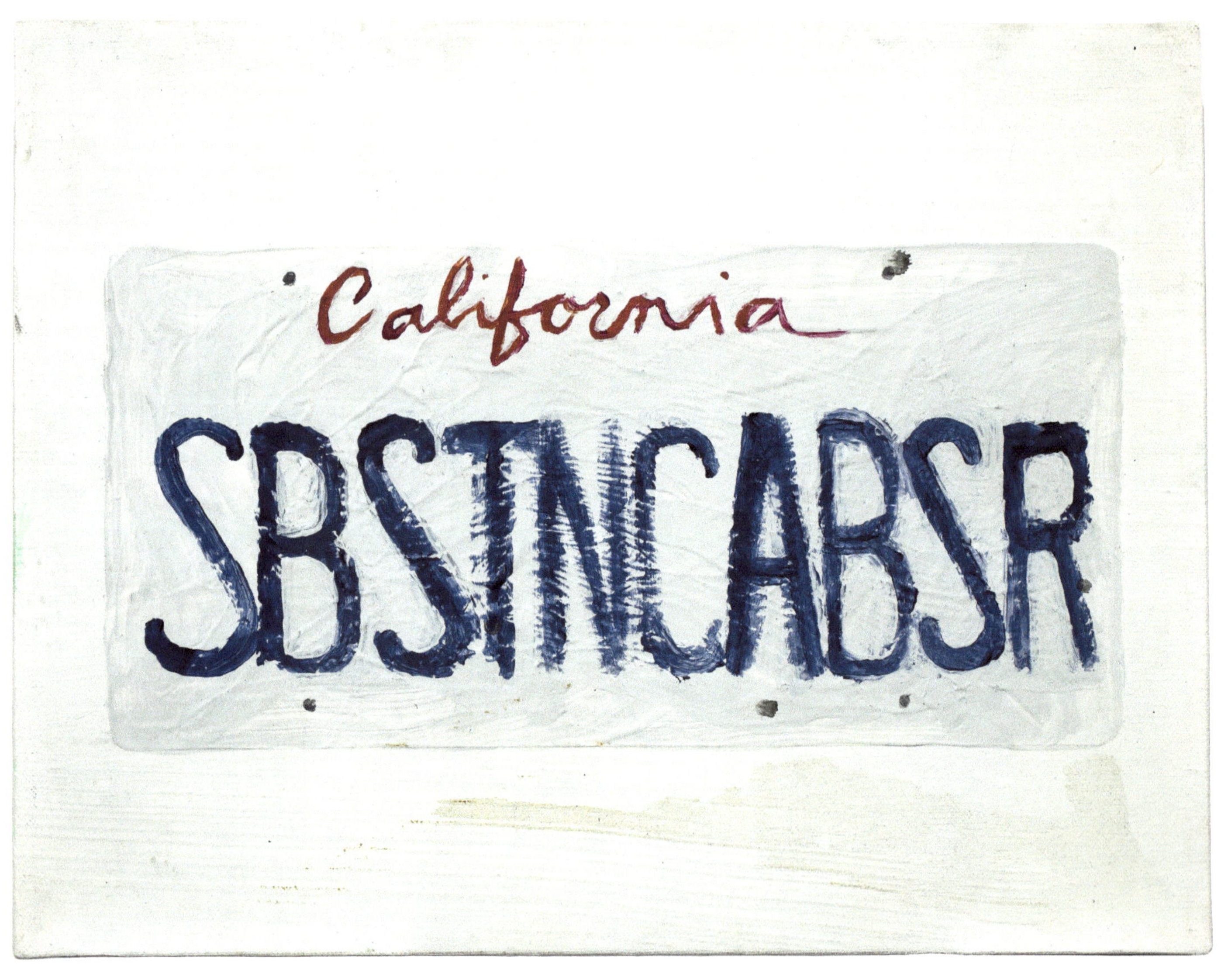

Plate 42
California Substance Abuser
2005

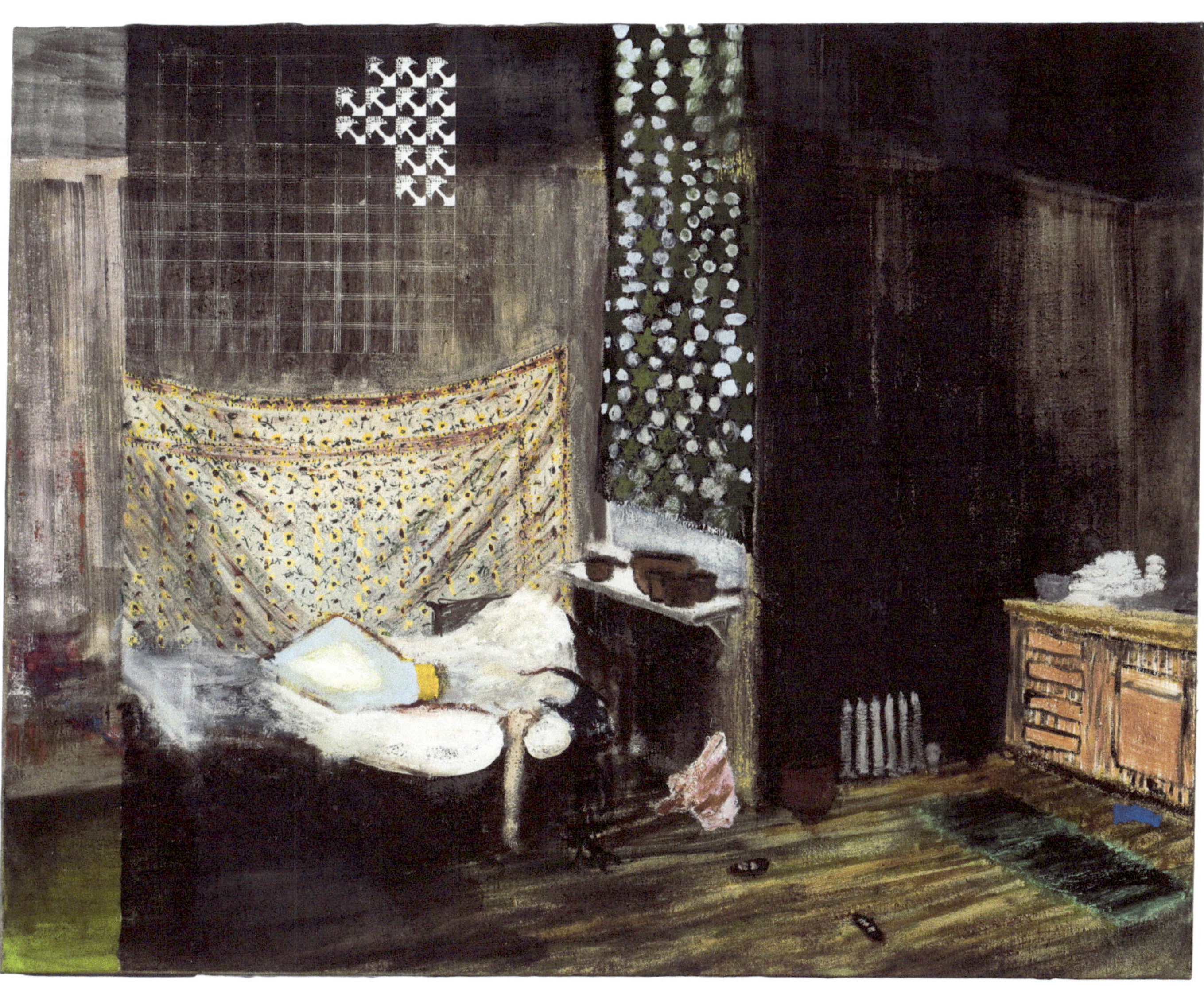

Plate 43
Information Overload Syndrome
2005

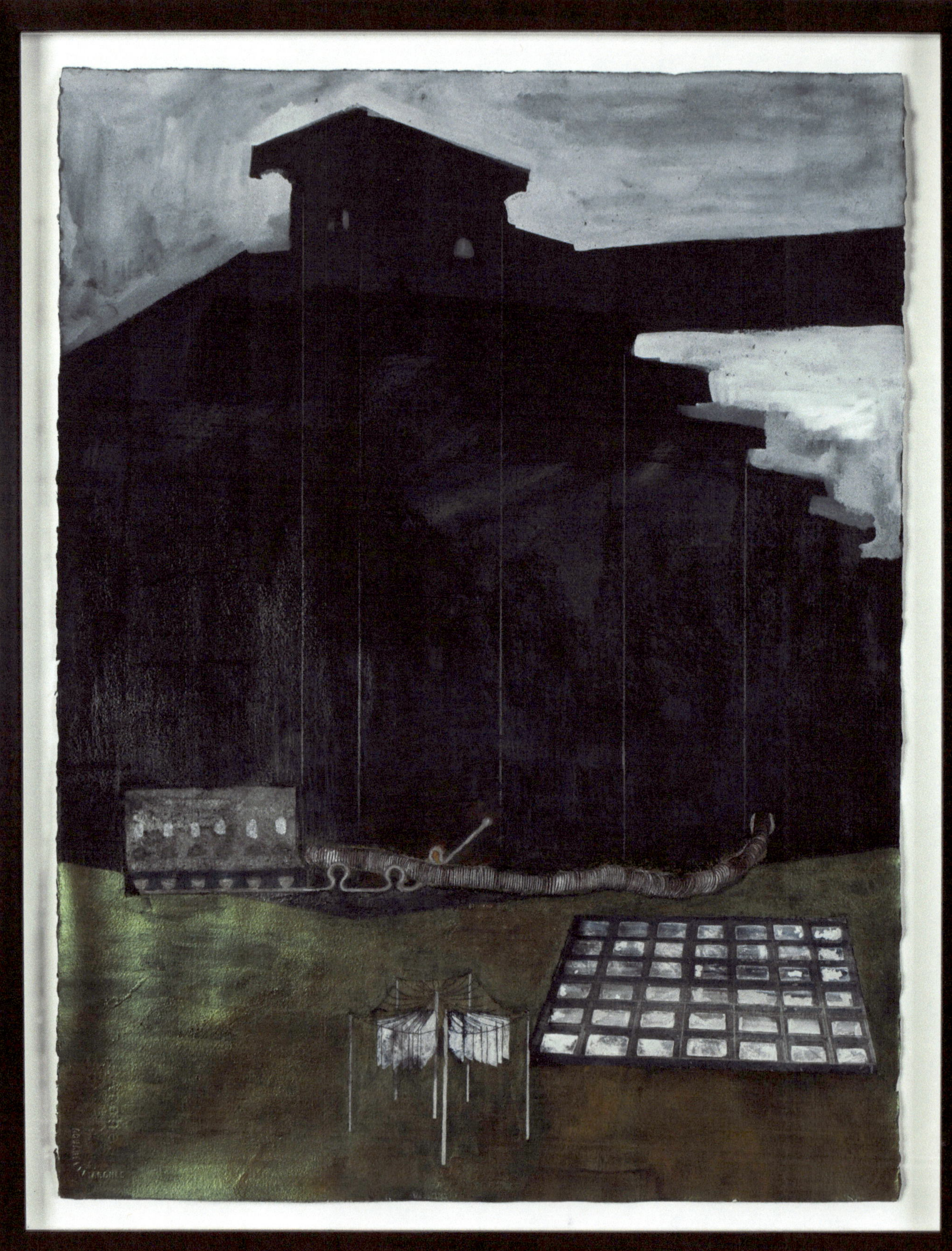

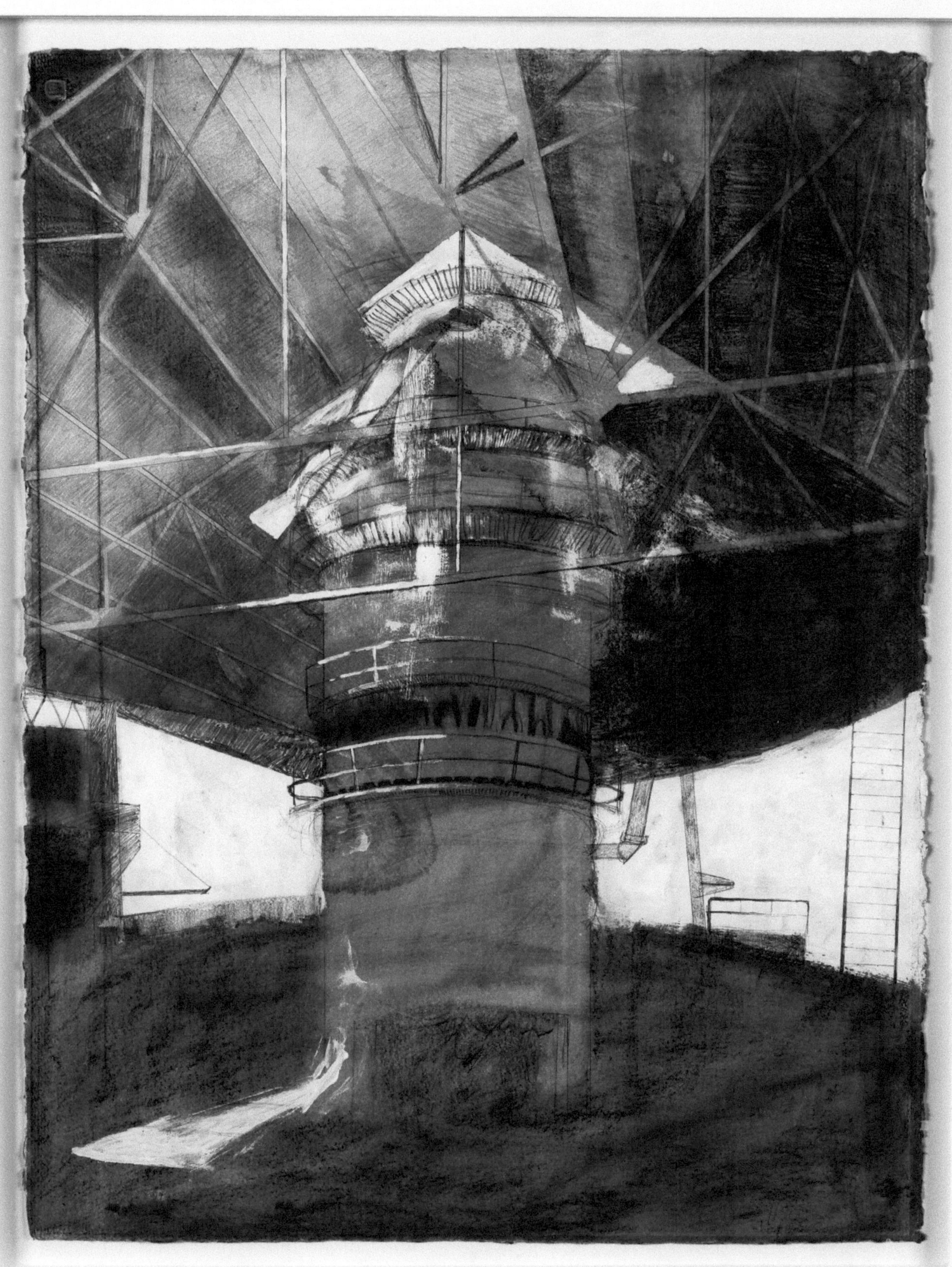

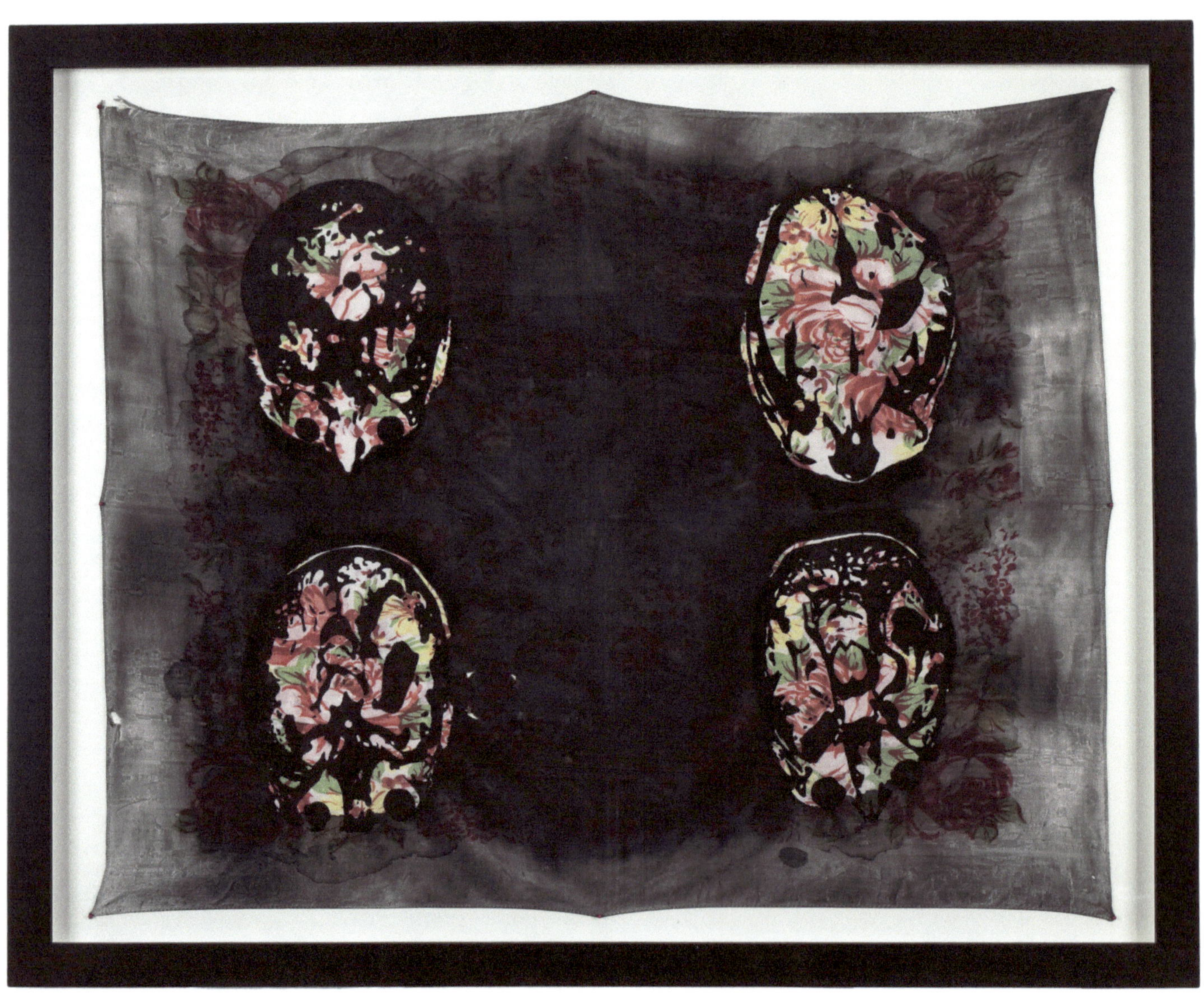

Plate 44
(previous spread, left side)
Paper Factory
2005

Plate 45
(previous spread, right side)
Sloss Furnace
2004

Plate 46
Head Scarf
2001

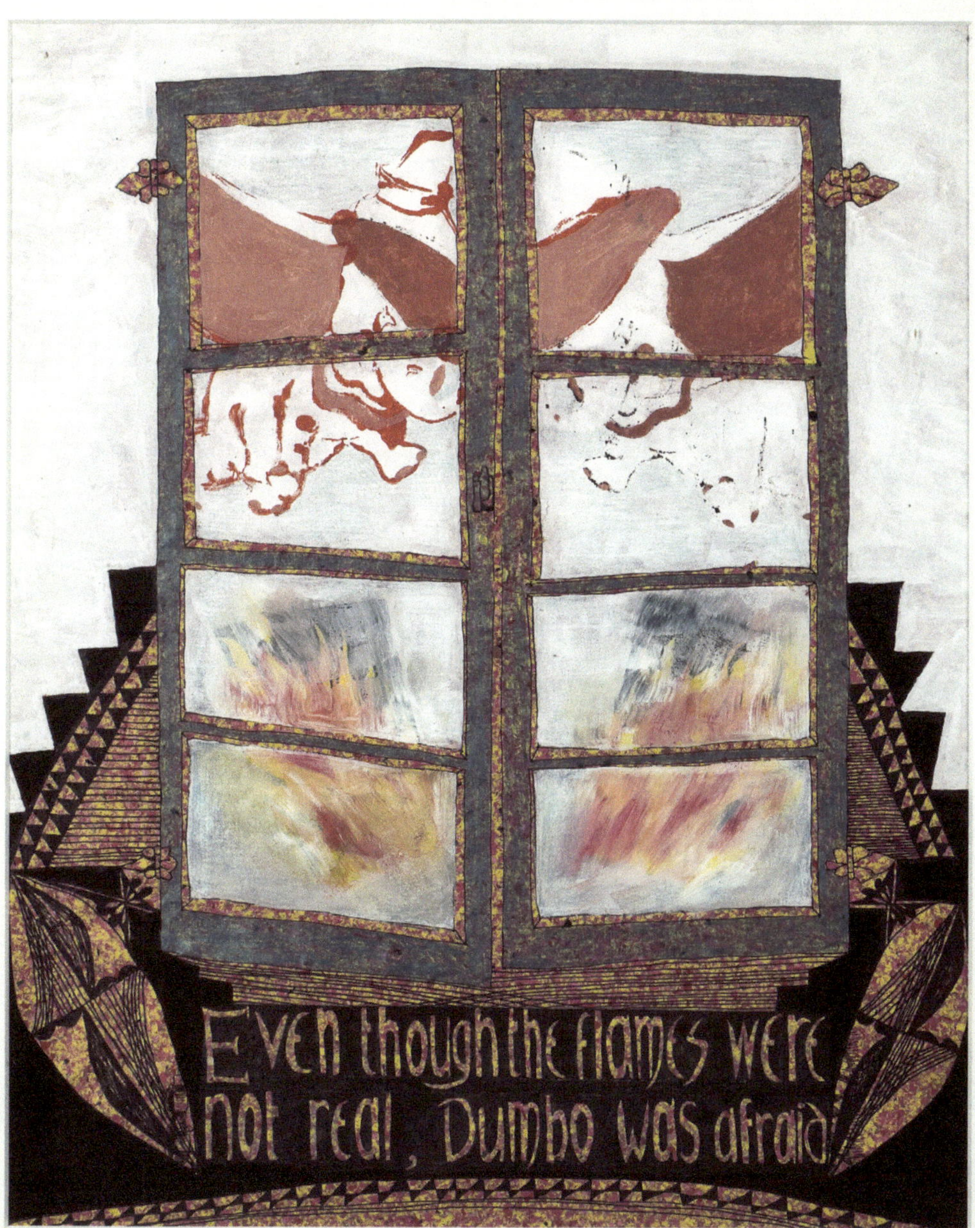
Even though the flames were
not real, Dumbo was afraid

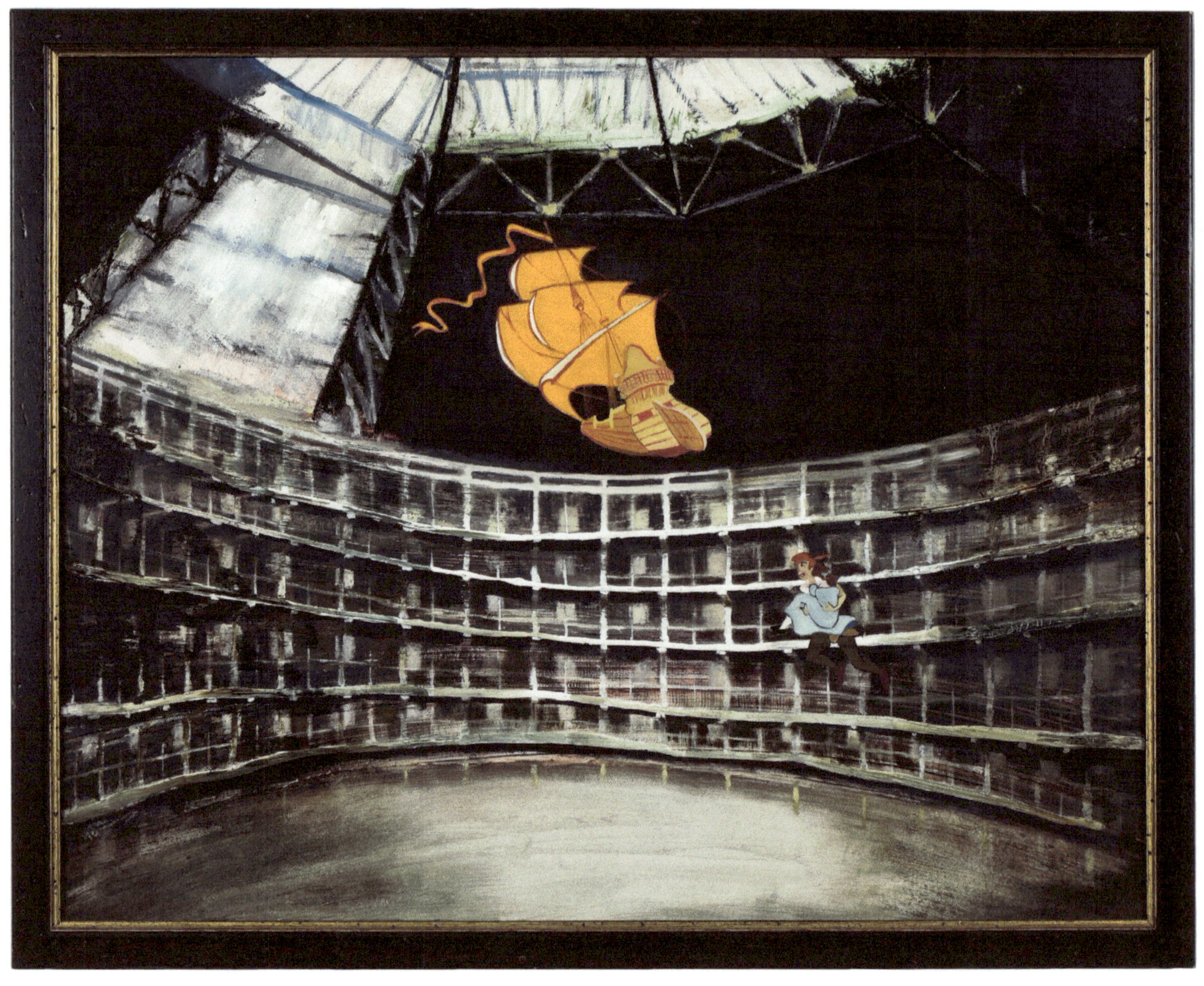

Plate 47
(previous spread, right side)
Even Though The Flames Were Not Real, Dumbo Was Afraid
2000

Plate 48
Peter Panopticon
2000

Installation Views

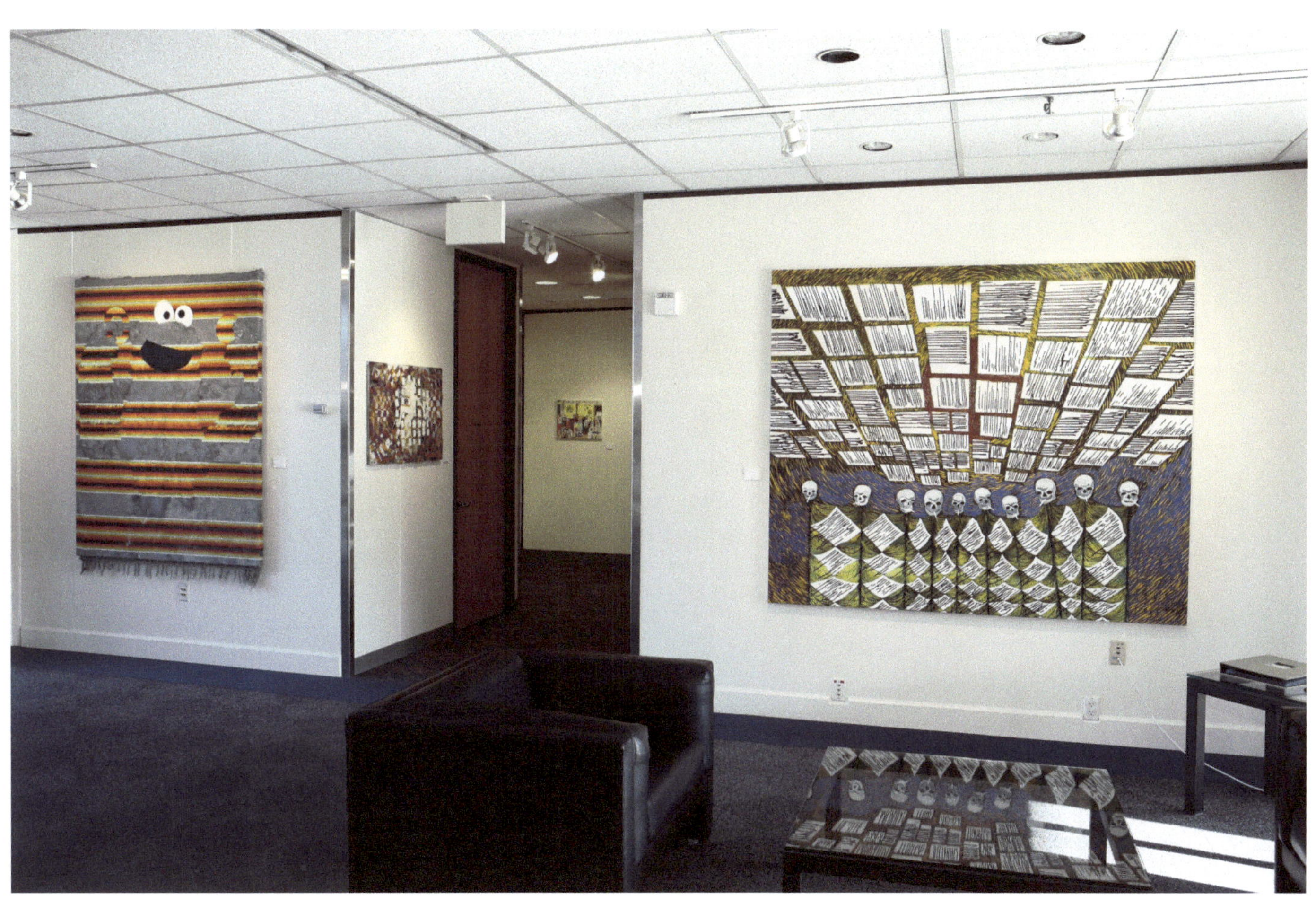

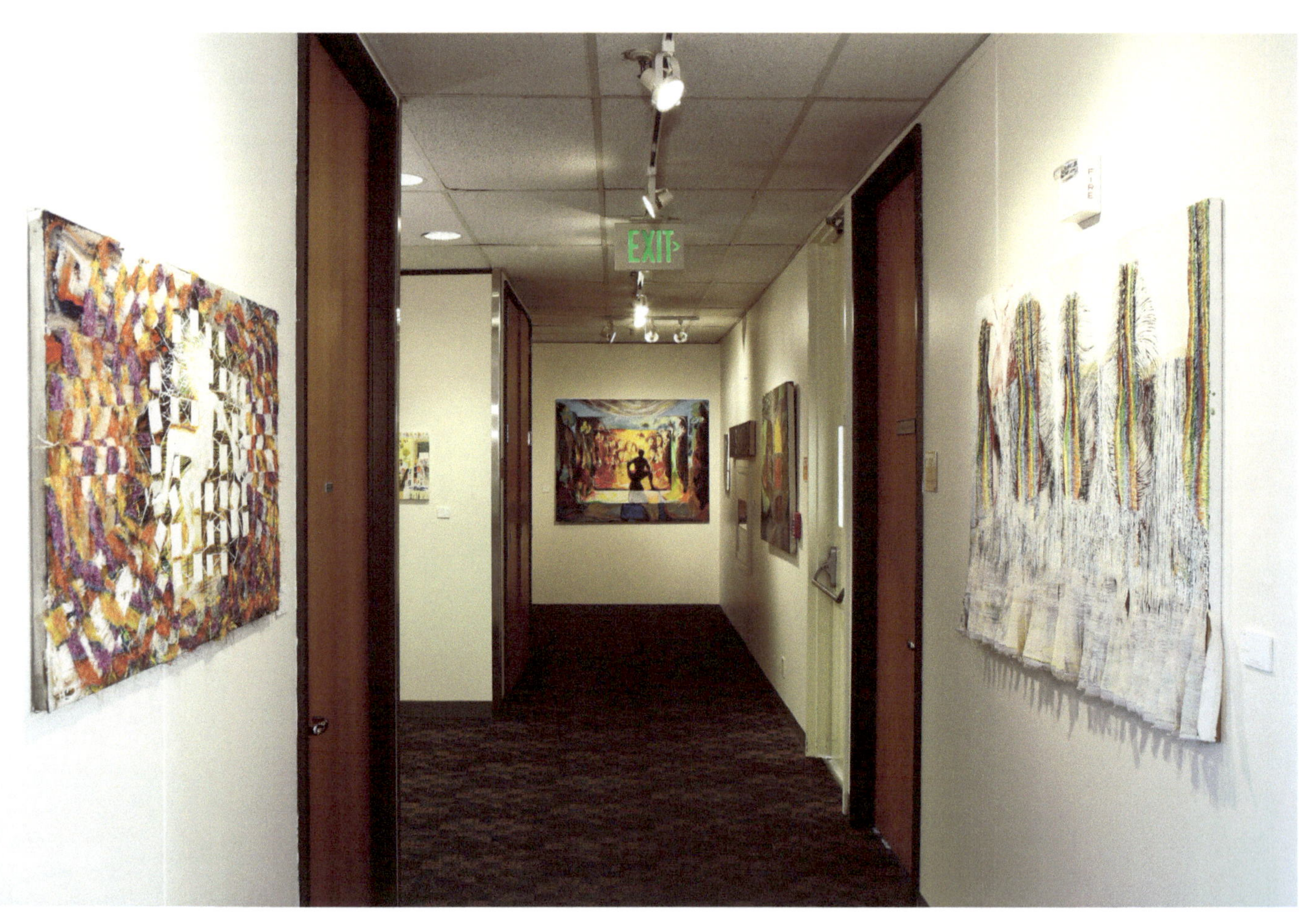
EXIT

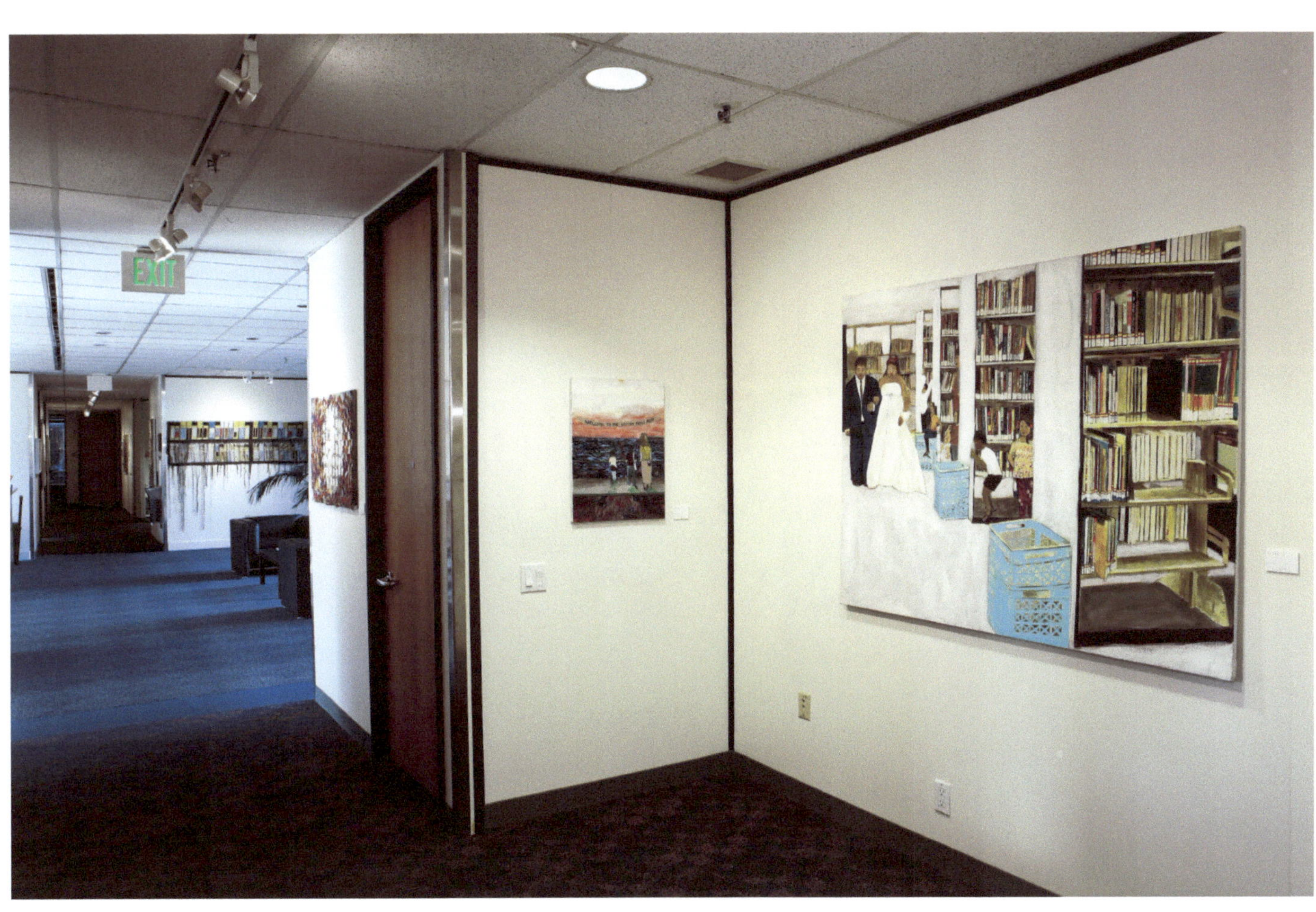
EXIT

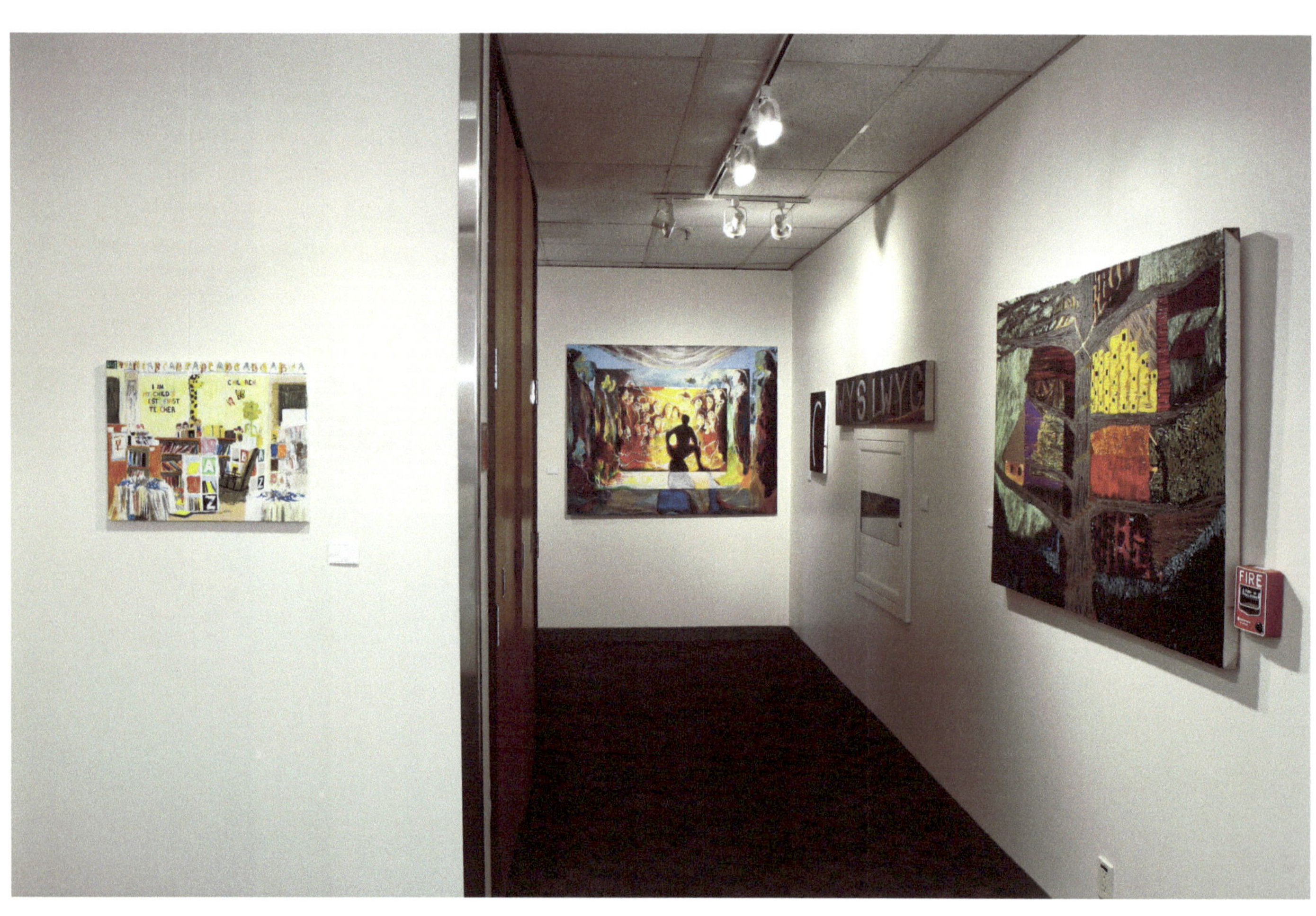
FIRE

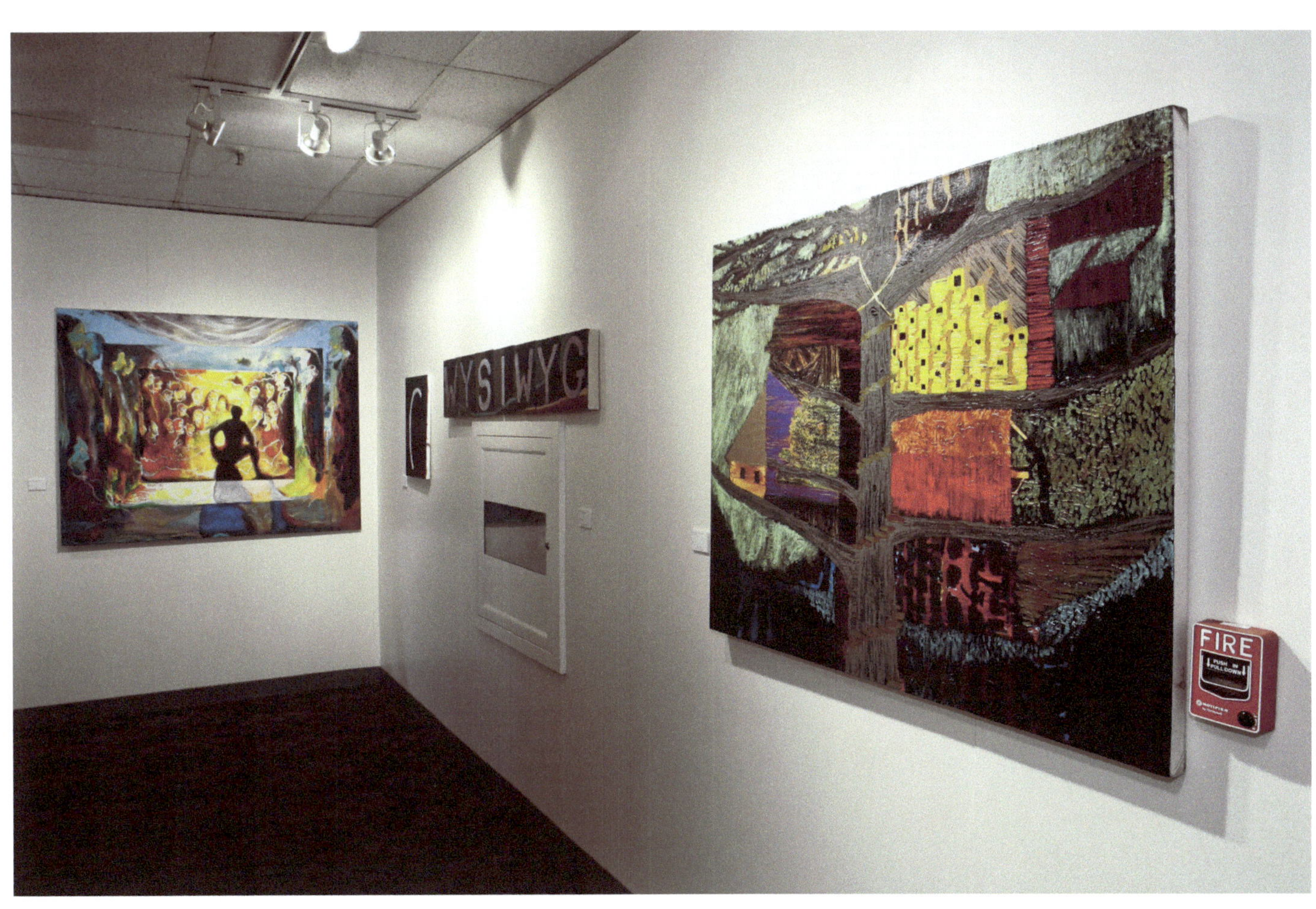
C
WYSIWYG
FIRE

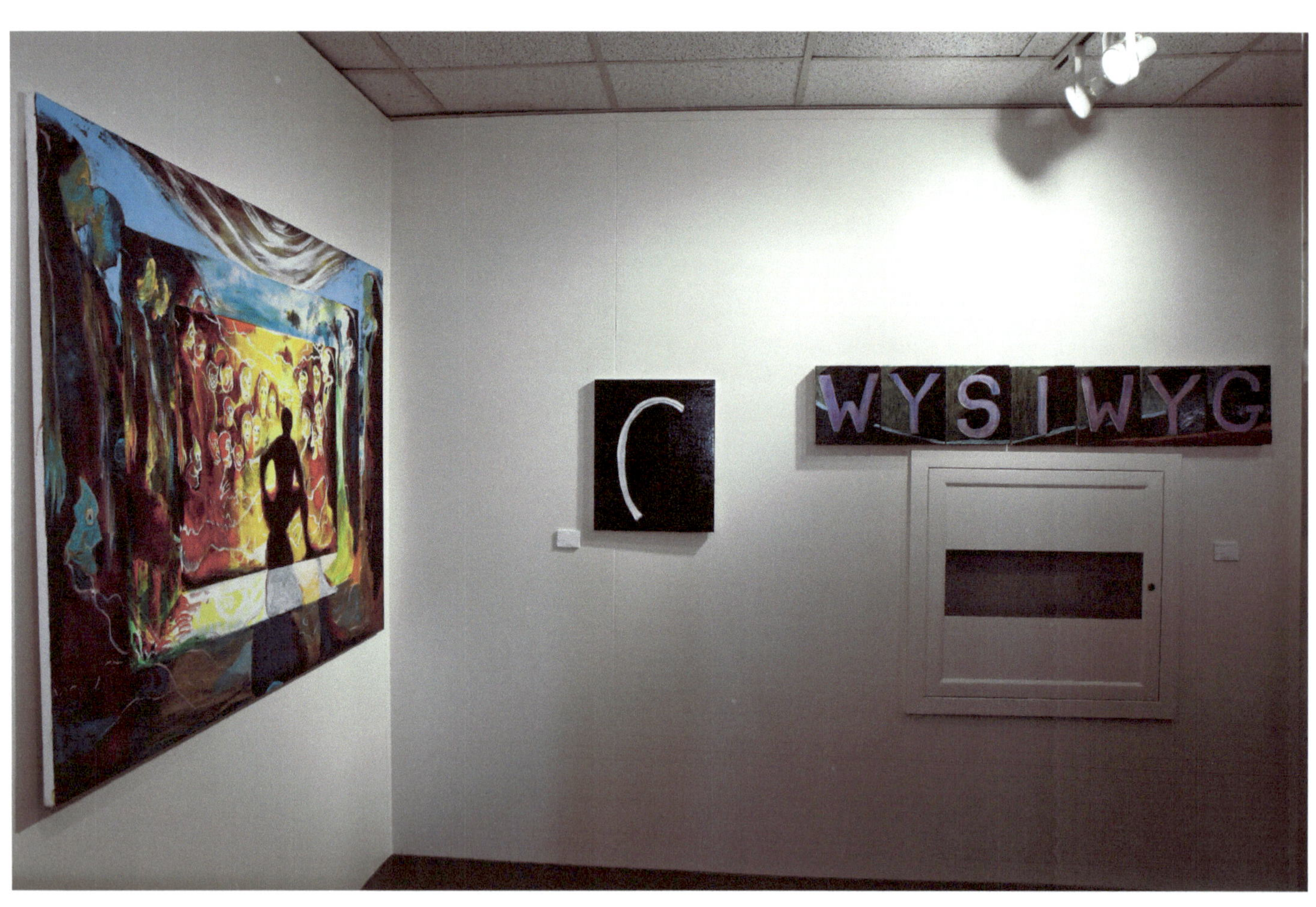
WYSIWYG

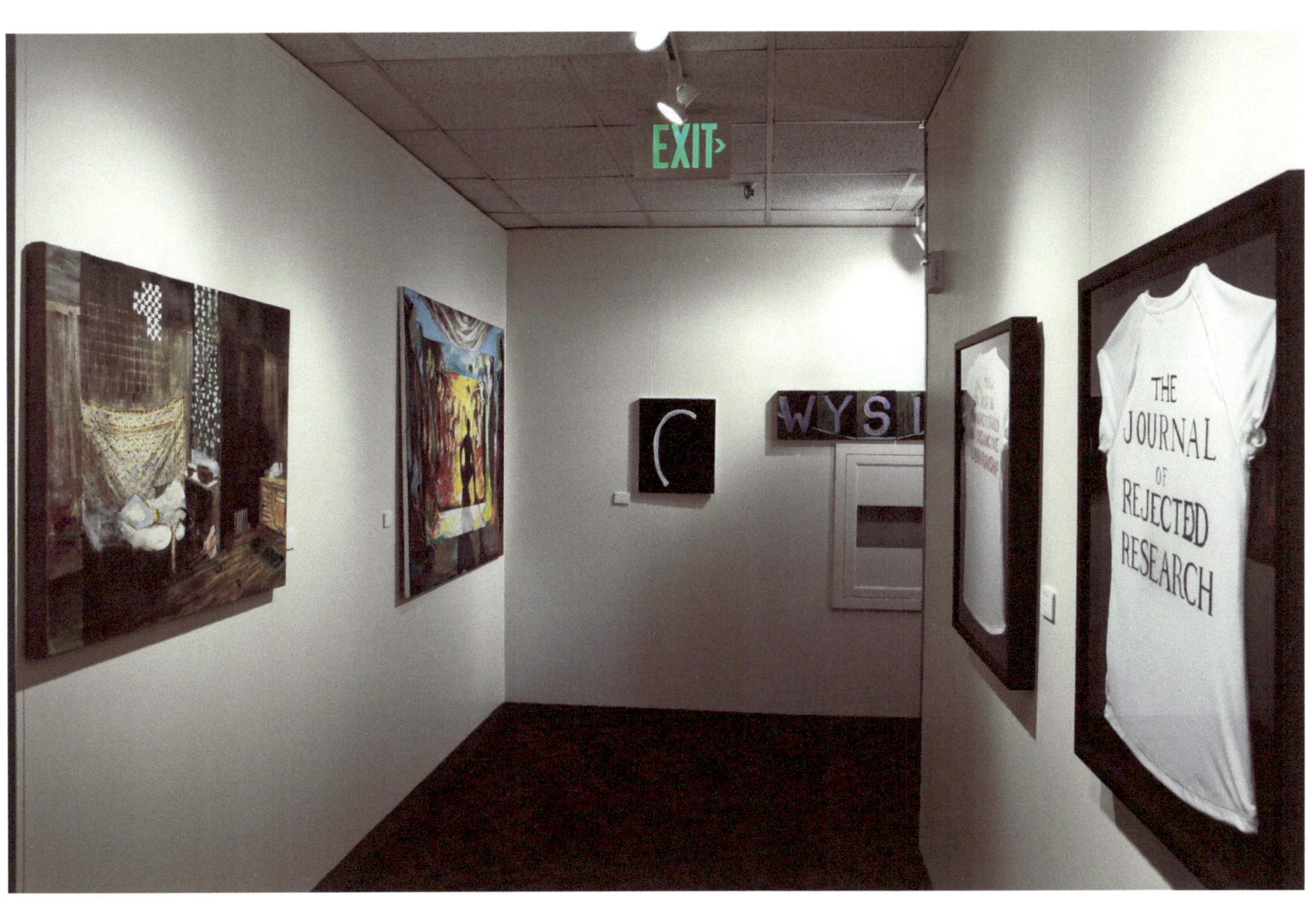
EXIT
WYSI
THE
JOURNAL
OF
REJECTED
RESEARCH

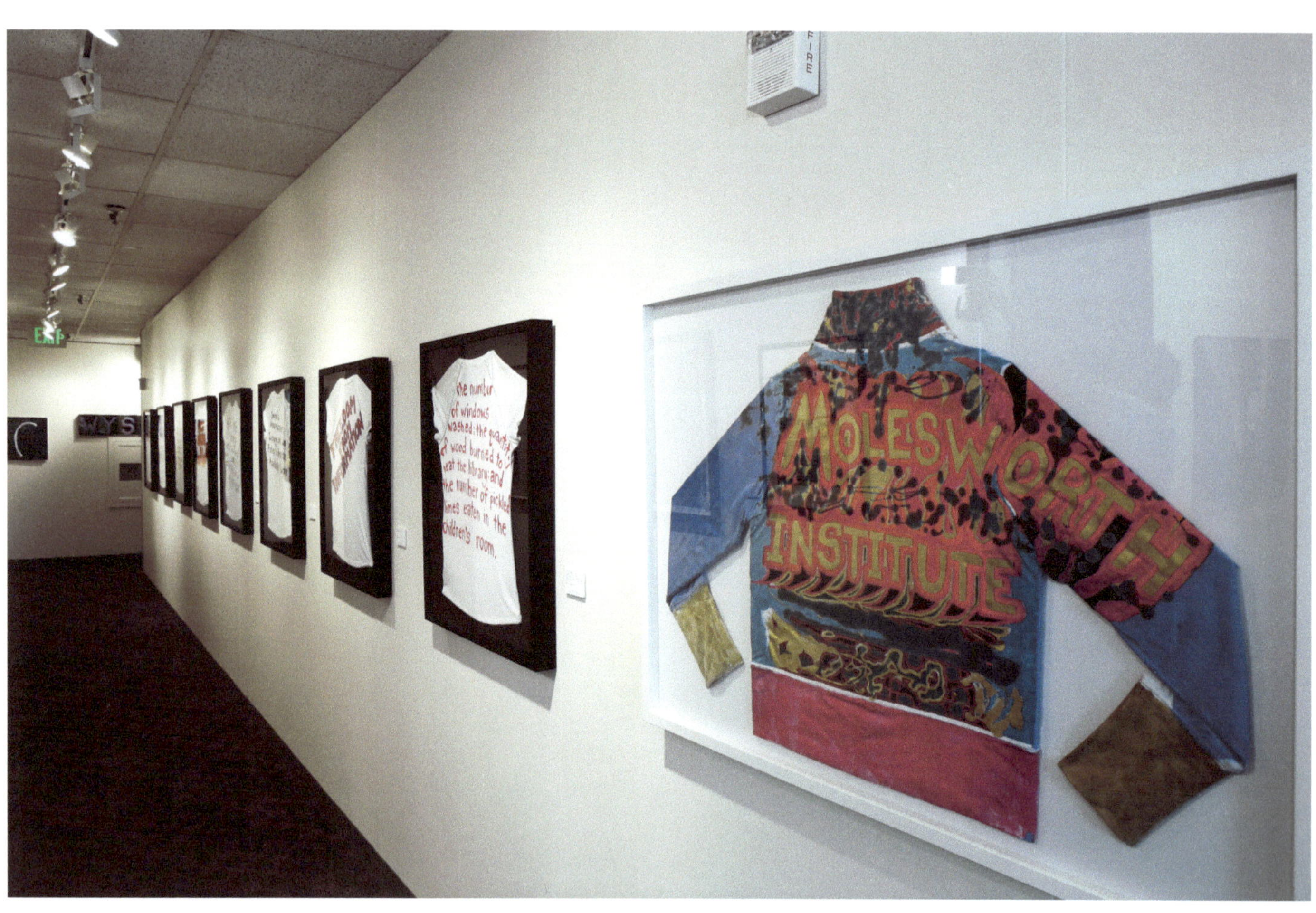
MOLESWORTH
INSTITUTE

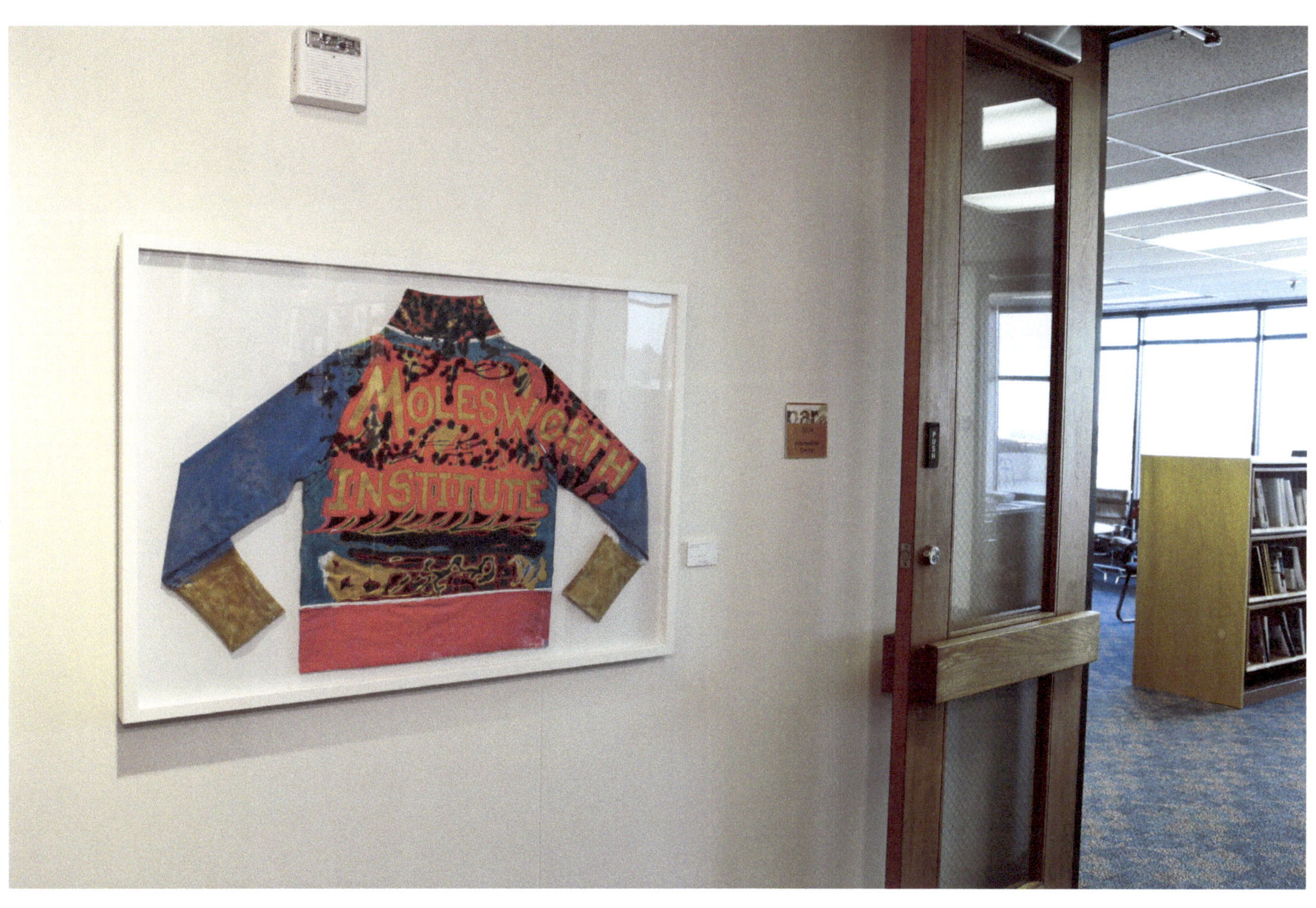
MOLESWORTH
INSTITUTE

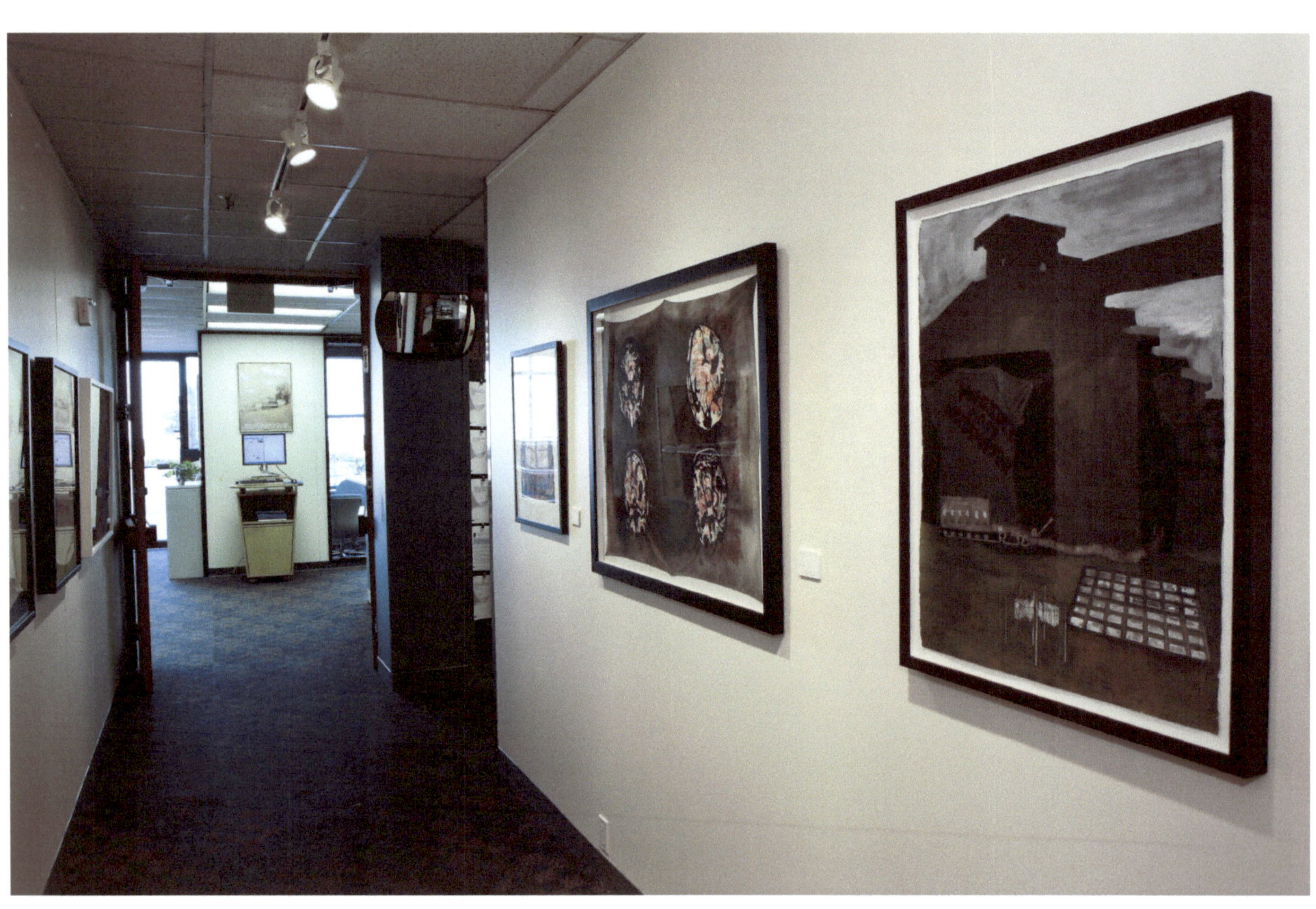

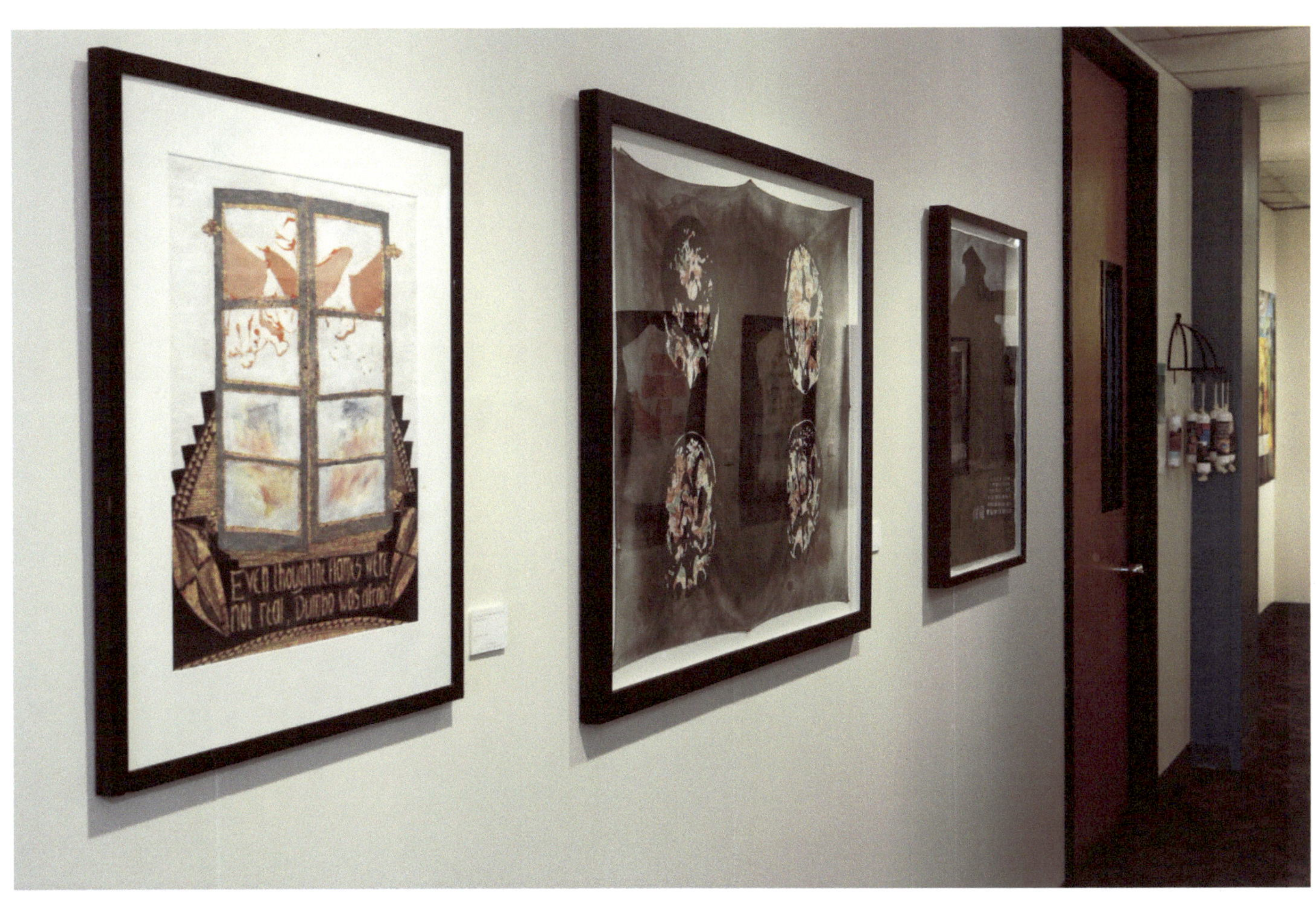

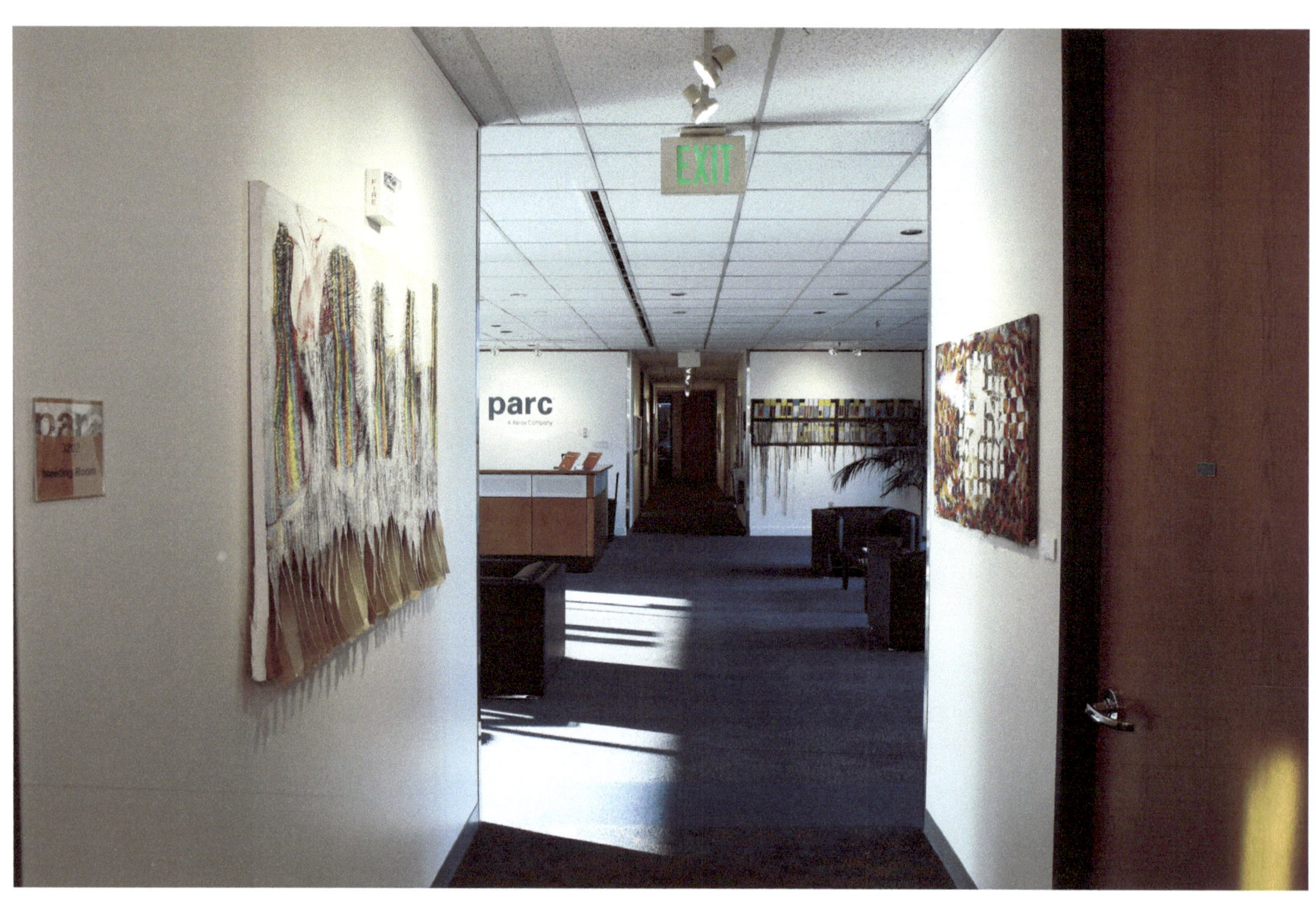
EXIT
parc

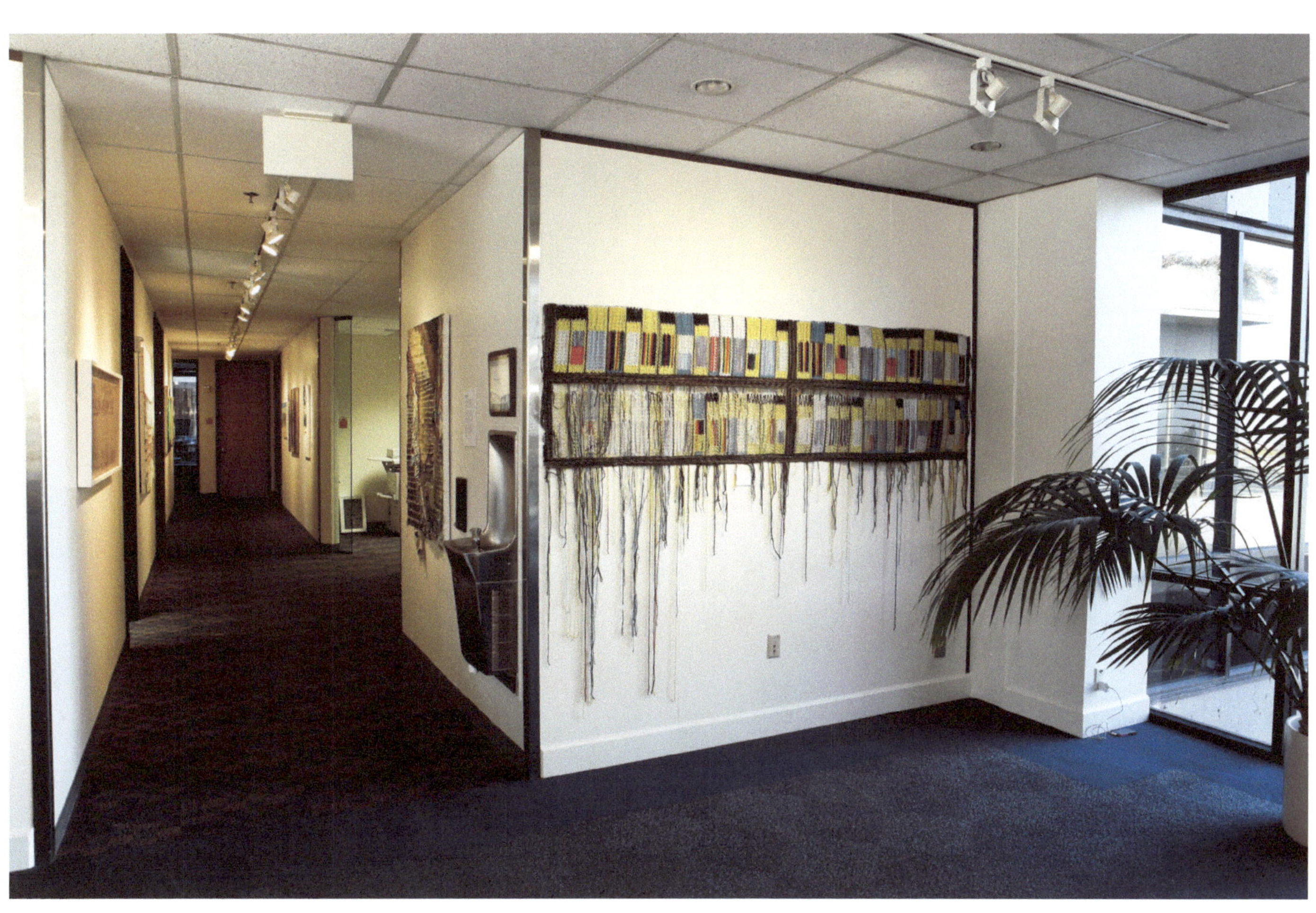

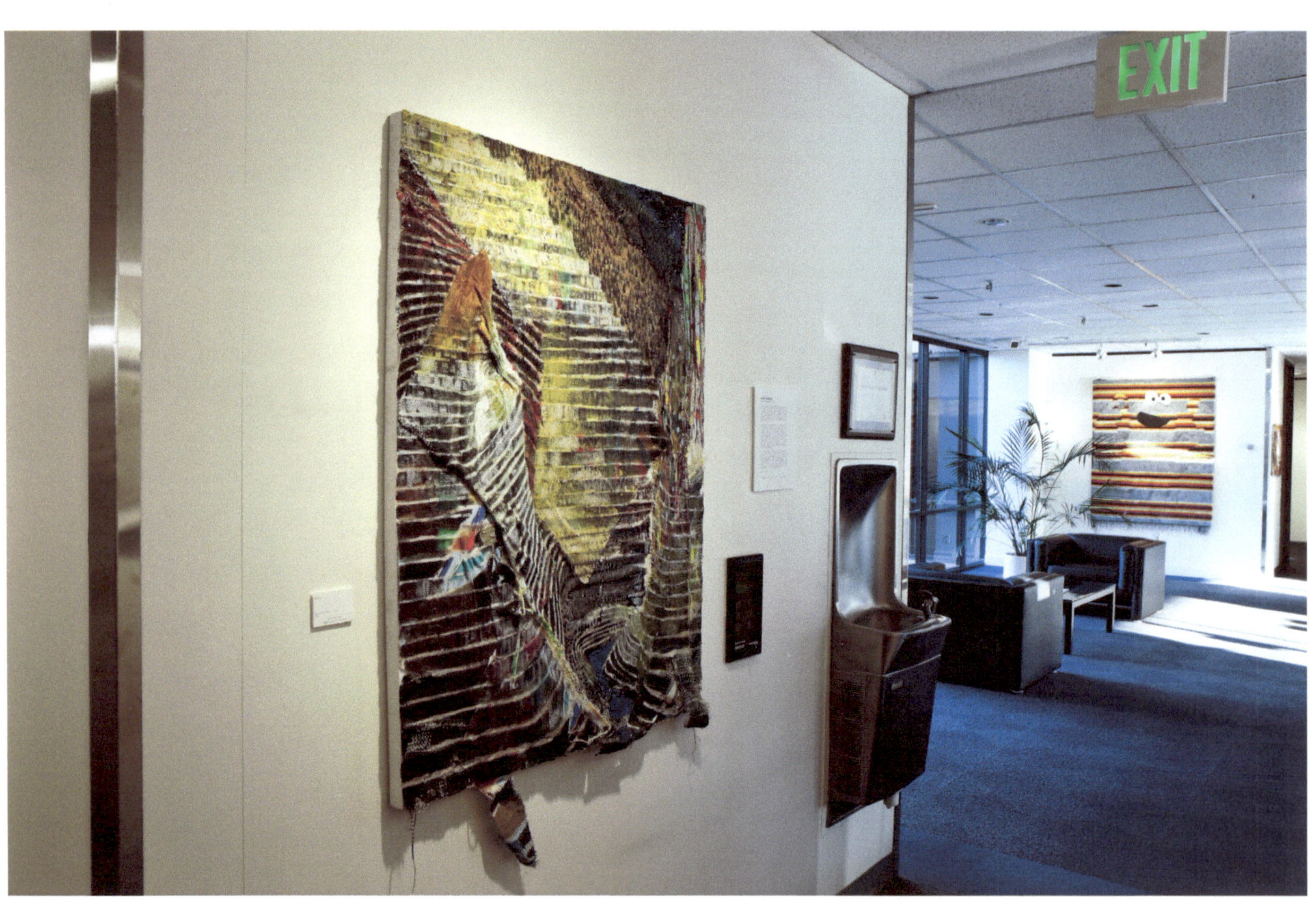
EXIT

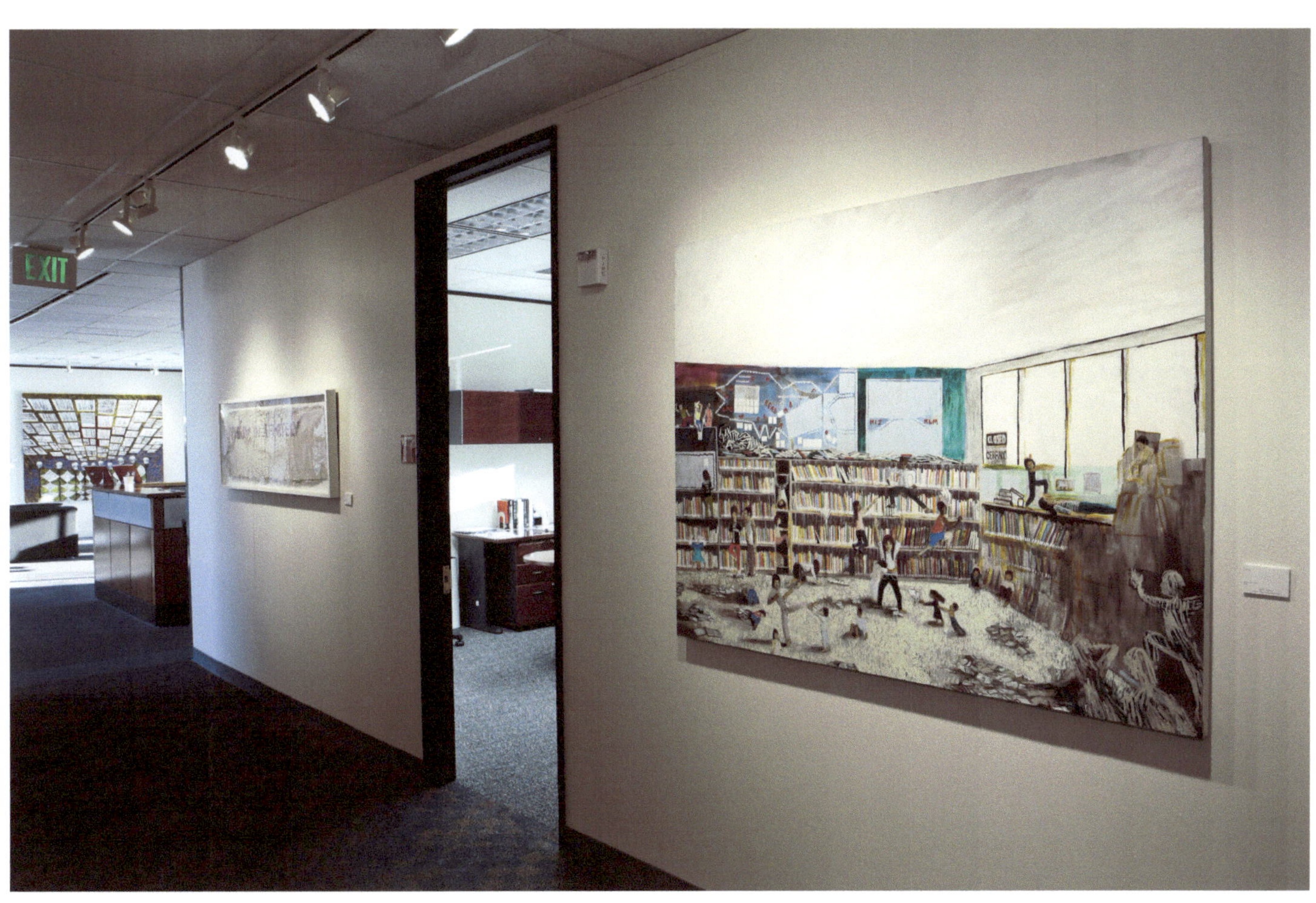
EXIT

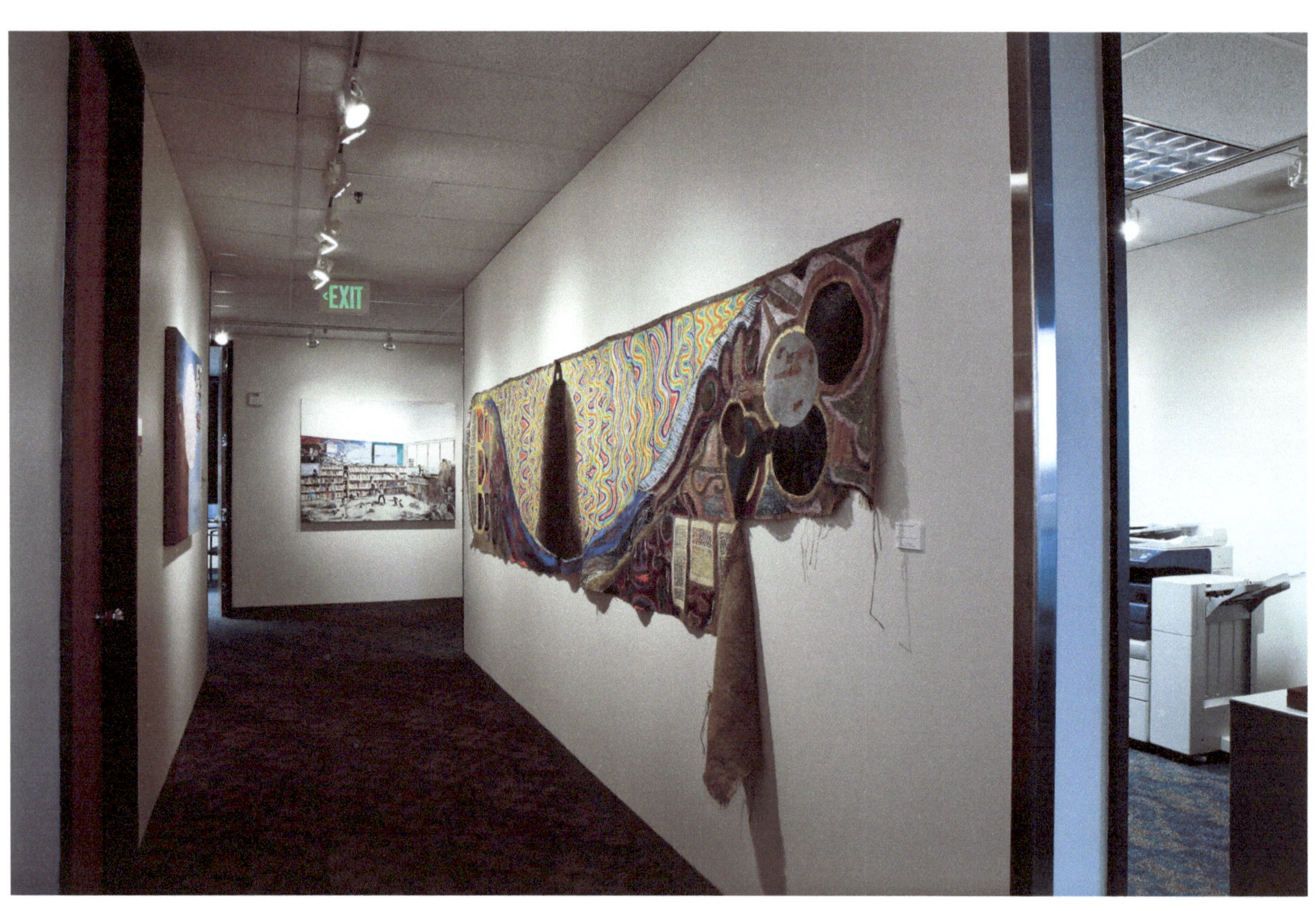
EXIT

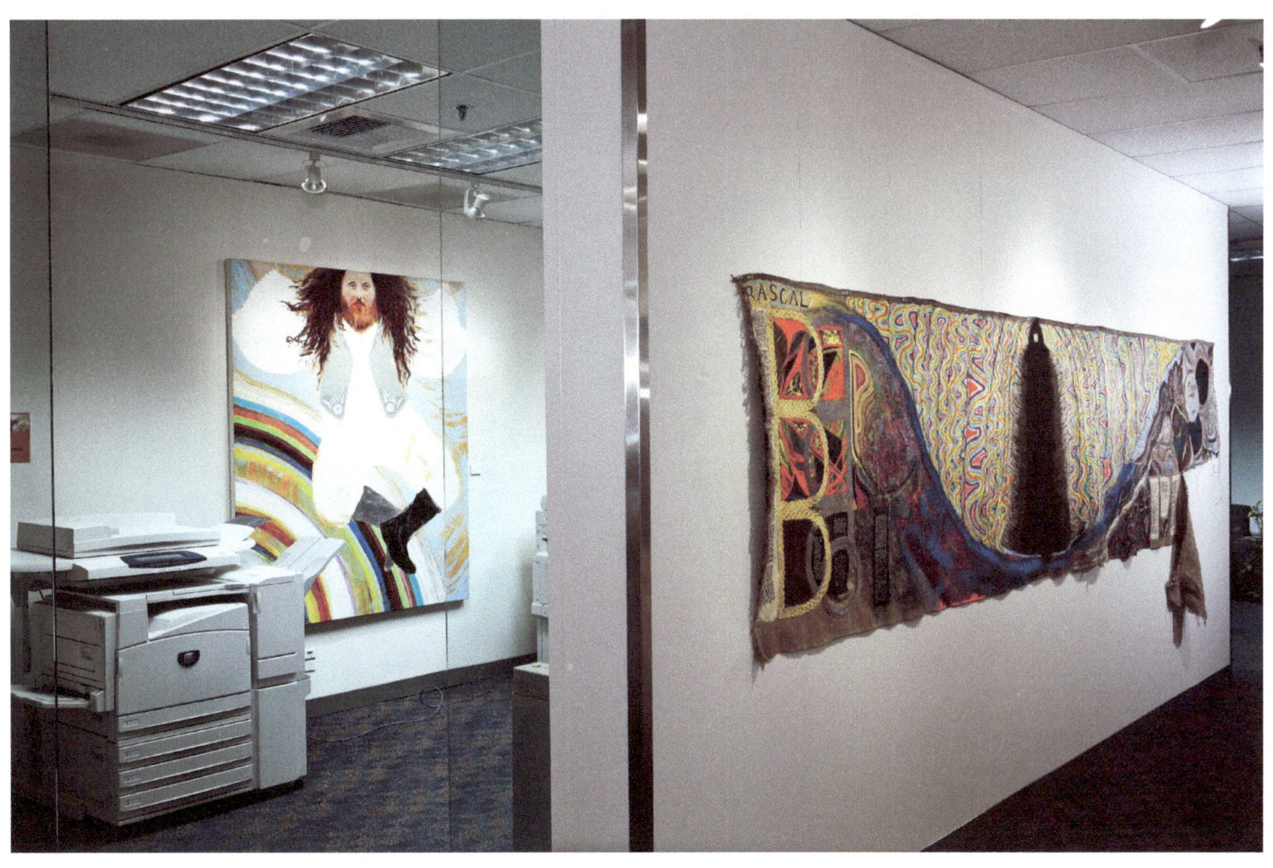
RASCAL

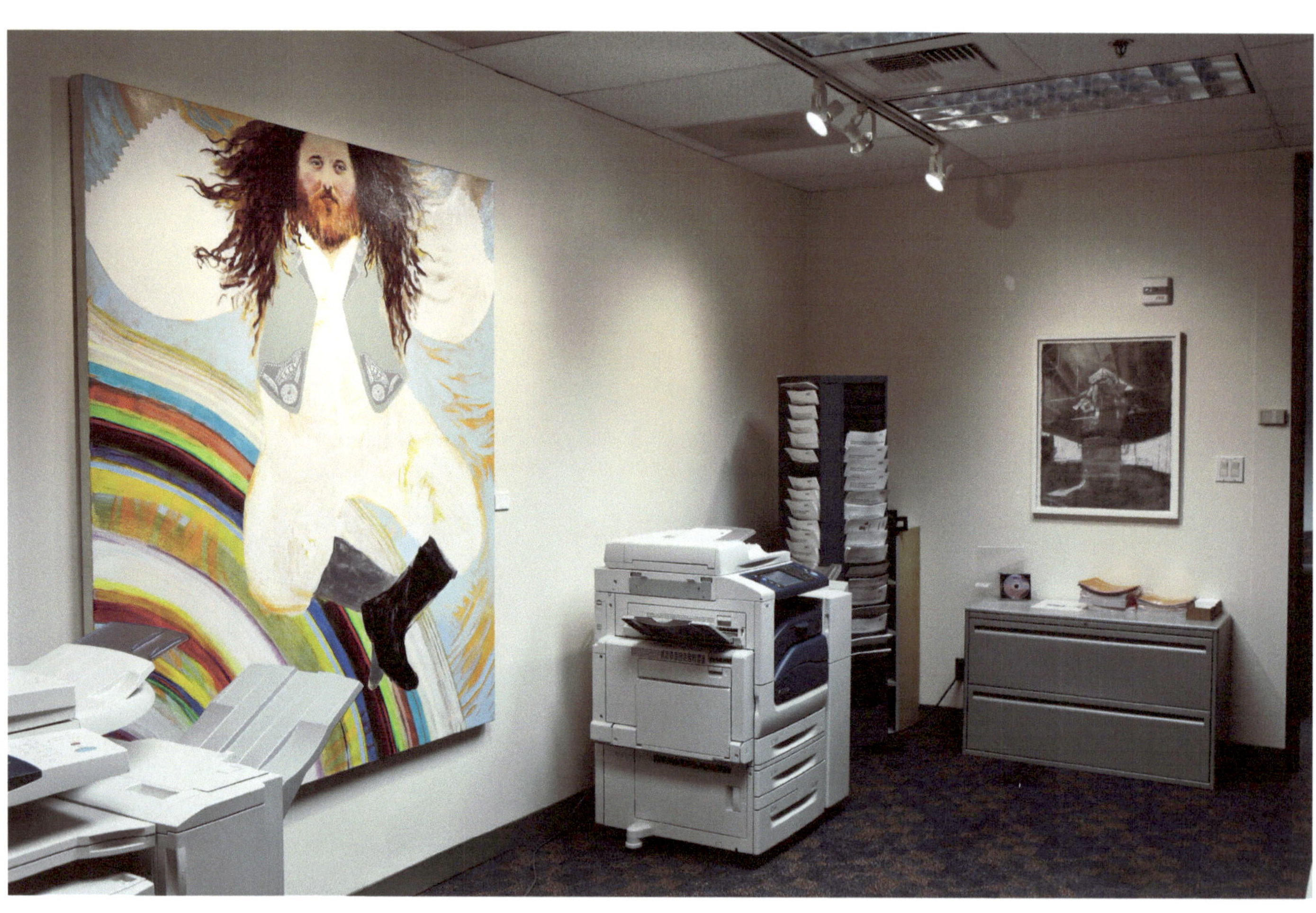

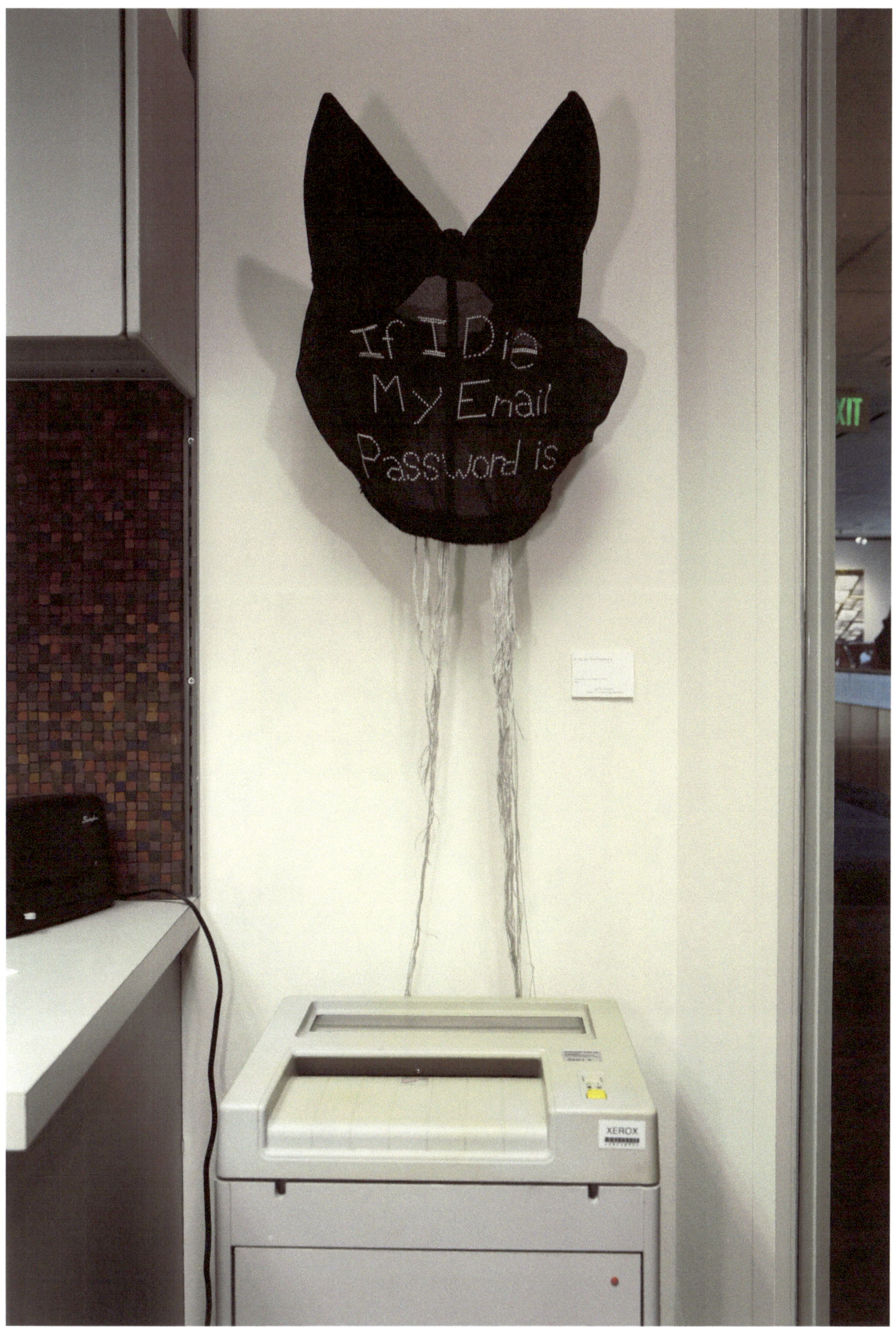
If I Die
My Email
Password is
EXIT
XEROX

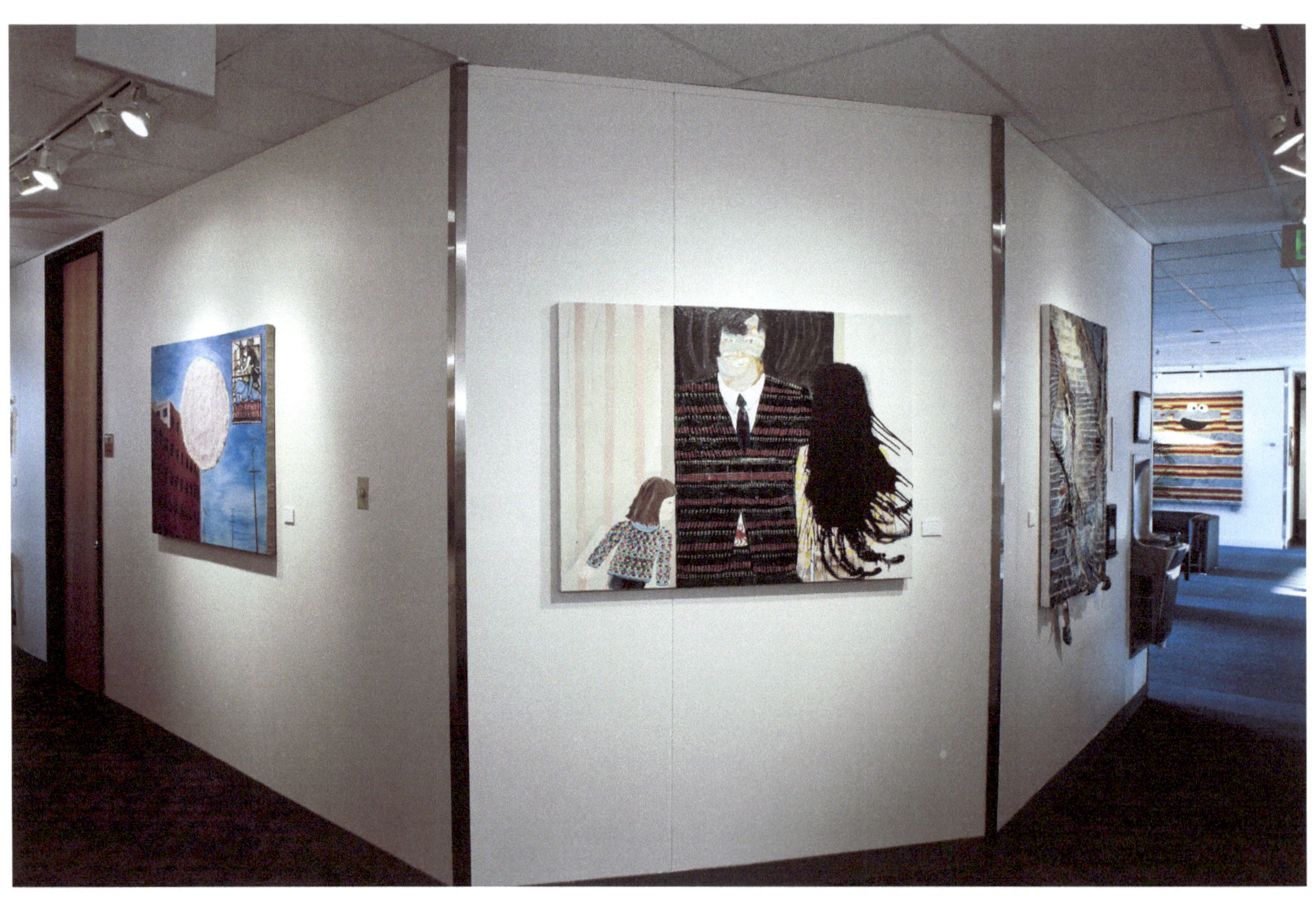

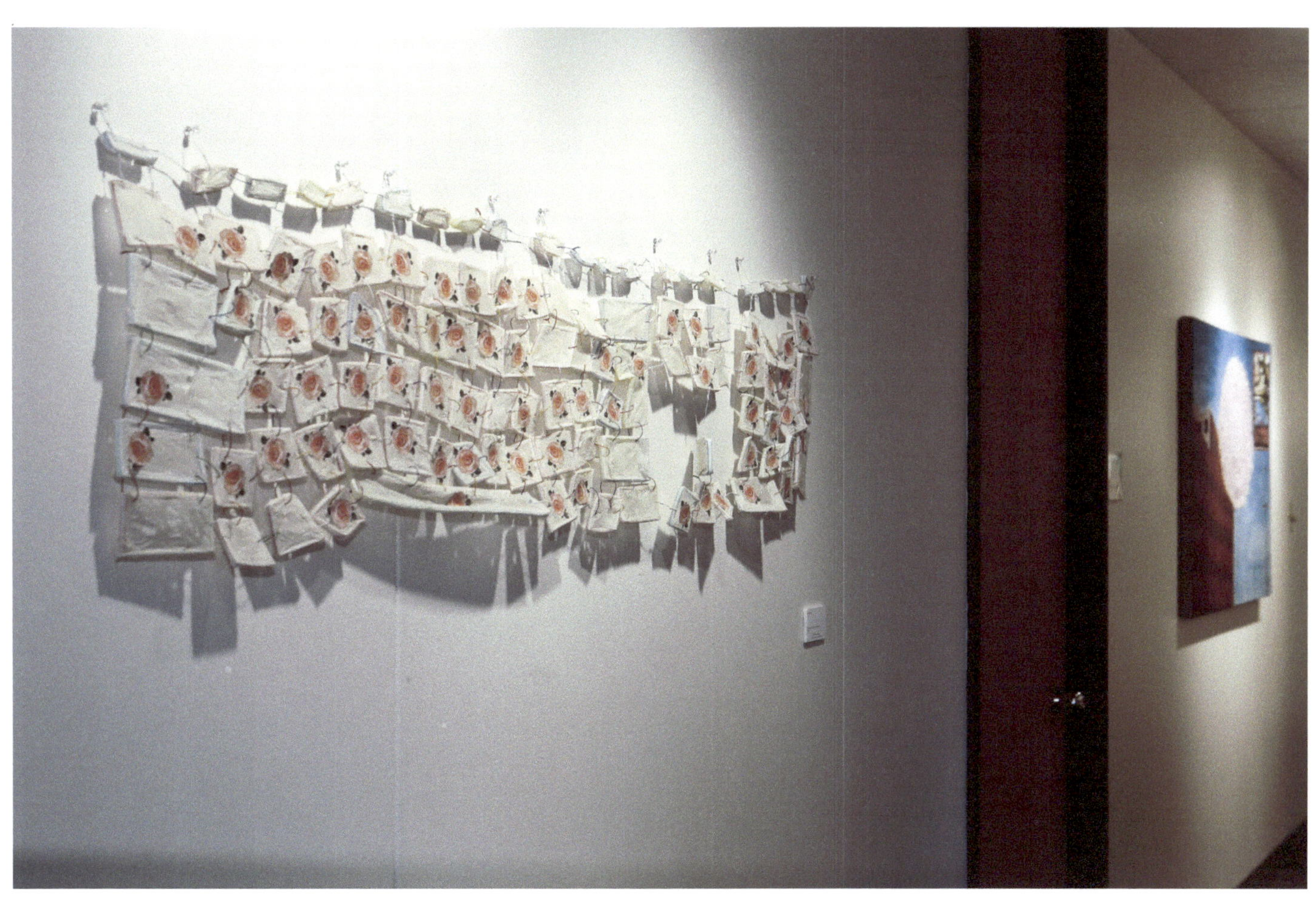

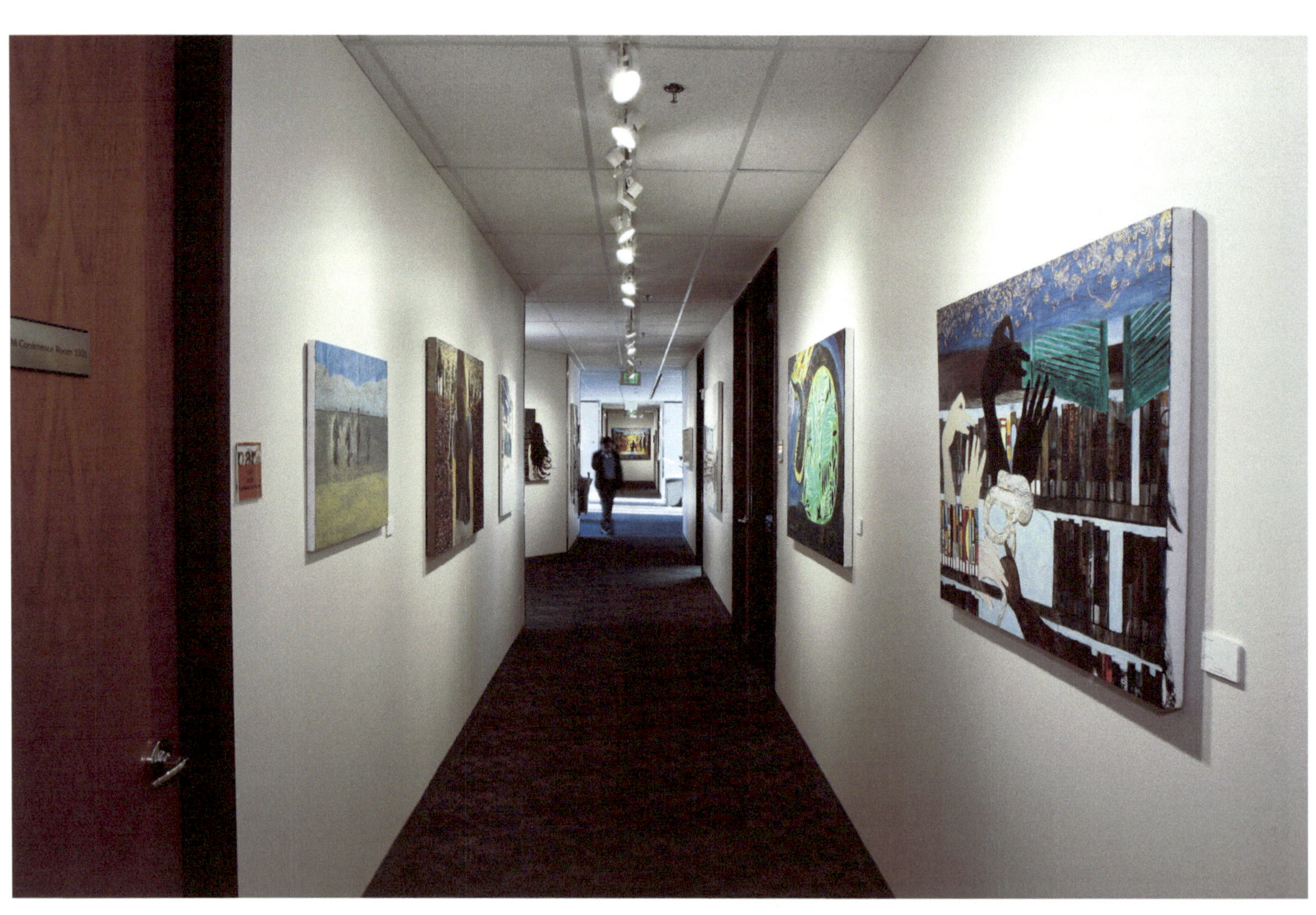

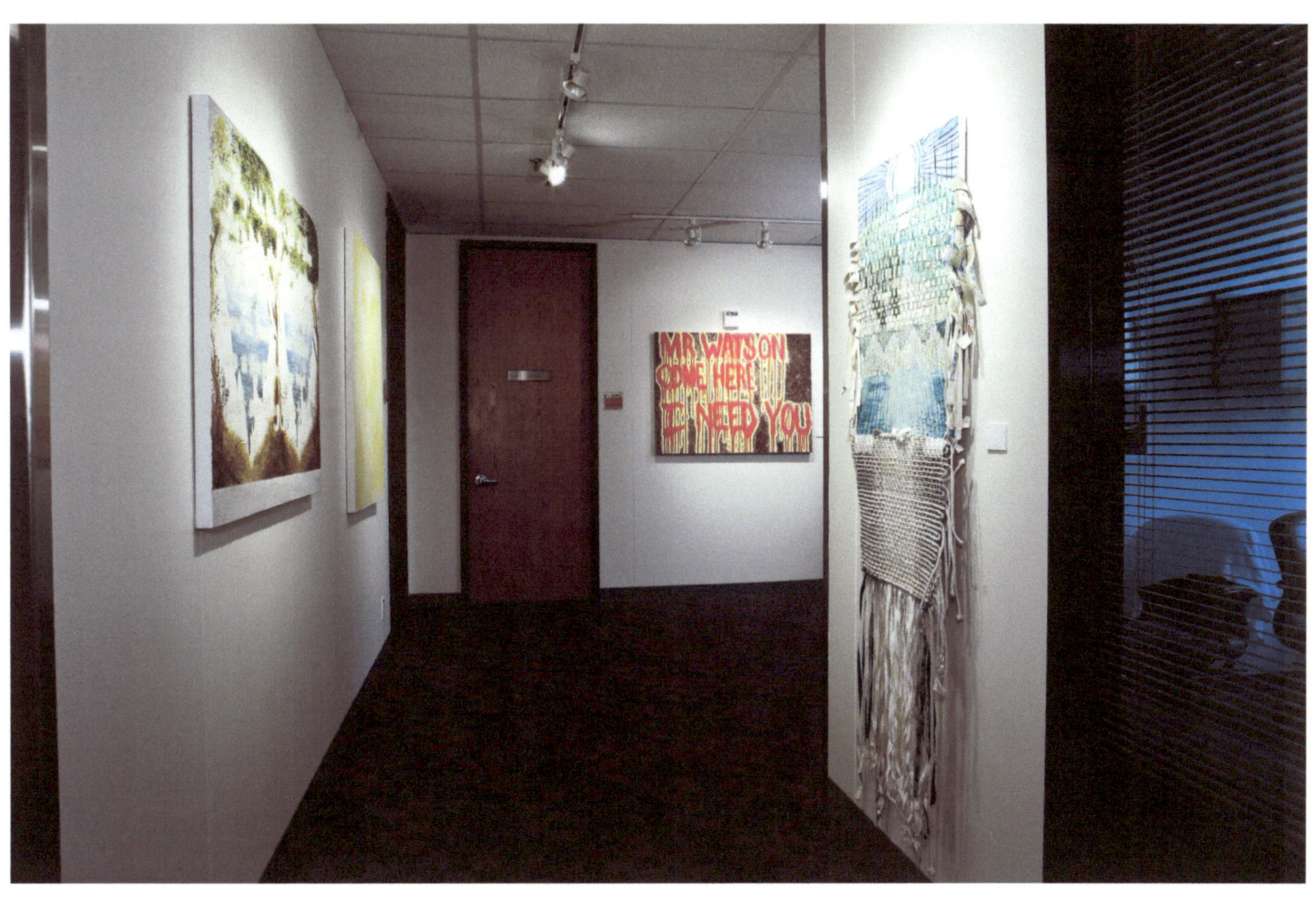
MR WATSON
COME HERE
I NEED YOU

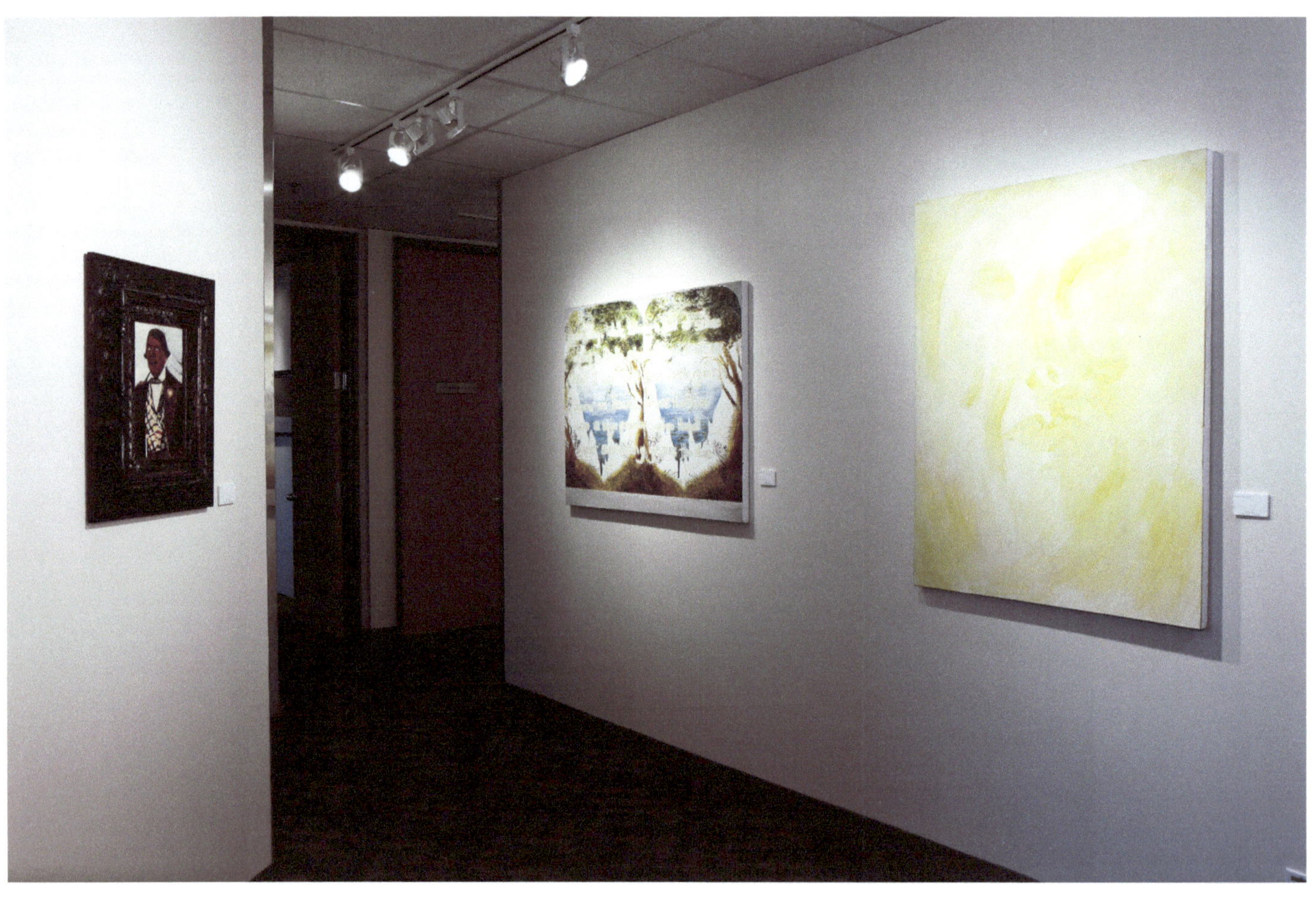

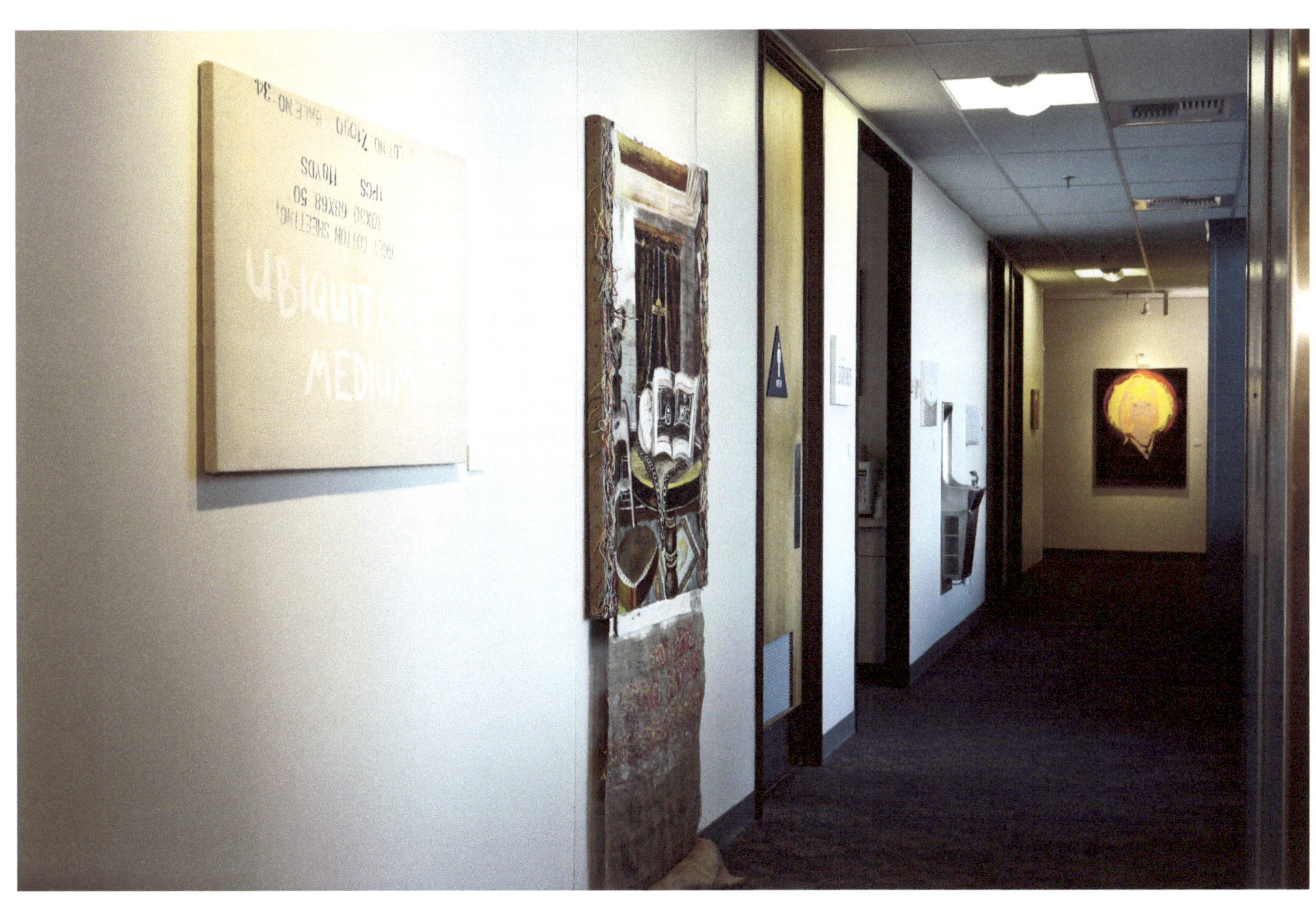
MEDIUM

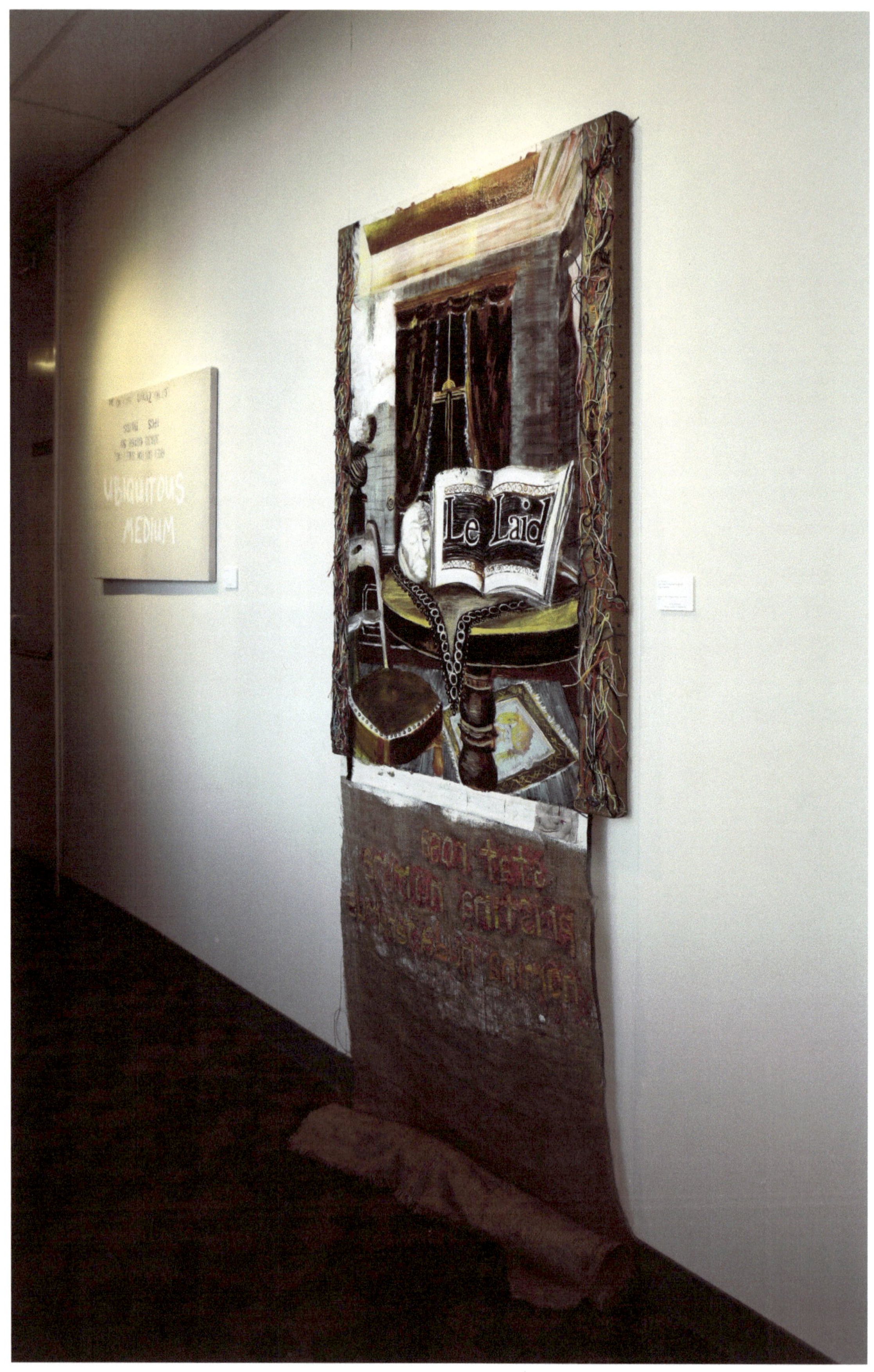
UBIQUITOUS
MEDIUM
Le Laid

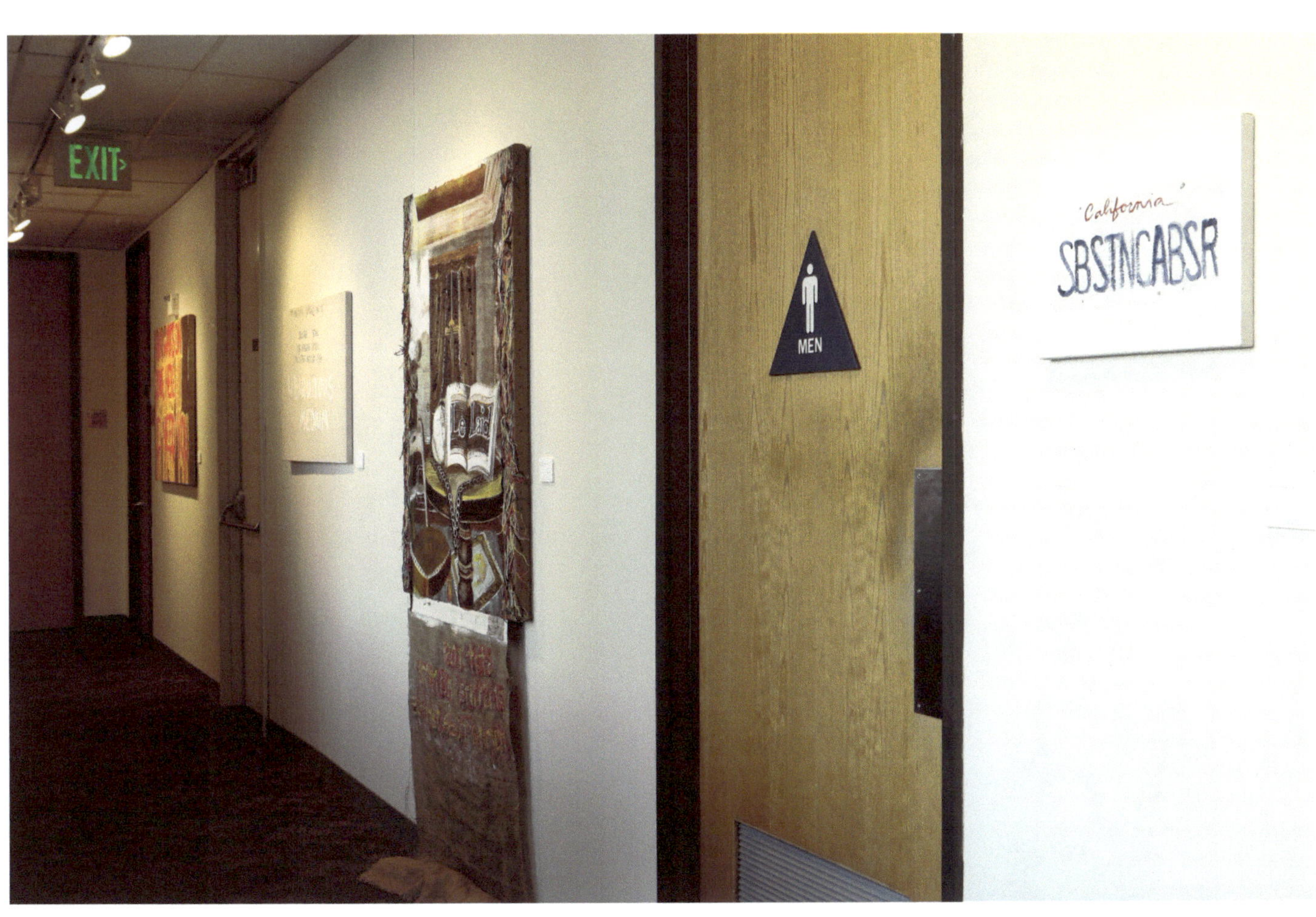
EXIT
MEN
California
SBSTNCABSR

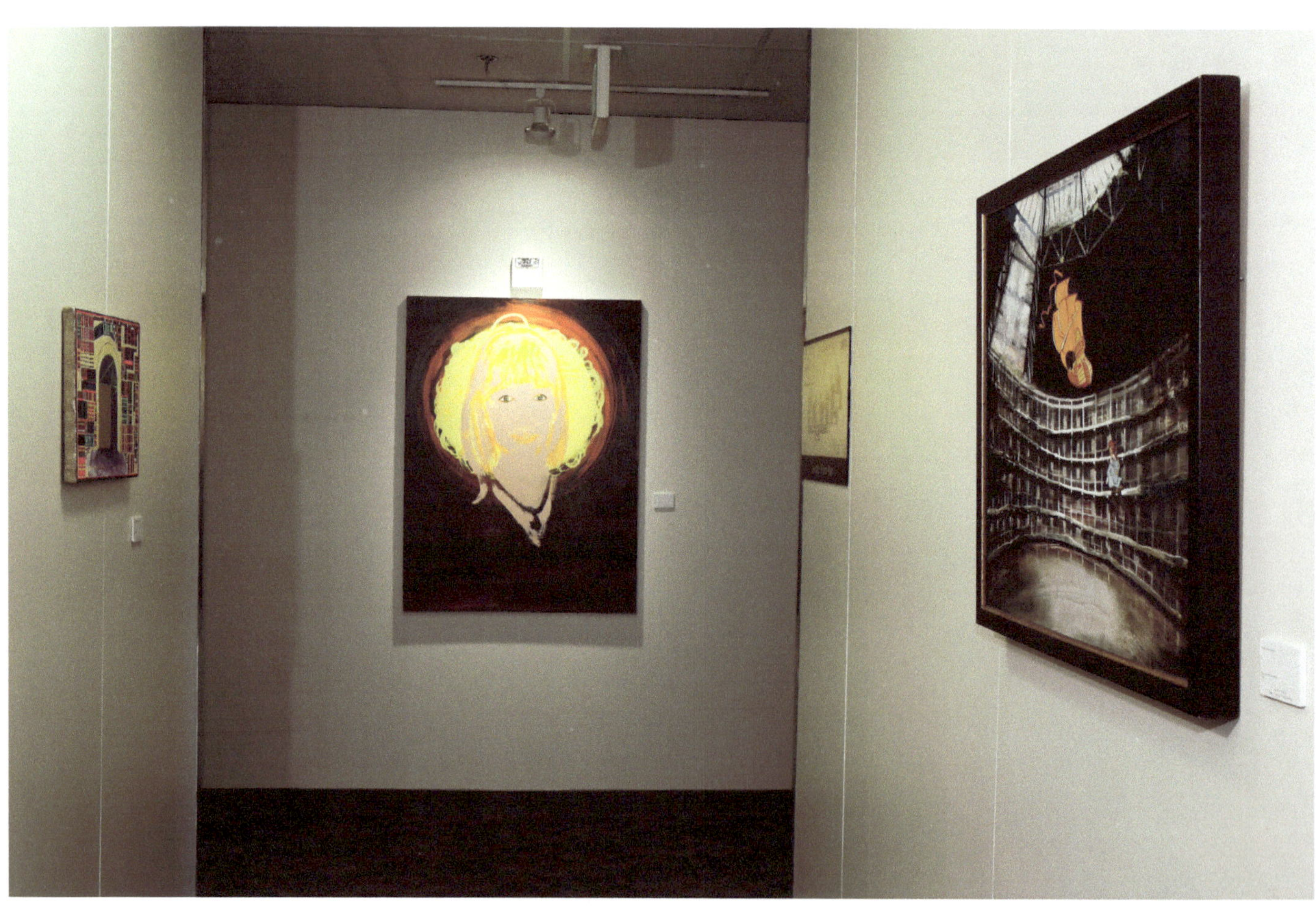

Exhibition Checklist

• *works not illustrated*

Plate 1
C is for Cookie (PARC)
2011
acrylic on wool blanket
54 x 68 inches (unframed)

Plate 2
Documents (Heads You Lose)
2011
acrylic on canvas
66 x 78 inches (unframed)

Plate 3
Door to Door Encyclopedia Salesman
2011
acrylic & mica powder on canvas
36 x 48 inches (unframed)

Plate 4
Mr. Watson Come Here I Need You
2011
acrylic and garnets on canvas
36 x 48 inches (unframed)

Plate 5
Pío Pico
2011
acrylic on paper
19 x 24 inches (framed)

Plate 6
Doug Engelbart, Red Cross Library, The Philippines
2011
acrylic on canvas
38 x 48 inches (unframed)

Plate 7
Lynn Conway
2011
acrylic on canvas
36 x 48 inches (unframed)

Plate 8
Melvil's Rib (Dewey)
2011
acrylic on canvas
16 x 20 inches (unframed)

Plate 9
Digital Gender Divide
2011
acrylic & mica powder on canvas
36 x 48 inches (unframed)

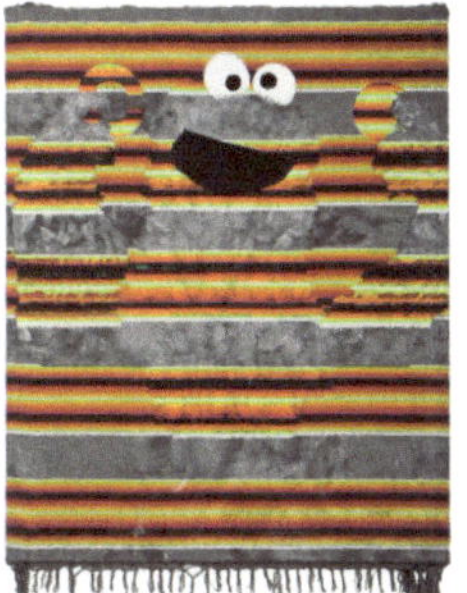
Plate 1

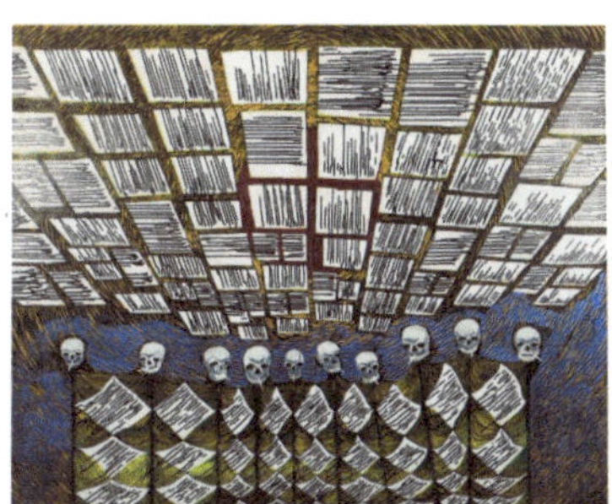
Plate 2

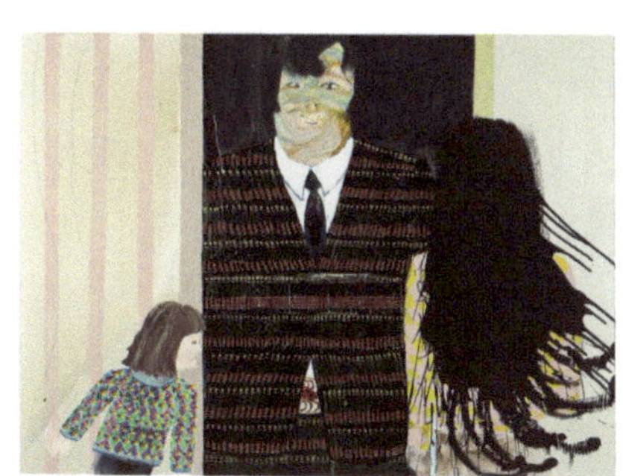
Plate 3

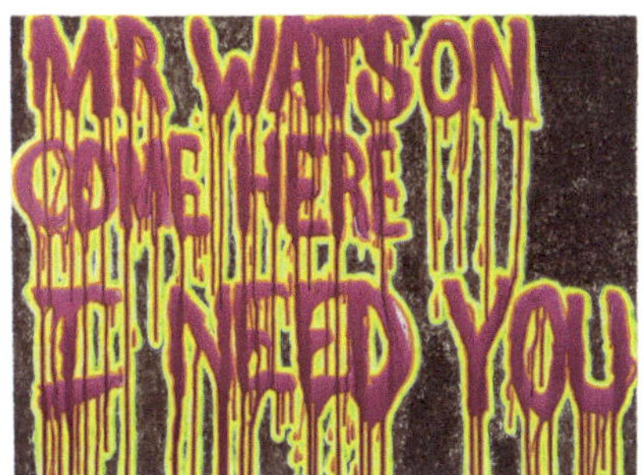

Plate 4

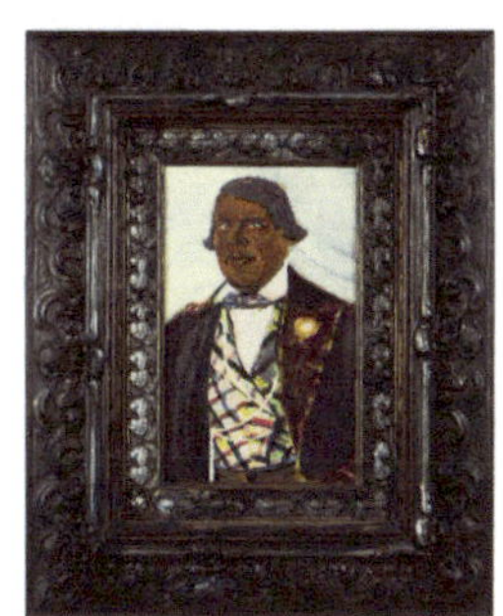
Plate 5

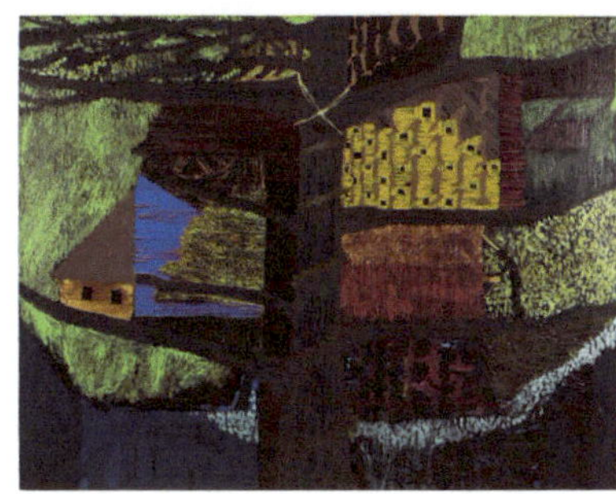
Plate 6

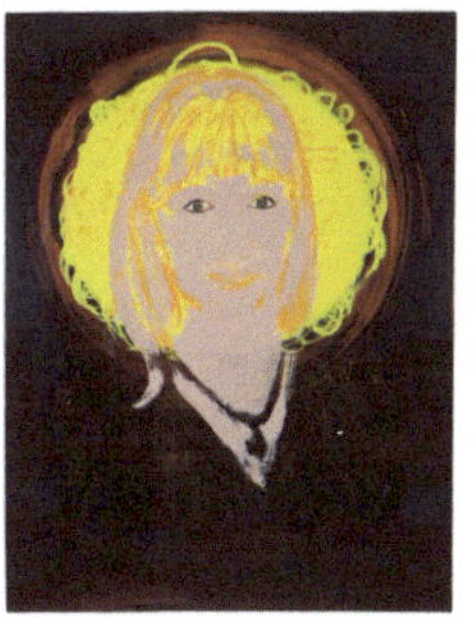
Plate 7

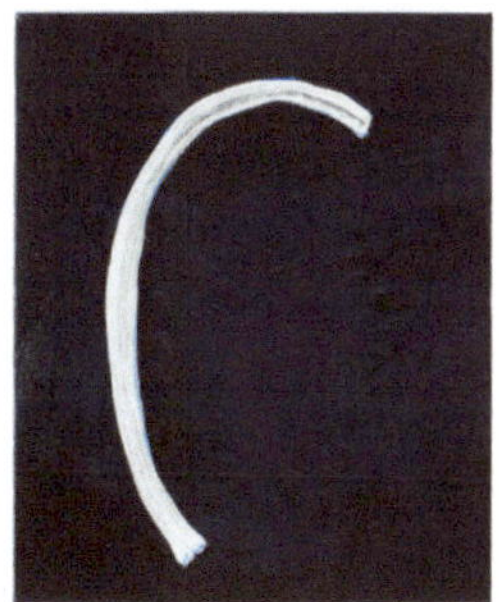
Plate 8

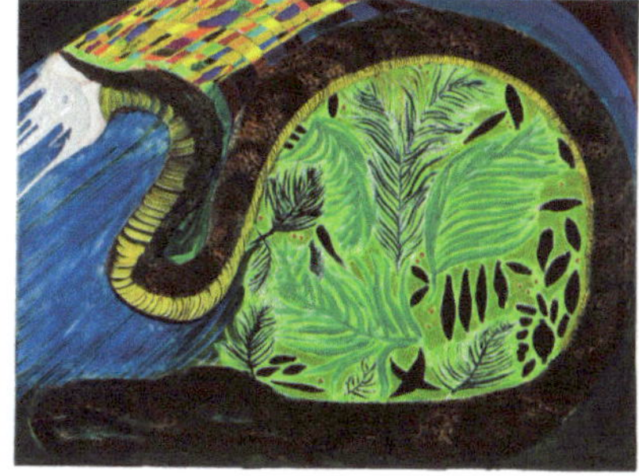
Plate 9

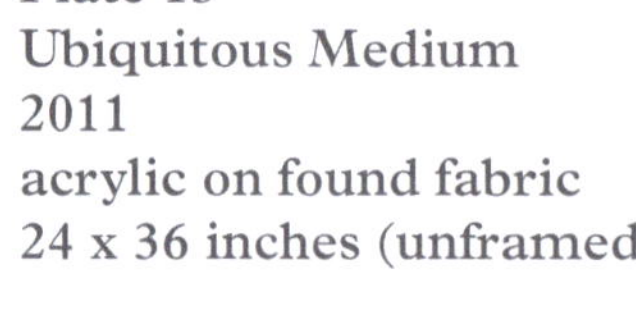

Plate 10
The Owners Historic Lesson
(Flag 1954 - 1955)
2011
acrylic on canvas
48 x 60 inches (unframed)

Plate 11
If I Die My Email Password Is
2011
embroidery on horse fly mask
approx. 16 x 10 x 48 inches

Plate 12
Golden Ratio Microprocessor
2011
acrylic on burlap and canvas
14 x 18 inches (unframed)

Plate 13
Ubiquitous Medium
2011
acrylic on found fabric
24 x 36 inches (unframed)

Plate 14
Cycling for Libraries, Molesworth Institute Jacket
2011
fabric paint on polyester jacket
30.5 x 41.5 inches (framed)

Plate 15
Cycling for Libraries Jersey: "A Cost Analysis Of A Cost Analysis"
2011
fabric paint on polyester shirt
26.5 x 30.5 inches (framed)

Plate 16
Cycling for Libraries Jersey: "Freedom From Information"
2011
fabric paint on polyester shirt
26.5 x 30.5 inches (framed)

Plate 17
Cycling for Libraries Jersey: "Our view can best be characterized as disjunctive librarianship"
2011
fabric paint on polyester shirt
26.5 x 30.5 inches (framed)

Plate 18
Cycling for Libraries Jersey: "The Journal of Rejected Research"
2011
fabric paint on polyester shirt
26.5 x 30.5 inches (framed)

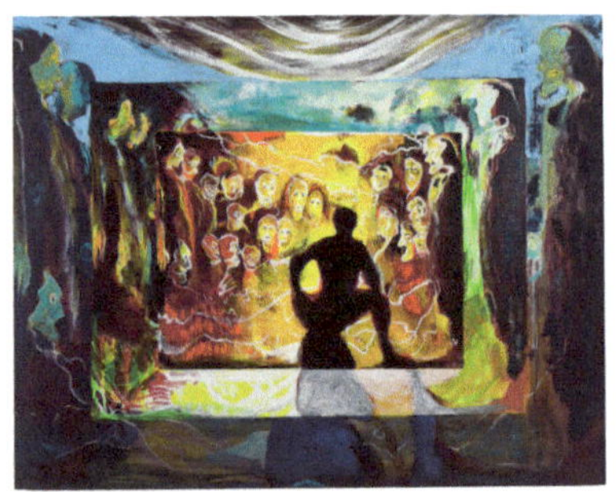

Plate 10

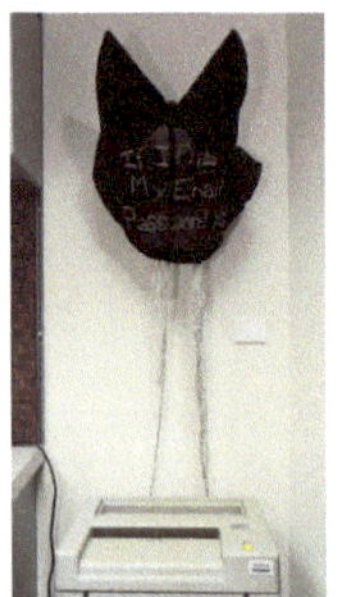

Plate 11

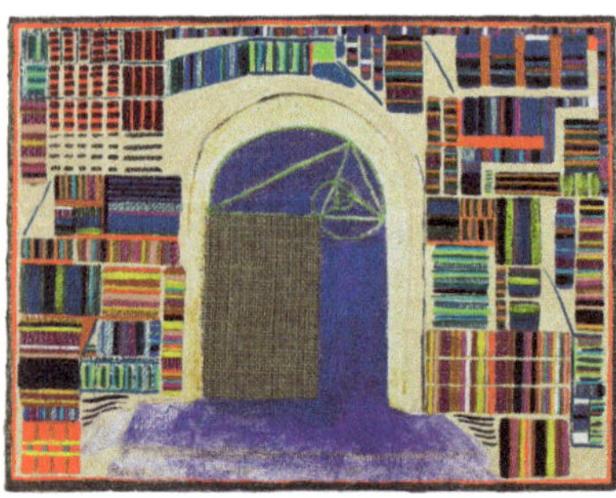

Plate 12

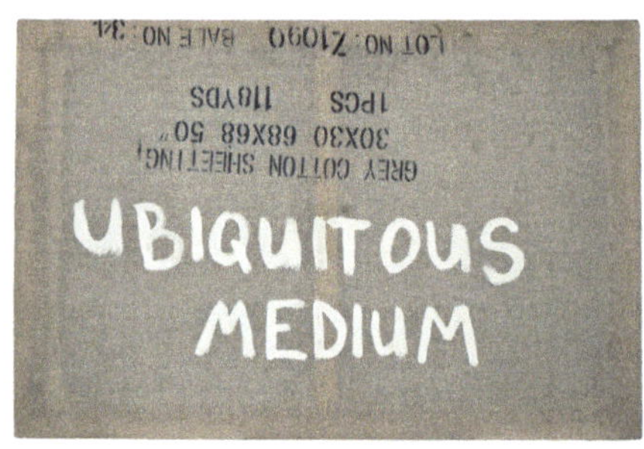

Plate 13

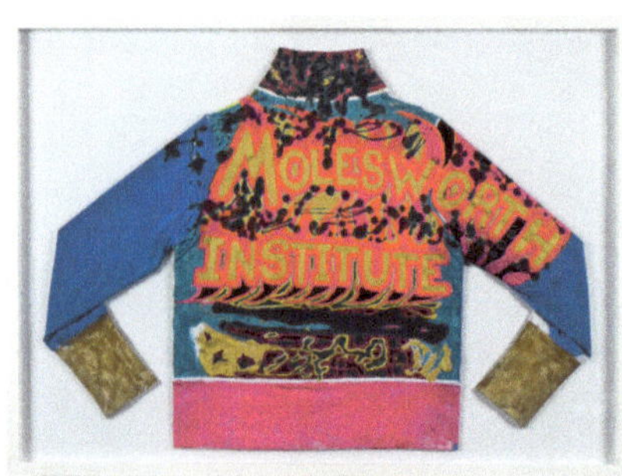

Plate 14

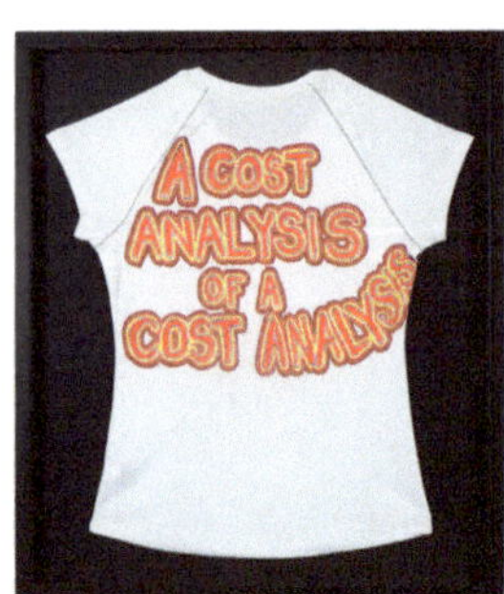

Plate 15

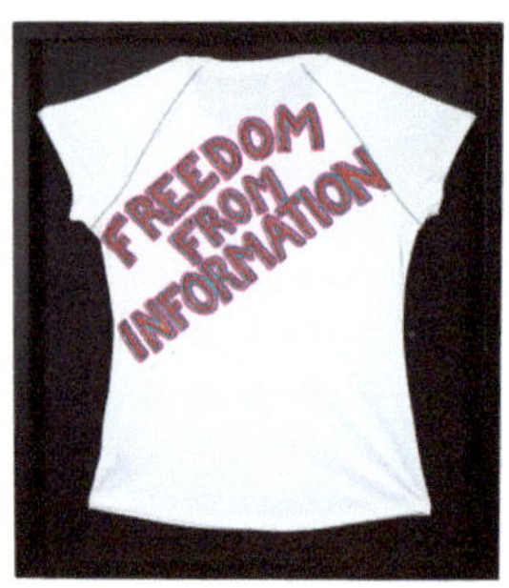

Plate 16

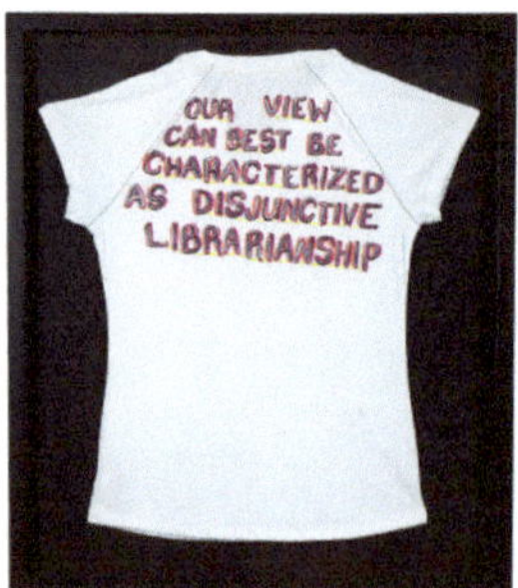

Plate 17

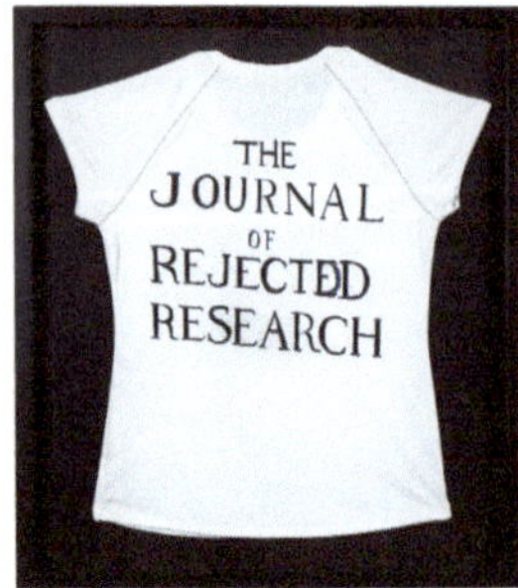

Plate 18

Plate 19
Cycling for Libraries Jersey: "The number of windows washed; the quantity of wood burned to heat the library; and the number of pickled limes eaten in the children's room."
2011
fabric paint on polyester shirt
26.5 x 30.5 inches (framed)

Plate 20
Cycling for Libraries Jersey: "The original purpose of this organization has long since been forgotten and the origins of its name are likewise shrouded in mystery"
2011
fabric paint on polyester shirt
26.5 x 30.5 inches (framed)

Plate 21
Cycling for Libraries Jersey: "Umbrella Disappearance, Echange, and Loss Rates in American Academic Libraries"
2011
fabric paint on polyester shirt
26.5 x 30.5 inches (framed)

Plate 22
Cycling for Libraries Jersey: "We find the library world, like the real world, impossible to understand on a rational basis"
2011
fabric paint on polyester shirt
26.5 x 30.5 inches (framed)

•
Literaturwurst
2011
printed texts, sausage casing, hog rings, string
approx. 2 x 2 x 12 inches each

•
What You See Is What You Get
2011
acrylic on found fabric
10 x 57.5 inches (unframed)

Plate 23
I Am My Child's Best First Teacher
2010
acrylic on canvas
16 x 20 inches (unframed)

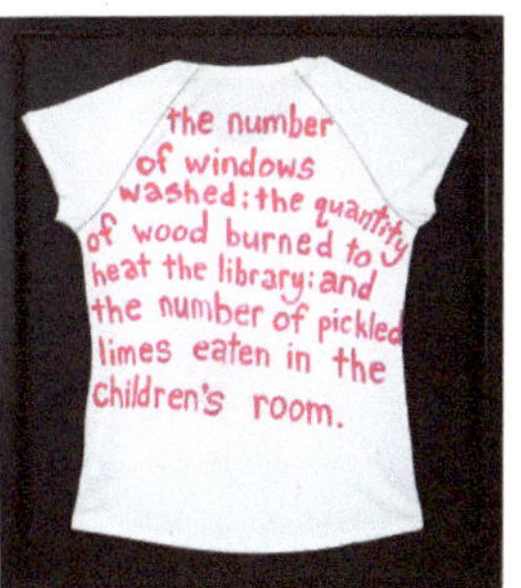

Plate 19

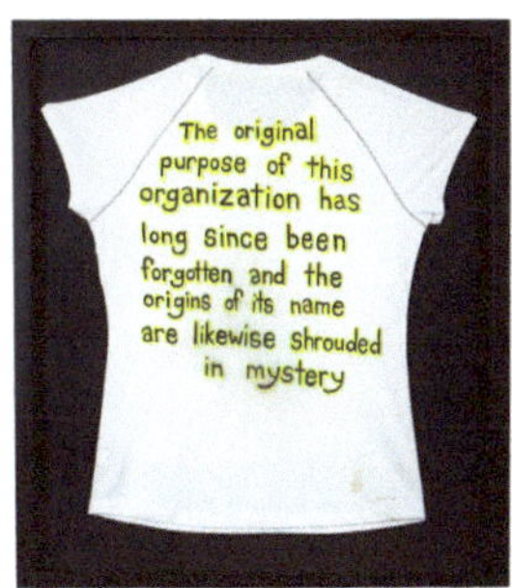

Plate 20

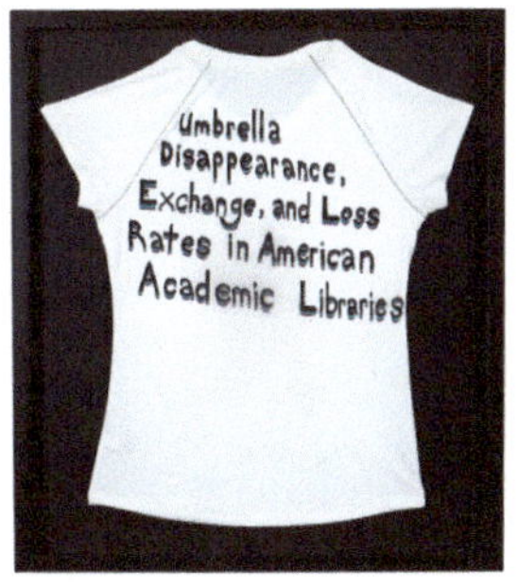

Plate 21

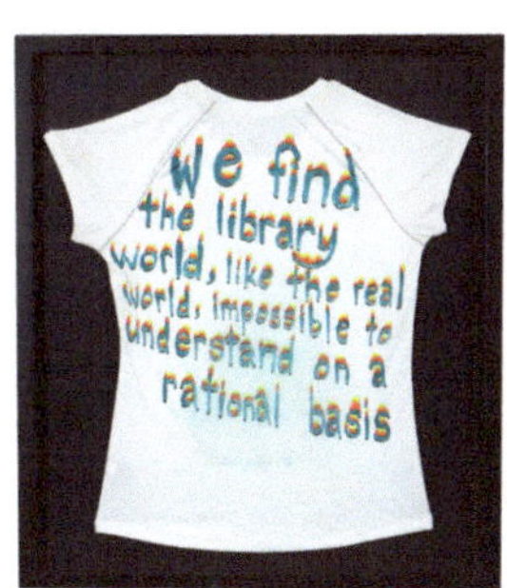

Plate 22

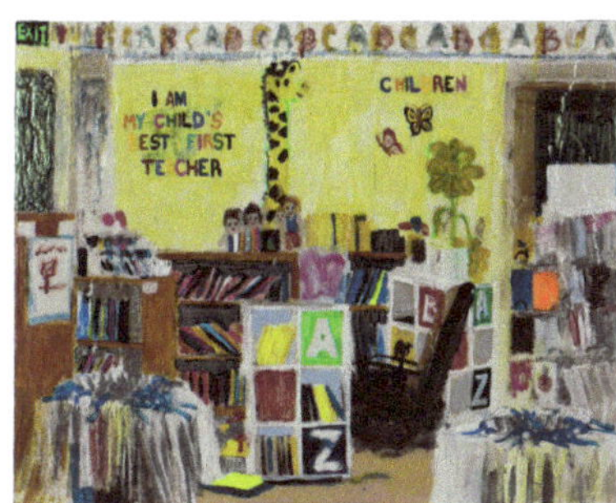
Plate 23

Plate 24
Memory School Dropout
2010
acrylic on canvas
36 x 48 inches (unframed)

Plate 25
On Denoting (stat rosa pristina nomine nomina nuda tenemus)
2010
acrylic and wax strings on burlap and canvas
36 x approx. 84 inches (unframed)

Plate 26
Encyclopedia Book Cover Set (Lithium Indefinitely)
2009
embroidery on linen
22 x 62 inches (framed)

Plate 27
Tracey Emin Library, Uganda
2009
acrylic on canvas
14 x 18 inches (unframed)

Plate 28
Whittier Public Library (entrance)
2009
acrylic on canvas
24 x 36 inches (unframed)

Plate 29
Information Entropy
2009
acrylic and fiber on canvas
24 x 36 inches (unframed)

Plate 30
Quarry
2009
acrylic on found fabric on canvas
36 x 48 inches (unframed)

•
Psychedelic Illuminated Manuscript
2009
acrylic, pastel, wax strings, gold leaf, on burlap
approx. 42 x 180 inches (unframed)

Plate 31
Freedom (Richard Stallman Folk Dancing)
2008
acrylic on canvas
60 x 72 inches (unframed)

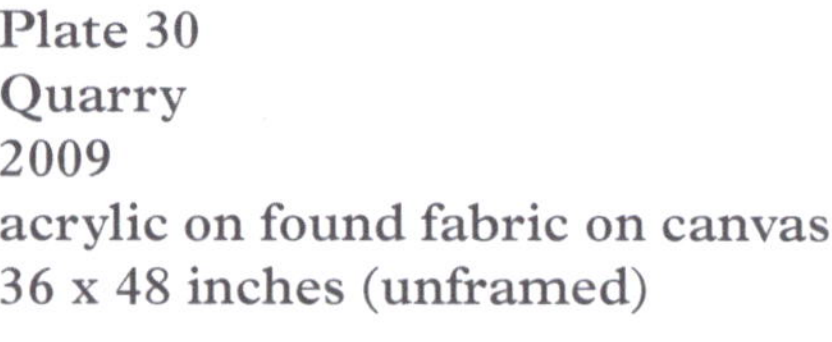

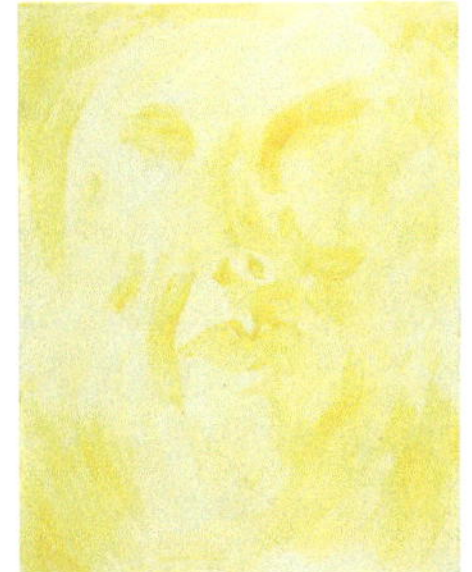

Plate 24

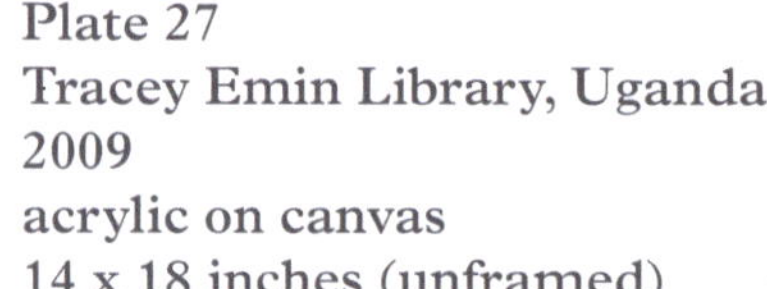

Plate 27

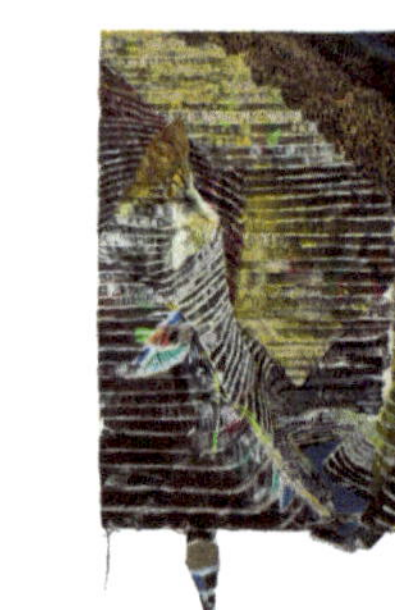

Plate 30

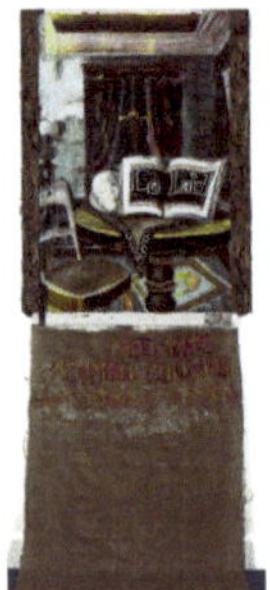

Plate 25

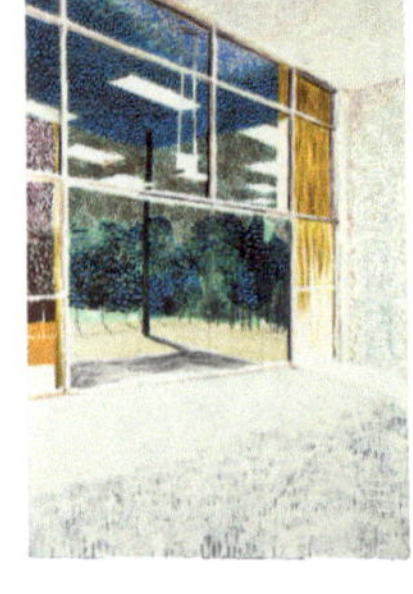

Plate 28

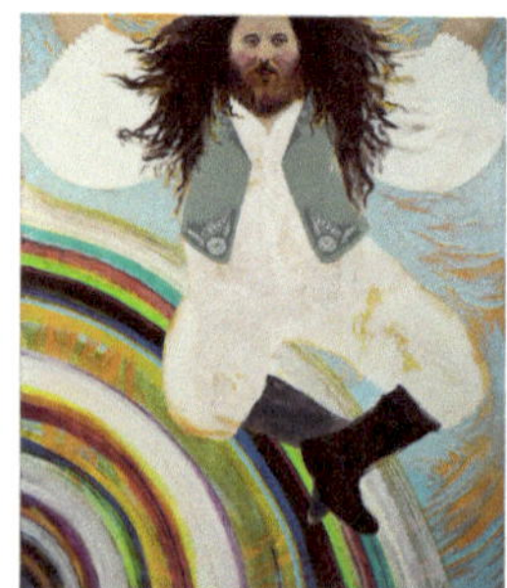

Plate 31

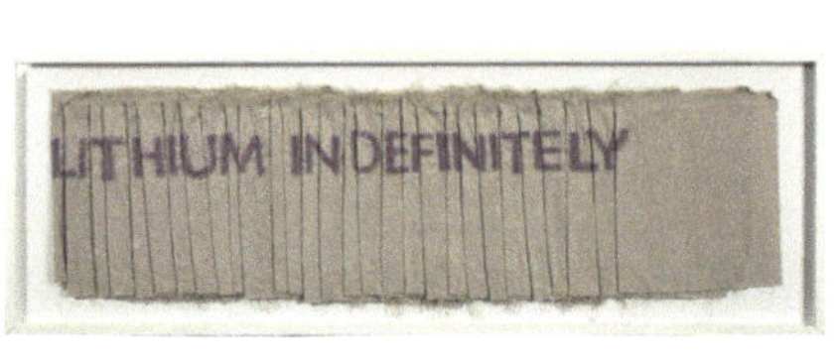

Plate 26

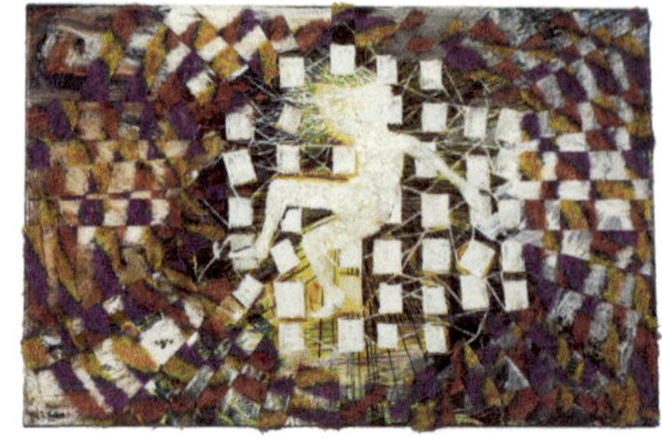

Plate 29

Plate 32
Urinalysis
2008
acrylic on canvas
36 x 48 inches (unframed)

Plate 33
Stereopticon (One day, while taking a look at some vistas in Dad's stereopticon, it hit me that I was just this little girl, born in Texas, whose father was a sign painter, who had just so many years to live)
2008
oil and acrylic on canvas
36 x 48 inches (unframed)

Plate 34
Don't Turn Away From Love, Sailor
2008
acrylic and fiber on canvas
36 x 48 inches (unframed)

Plate 35
Lux Aeterna
2008
mixed media on linen
36 x 48 inches (unframed)

Plate 36
Dead Coyotes on a Fence
2008
acrylic on canvas
22 x 28 inches (unframed)

Plate 37
You Are Here
2008
mixed media
28 x 70 inches (unframed)

•

Keyboard
2008
KFC straws, napkins, wire, stickers, glue
approx. 18 x 57 inches

•

Phone Books
2008
yarn on metal lath
approx. 72 x 96 inches

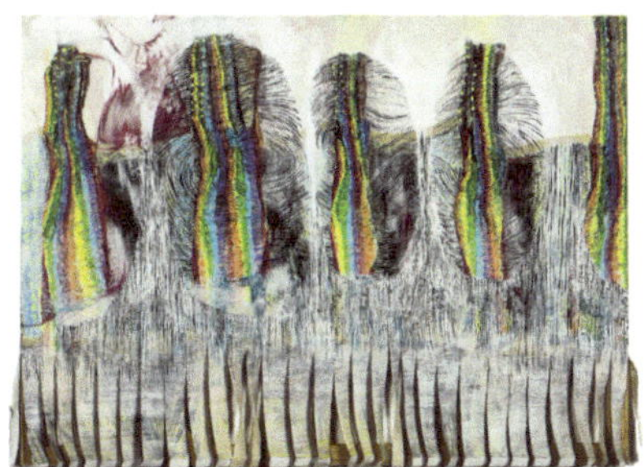

Plate 32

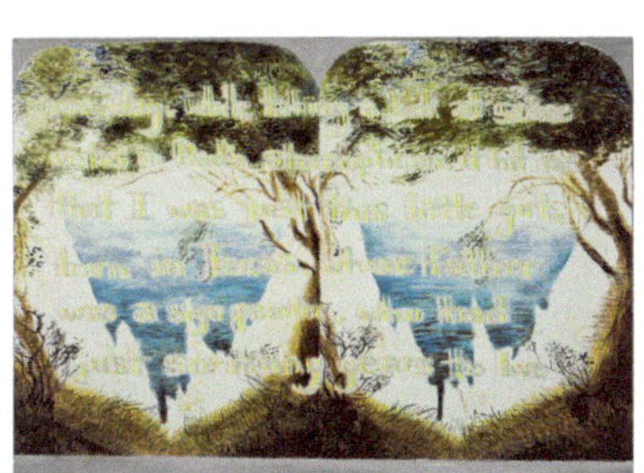

Plate 33

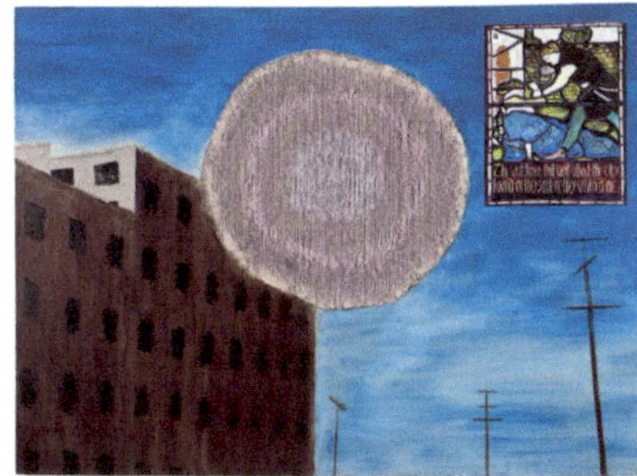

Plate 34

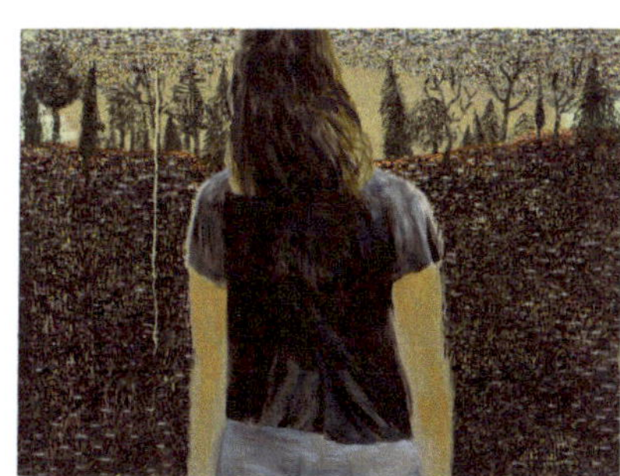

Plate 35

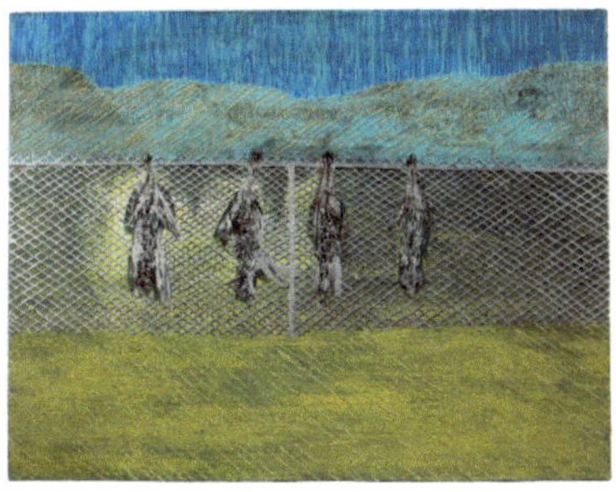

Plate 36

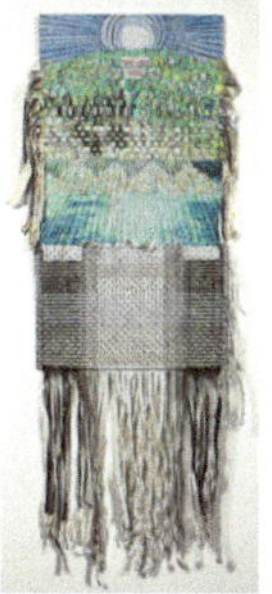

Plate 37

Plate 38
Today The Library Was Ripped A New Asshole
2007
acrylic on canvas
48 x 60 inches (unframed)

•

A Disturbance of Memory on the Acropolis (Sigmund, Me, and Alexander)
2007
acrylic on canvas
54 x 68 inches (unframed)

Plate 39
Library Wedding
2006
acrylic on canvas
48 x 60 inches (unframed)

Plate 40
Swan Shadow
2006
acrylic on canvas
30 x 40 inches (unframed)

Plate 41
United States Mint
2006
acrylic on canvas
24 x 36 inches (unframed)

Plate 42
California Substance Abuser
2005
acrylic on canvas
11 x 14 inches (unframed)

Plate 43
Information Overload Syndrome
2005
oil on linen
32 x 40 inches (unframed)

Plate 44
Paper Factory
2005
charcoal, graphite, and acrylic on paper
26 x 33.5 inches (framed)

Plate 45
Sloss Furnace
2004
graphite and gesso on paper
23 x 30 inches (framed)

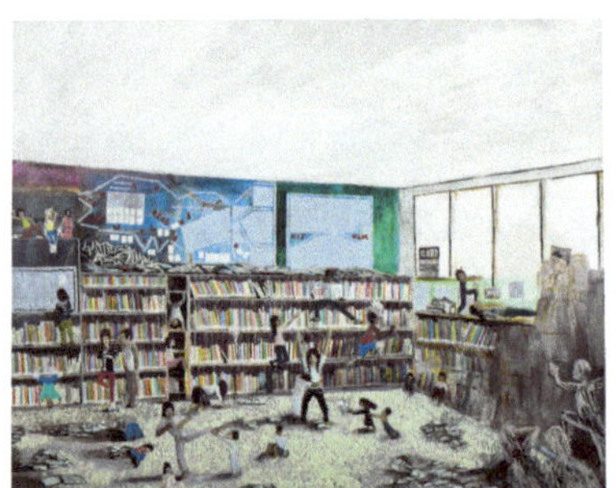

Plate 38

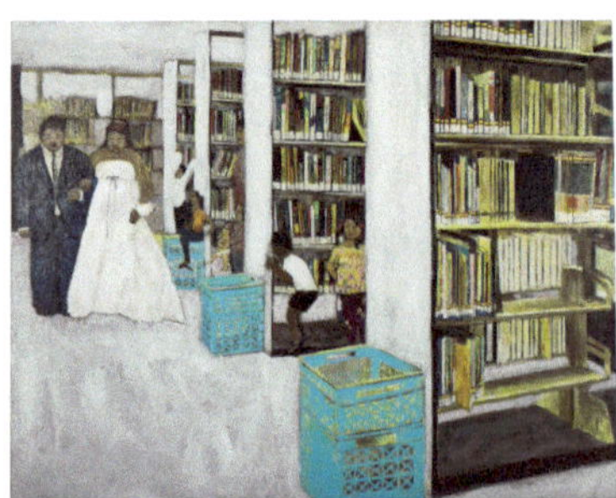

Plate 39

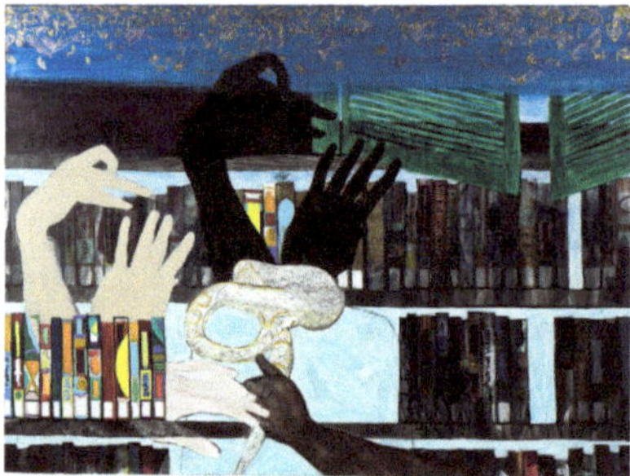

Plate 40

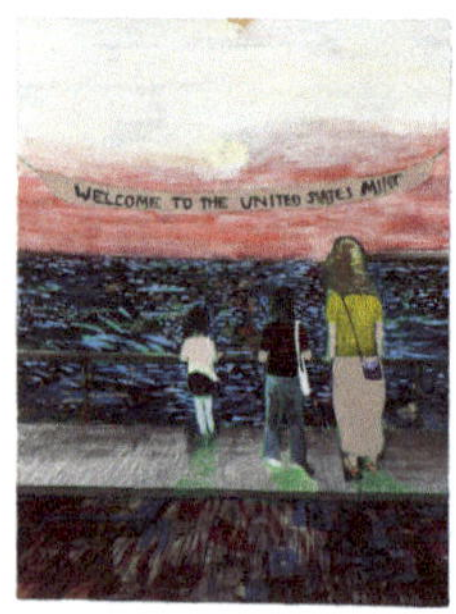

Plate 41

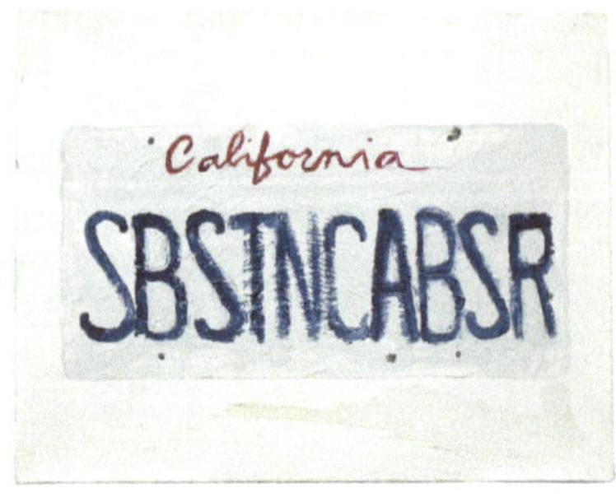

Plate 42

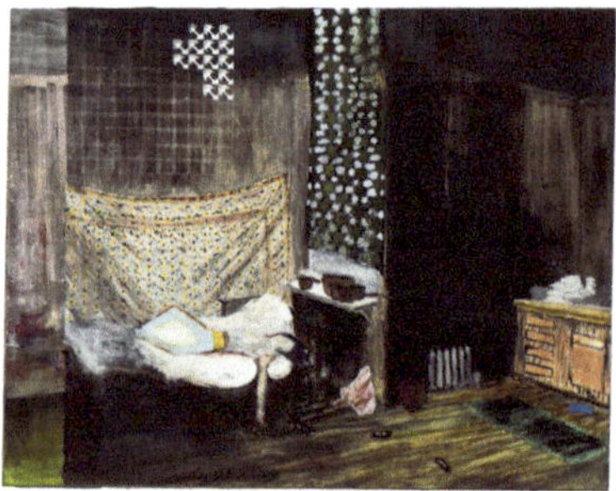

Plate 43

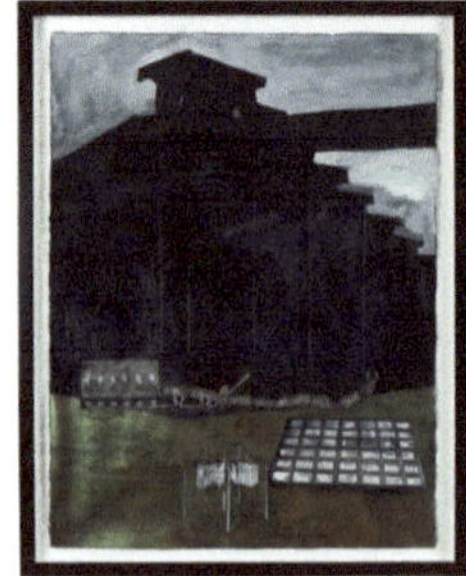

Plate 44

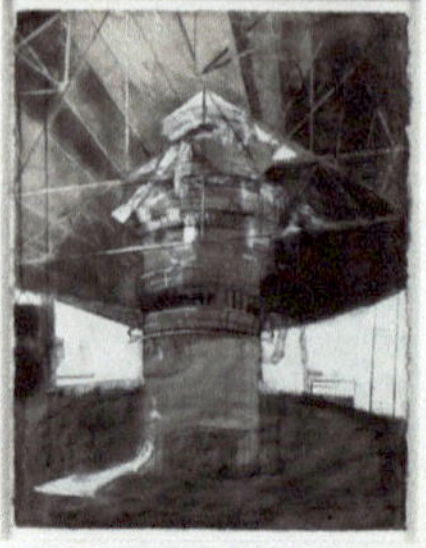

Plate 45

•
Haystack
2004
photo copy installation
approx. 40 x 60 inches (framed)

Plate 46
Head Scarf
2001
ink on found scarf
34.5 x 42.5 inches (framed)

Plate 47
Even Though The Flames Were
Not Real, Dumbo Was Afraid
2000
ink and acrylic on paper
22 x 27 inches (framed)

Plate 48
Peter Panopticon
2000
mixed media on canvas
26 x 32 inches (framed)

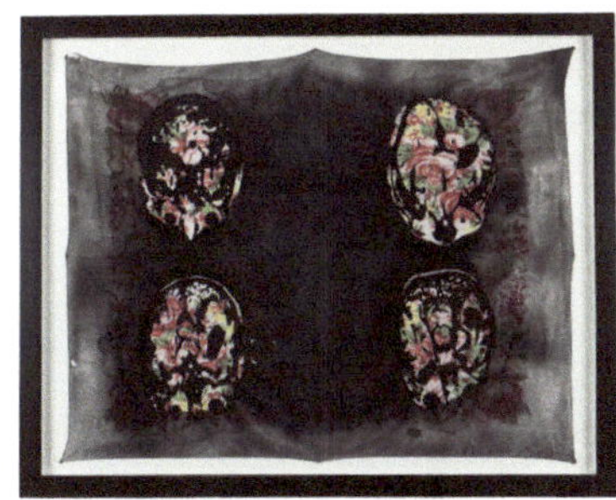

Plate 46

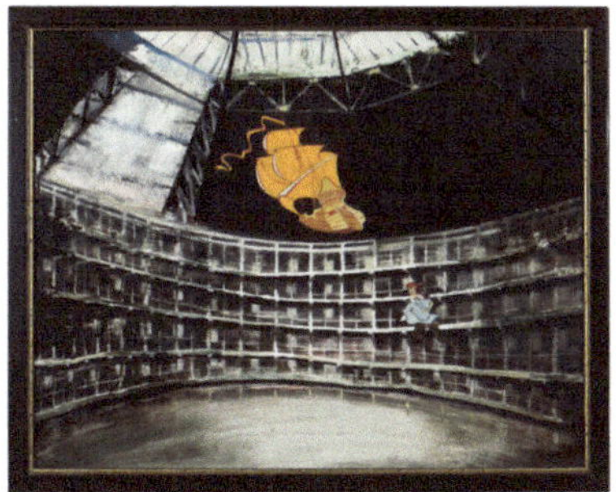

Plate 48

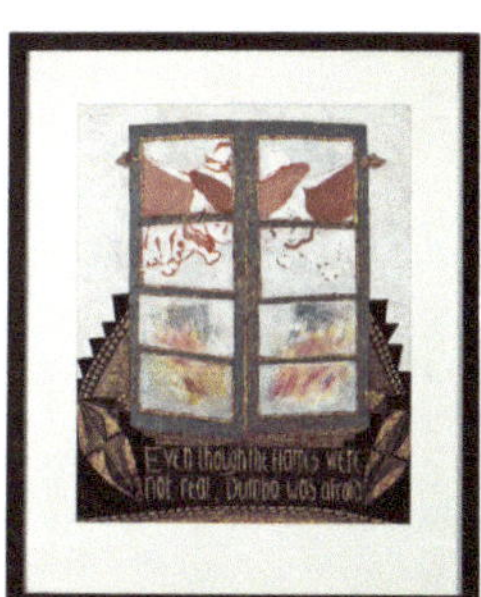

Plate 47

www.ingramcontent.com/pod-product-compliance
Lightning Source LLC
LaVergne TN
LVHW071632100826
845154LV00008BA/136

9780981462363